Adobe Photoshop for Beginners

How to create simple drawings and forms

Stephanie Lane

Keywords: photoshop, photoshop elements 2018, photoshop cc 2018 book, adobe photoshop elements 2018, photoshop books, photoshop 2018, photoshop 2018 for dummies, photoshop books 2018, adobe photoshop cc classroom in a book 2018, drawing photoshop, drawing in photoshop.

Table of Contents

Disclaimer

While all attempts have been made to verify the information provided in this book, the author does assume any responsibility for errors, omissions, or contrary interpretations of the subject matter contained within. The information provided in this book is for educational and entertainment purposes only. The reader is responsible for his or her own actions and the author does not accept any responsibilities for any liabilities or damages, real or perceived, resulting from the use of this information.

The trademarks that are used are without any consent, and the publication of the trademark is without permission or backing by the trademark owner. All trademarks and brands within this book are for clarifying purposes only and are the owned by the owners themselves, not affiliated with this document.

Introduction

Drawing is probably one of the oldest forms of art in human history. Humans have been drawing pictures since some ancient man drew something on the ground or on the walls of his cave. These images were representations of their life. The very first drawings may have been drawn using a stick or a rock. Their canvas: the walls of the cave they dwell in. There are many examples of cave paintings portraying animals and humans. Some also show the activities of these ancient humans.

The pictures we have drawn have evolved along with the human brain. As the brain grew more sophisticated, so did the drawings and pictures. Some became more realistic; showing what the artist sees in reality. Others tried to draw and paint the emotions they have. There have been scores of great painters in history. They have created wonderful, awe-inspiring, and truly magnificent works of art.

As time moved forward, technology developed and progressed. So, too, did the tools and mediums that were used for drawing. Humans progressed from traditional paints and canvas to one of this age's most powerful tools: the computer. The rise of digital art brought about by the development of computers. Artists all over the world now have a new medium for creating their paintings. Computers allowed a wider range of colors and styles for painting. It also had a key feature: the 'undo' action. This action is used for correcting mistakes or make changes in the work.

While there are many programs and tools available for artists to use, one of the most popular digital painting tools is Adobe Photoshop. This book may be a great help, especially for beginners, in creating basic shapes and drawings and to familiarize him with the program.

Learning the Basics of Photoshop

Adobe Photoshop is a photo editing software that allows artists to create stunning paintings, make amazing logos and designs, and edit photographs. The program gives a lot of options and freedom for its users.

- **Interface**

The very first thing you will see upon opening Photoshop for the first time is the "Start" workspace. This contains all the recent files that you have opened in the program. It also contains some presets and examples of other artists' works. This is also where the user is given the option to start a new project or open an old one.

Once a new, or old, project is opened, you are then taken to the main workspace of the program. The interface is similar across all versions of Photoshop with some minor visual and aesthetic changes, so once you are familiar with one version it is very easy to switch to another without any intimate knowledge of that version.

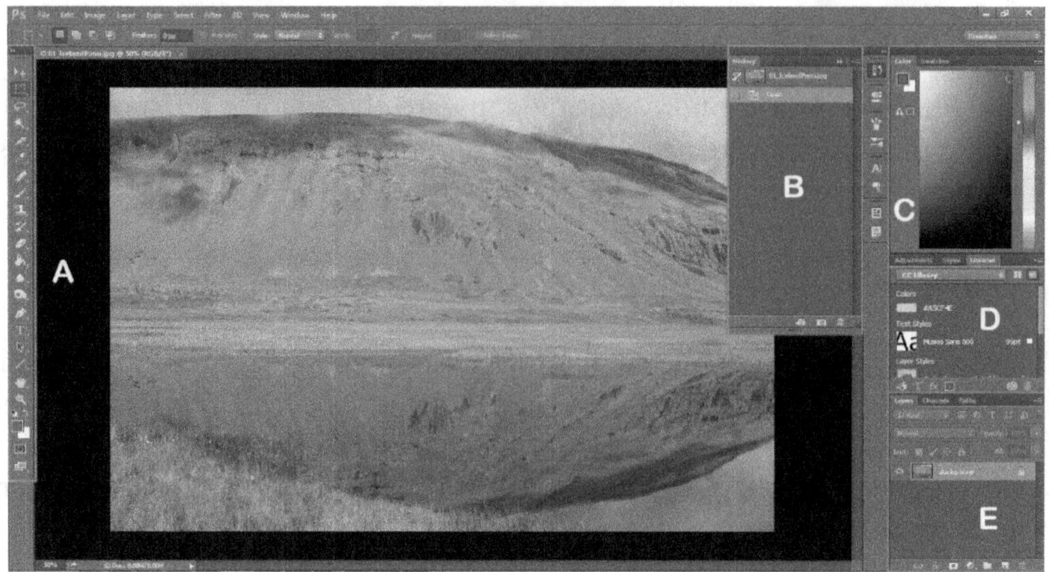

The "Tools Panel" is located at the far left of the screen, denoted by "A" in the image above. This panel contains tools for selecting parts of the image, painting, measuring, retouching, drawing and text input, and navigation. The items on this panel are probably the most common things you will use for the program as they are the most basic tools of Photoshop.

The "History Panel", shown as "B" on the image above, shows all the changes made on the project. This allows you to undo changes and retrace previous commands to adjust and refine the project.

"C" on the image above is the "Color Panel". This is where you can change and adjust the colors used in the project. There are options to select preset colors or a specific color can be chosen by adjusting the RGB, or CMYK levels.

The "Creative Cloud Library", marked as "D" above, is an online portal which allows you to access your Creative Cloud account. This lets you use your previous works on your current project. This also has all the custom assets that you downloaded.

The "Layer Panel", "E" on the image, is the panel that lets you control the layers of the project. This is one of the most used panels in the workspace, along with the "Tools Panel".

This allows you to make changes on a layer without affecting the others. This is very useful when making big, or drastic, changes on the project.

- **Basic Commands**

Photoshop is a very complicated program since it is used in making very complicated works. Because of this fact, commands and shortcuts were created to make things a bit easier for the users. These shortcuts let users use tools and commands without manually looking for them. Some commands are not even shown in the Workspace Panels.

Here are some of the most common keyboard shortcuts, their commands, and their functions:

FUNCTION	SHORTCUTS	
	WINDOWS	MAC
Make a new layer	Ctrl+Shift+N	Cmd+Shift+N
Adjust Brush Size	[(Decrease);] (Increase)	[(Decrease);] (Increase)
Fill Selection	Shift+F5	Shift+F5
Levels	Ctrl+L	Cmd+L
Render	Alt+Shift+Ctrl+R	Opt+Shift+Cmd+R
Zoom	Ctrl++ (In) Ctrl+- (Out)	Cmd++ (In) Cmd+- (Out)
Search	Ctrl+F	Cmd+F
Undo/Redo	Ctrl+Z	Cmd+Z
Step forward	Ctrl+Shift+Z	Cmd+Shift+Z
Step backward	Ctrl+Alt+Z	Cmd+Opt+Z

- **Layers**

Layers are an essential part of learning to use Photoshop. They are very similar to the acetates used by animators, especially in old cartoons. Layers allow you to make changes and edit your project without affecting the previous work you have done, provided that you have them on separate layers.

This means that you can make the changes on a certain layer without changing the others. You can even hide certain layers to focus on separate parts of the project.

Layers are also useful in making a painting. You can create a background for the painting on one layer, and on another, you can paint the mid and foregrounds. This makes editing and making changes a whole lot easier as you don't need to make space for any part of the painting, you can just paint it as a whole.

Basic Principles in Creating 3D Images for Beginners

Drawing something is very easy. Just make an arbitrary shape on a piece of paper, add a few colors and it can be considered a drawing. Not a very good one, but a drawing nonetheless. The real challenge is making the drawing more realistic. This does not mean that you only draw things that you see and real. This means that your drawings must obey the rules of reality for it to be considered realistic. This can be challenge since most drawing materials are two-dimensional while objects in the world are three-dimensional. It is not impossible though. With a few principles and tricks, we can trick the eye into thinking that it is looking at a three-dimensional image instead of a two-dimensional, or flat, representation of it. The two most important principles of three-dimensional drawing are **perspective** and **shading.**

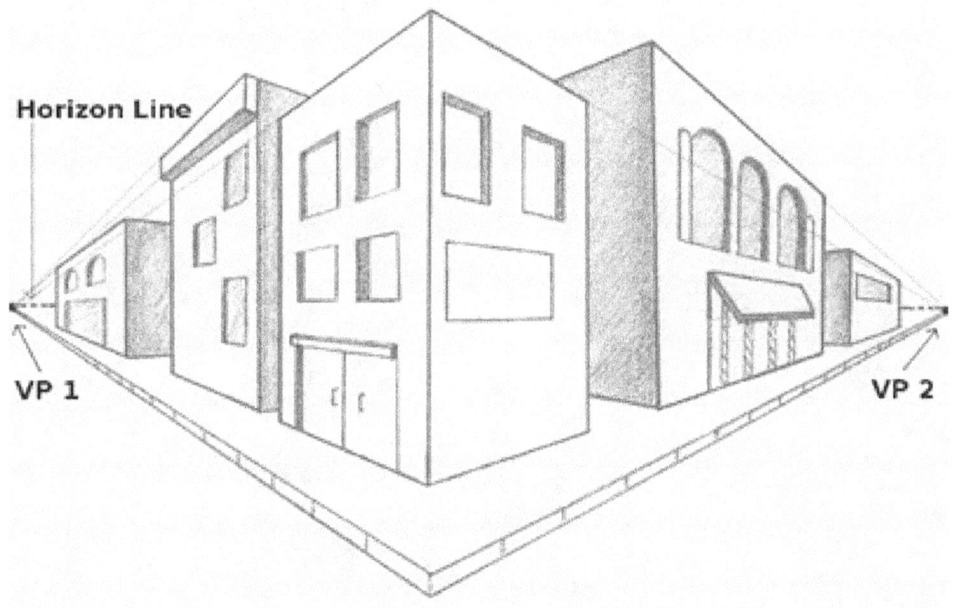

Perspective, as defined by the dictionary, is the "representation in a drawing or painting of parallel lines as converging in order to give the illusion of depth and distance." What this means is you have to keep in mind the relationships between objects in your drawings. Objects further from the viewer are smaller than those closer. It also affects the shape of objects. The closer an object is to the "vanishing point" – the point in which all lines of the drawing converge – the more skewed it will be.

Meanwhile, **shading** is the representation of the effects of light hitting the object in the drawing. To this effect, an object directly hit by light will be brighter while objects that are not will be darker. Applying this principle in drawing will make the object more realistic by giving it volume and texture. A simple cirlce will become a sphere or a ball with the application of correct shading.

Basic Shapes

Circle

1. Before drawing anything on Photoshop, make sure that you make a new layer for your drawing. Use this new layer and other succeeding layers in drawing. Click the Elliptical Marquee Tool and draw a circle. It is located on the Tools Menu. To draw a perfect circle, continuously press down the "Shift" key while moving the mouse to the desired radius of the circle. The dimensions of the circle will be shown while you are dragging the mouse.

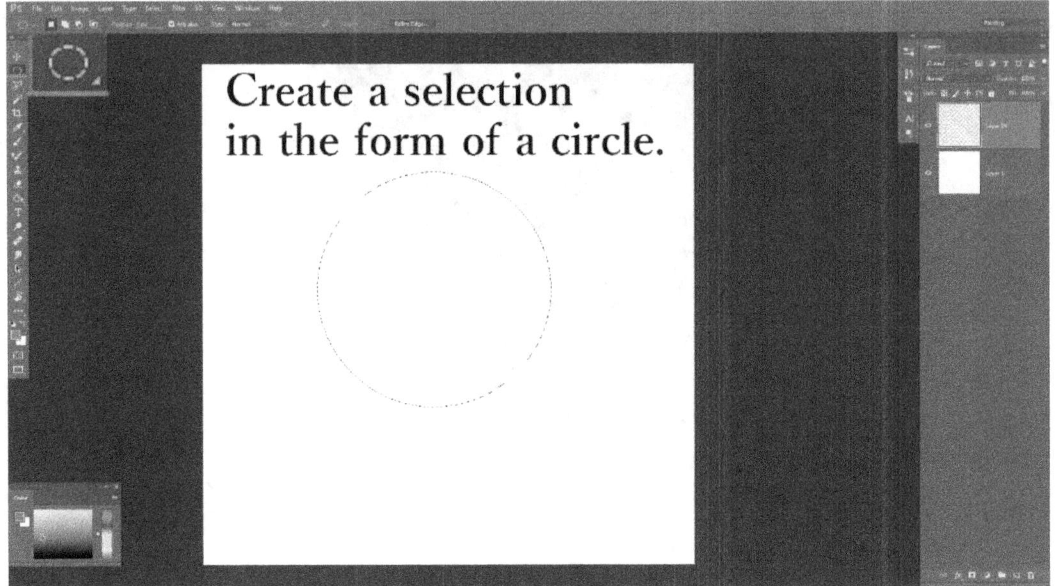

2. Click the Paint Bucket tool. Select a color and click inside the circle to fill it. The color can be selected form the Colors Panel. To fill in the shape, just click at any point inside the circle.

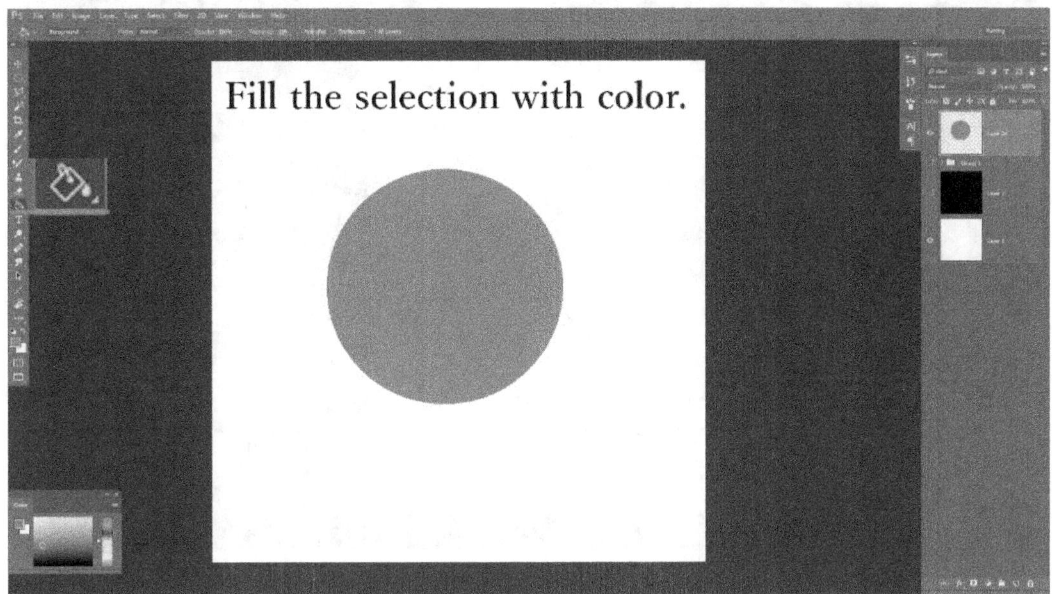

3. While holding down both the Ctrl and Alt keys simultaneously, drag the layer downwards to copy it and its contents.

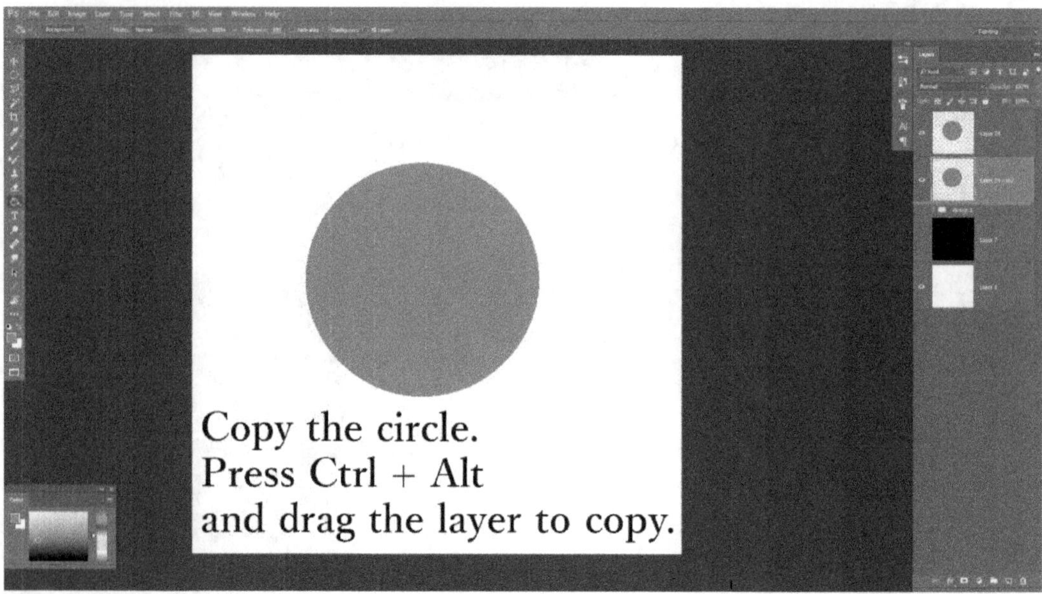

4. To select the circle, press Ctrl+T, as shown. This will open a transformation box around the drawing.

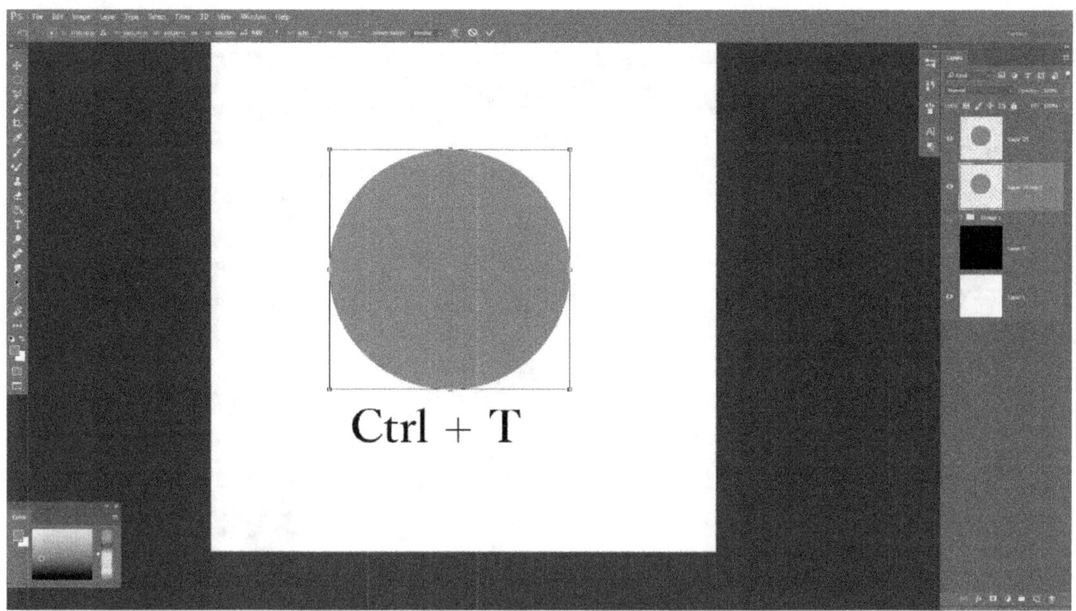

5. Using the nodes of the Transformation Box, adjust the circle to make it appear as if it is lying on a flat surface. Move this transformed circle directly under the first one.

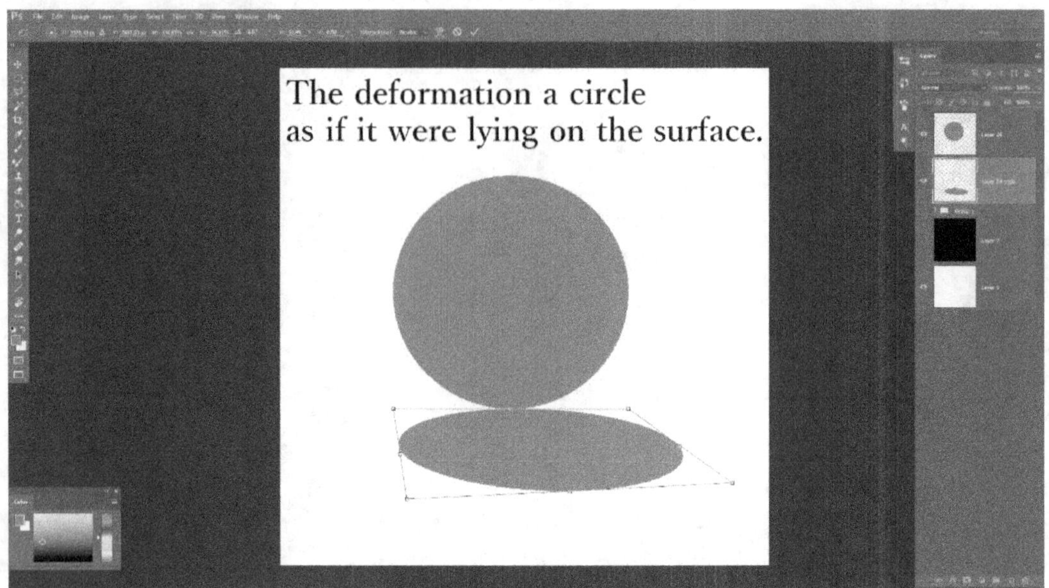

6. On the first circle, select it with the Magic Wand tool. While it is selected, pull up the Levels window by pressing Ctrl+L. Change the value highlighted to a number below 1.00 to darken it. On this image, 0.73 is used as the value.

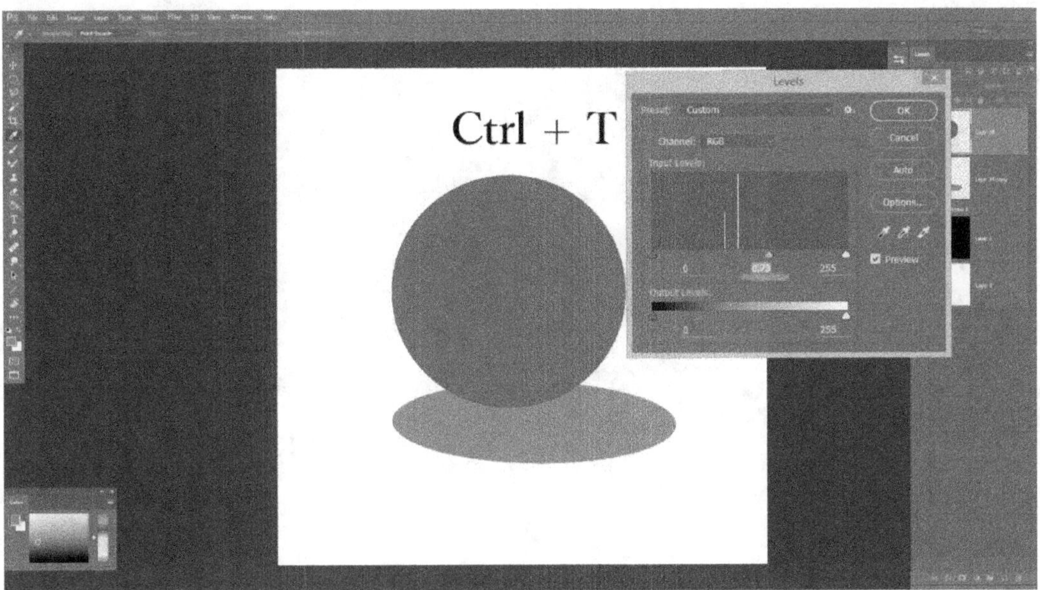

7. Select the Brush Tool and pull up the Brushes Menu. To pull it up, press the Right Mouse button on any point of the Workspace. Select the Soft Round Brush. Lock the current layer on the Layers Panel.

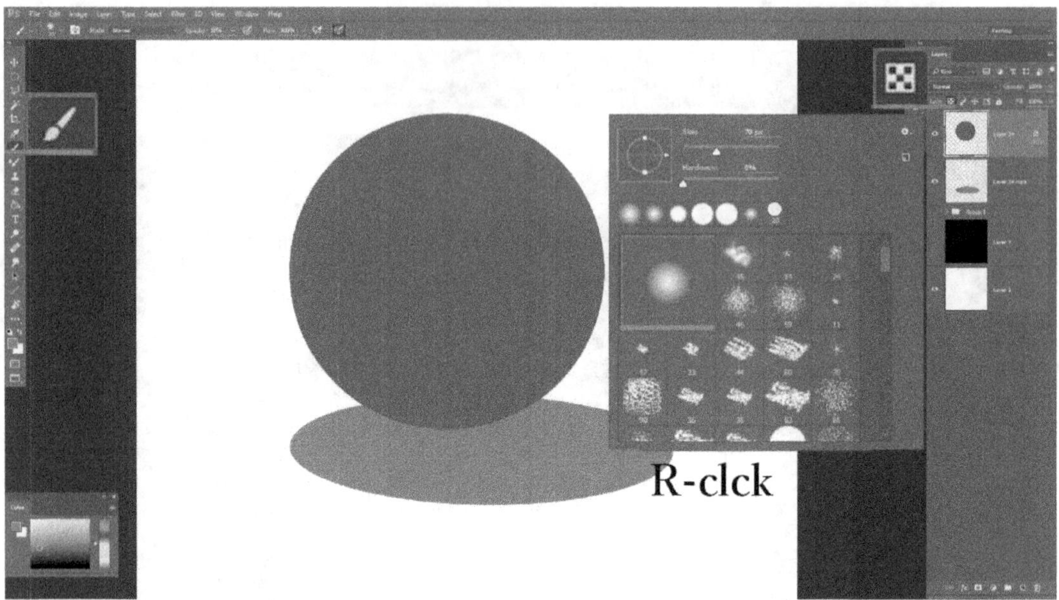

8. With the Dodge Tool, highlight the very top and two points in which the shadow intersects the circle. Use the Midtones Range with an Exposure of 42%.

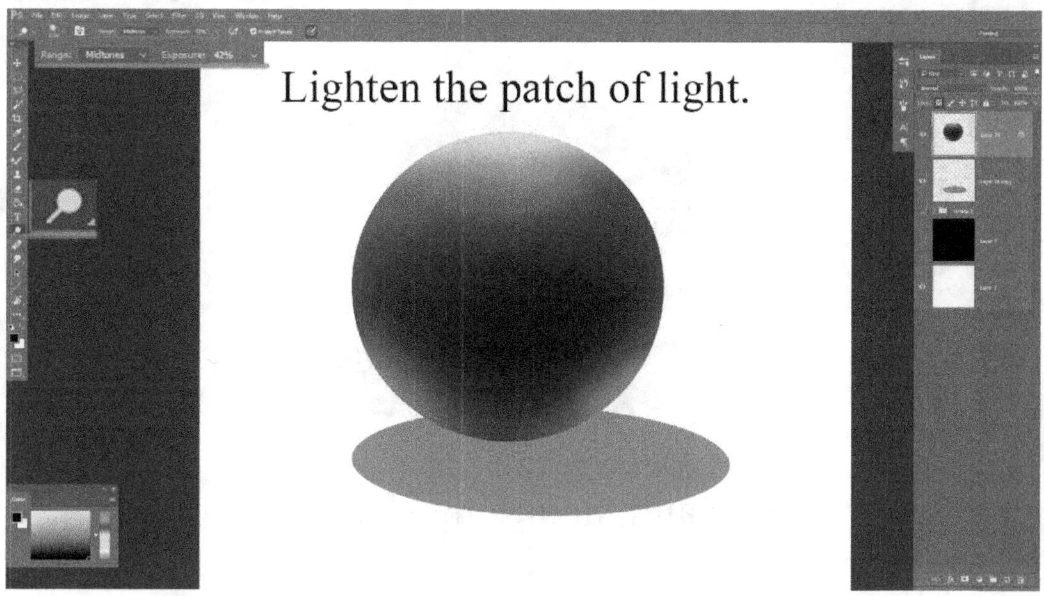

9. Darken the some parts of the circle and the shadow using the Burn Tool. Use Shadows for the Range and 16% for Exposure.

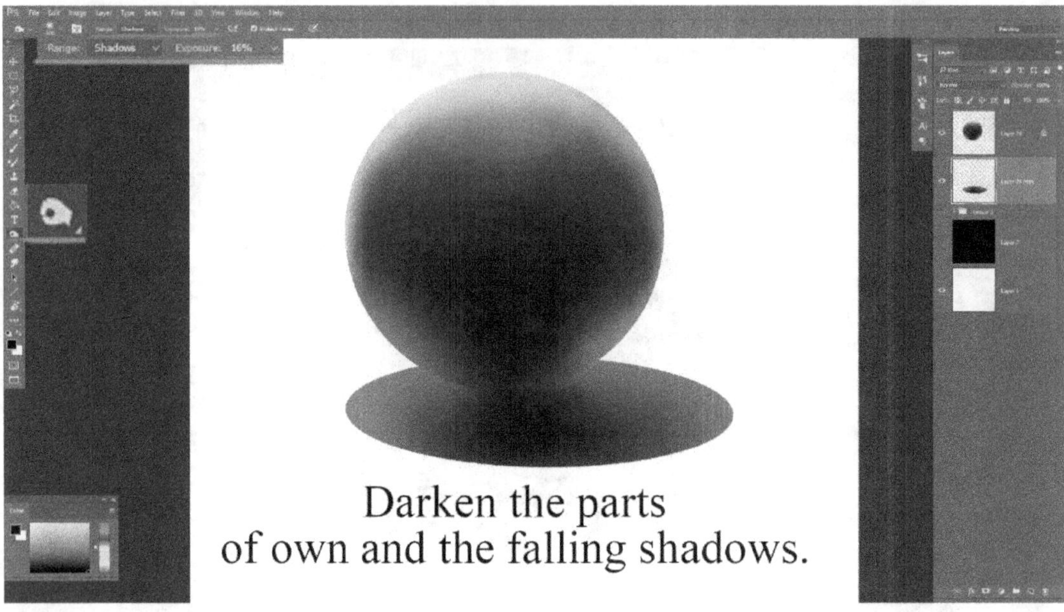

Darken the parts
of own and the falling shadows.

10. Copy the shadow's layer.

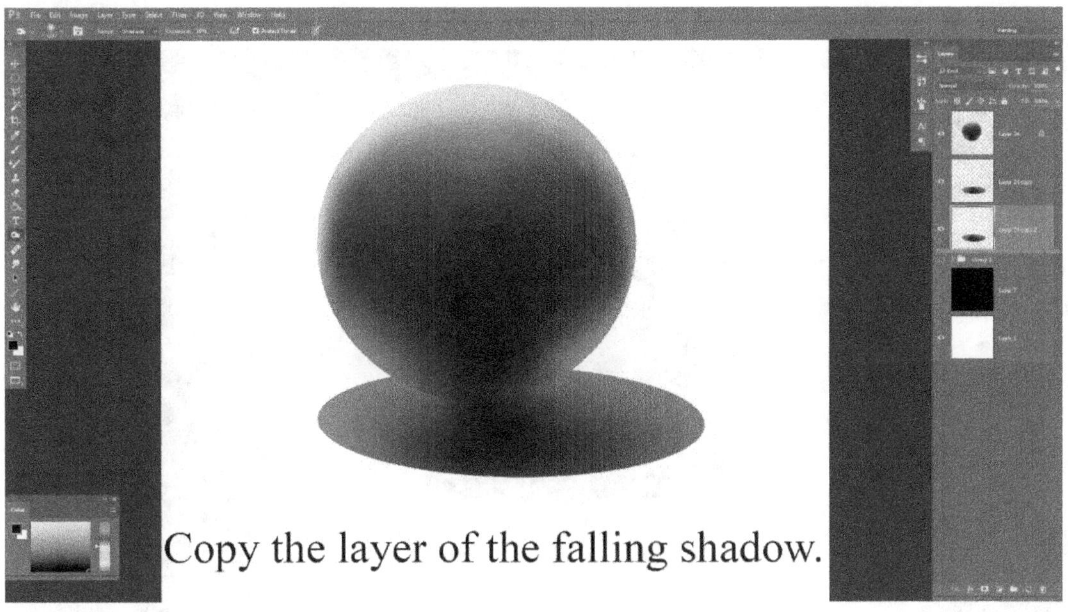

Copy the layer of the falling shadow.

11. On this copy apply the Gaussian Blur. This is found on the Menu bar. Follow Filter > Blur > Gaussian Blur.

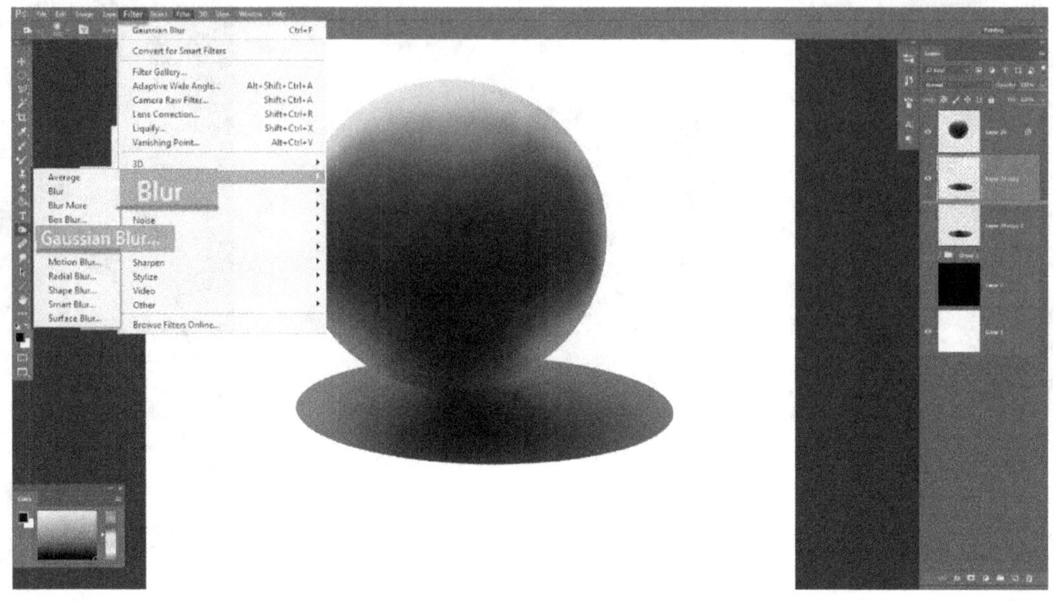

12. Set the Gaussian Blur's radius to 35.

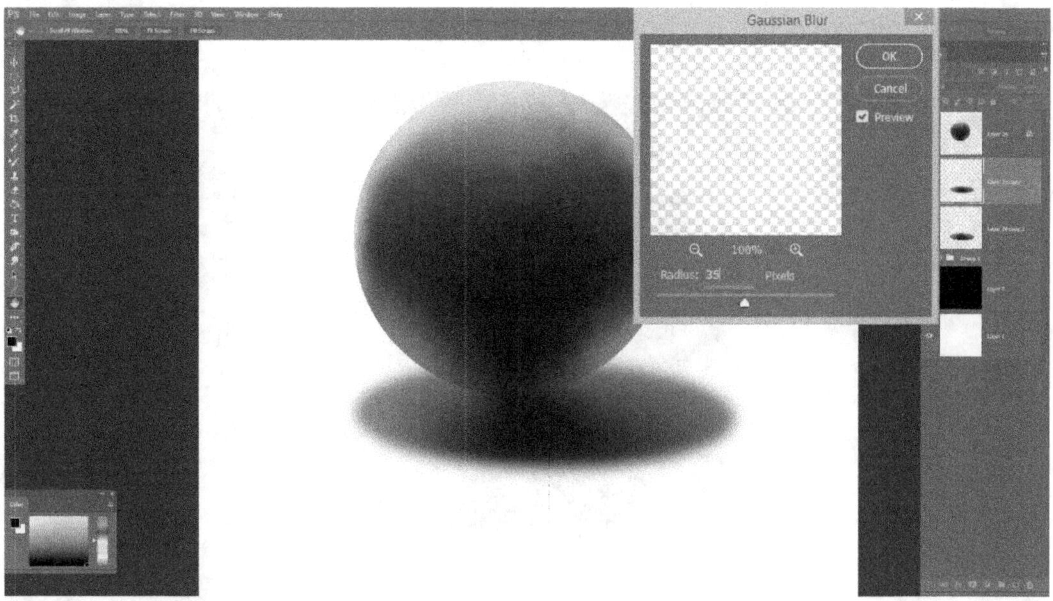

13. Hide the copy of the shadow's layer. Click the box with the eye icon next to the layer icon in the Layer Panel. With the Rectangle Marquee Tool, mark out a rectangle covering part of the shadow.

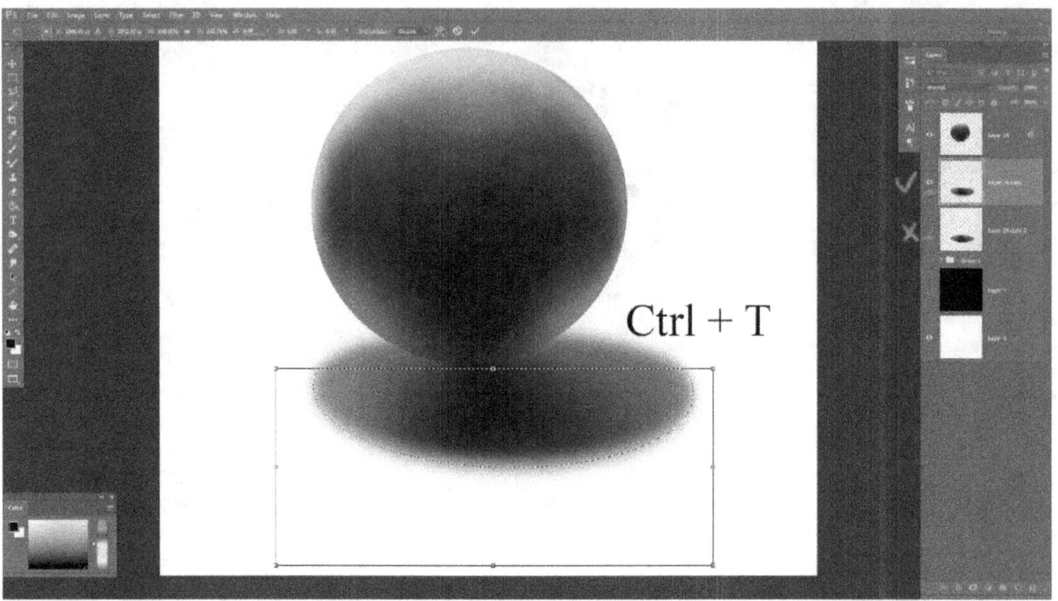

14. Erase a part of the blurred layer to expose some of the unchanged one.

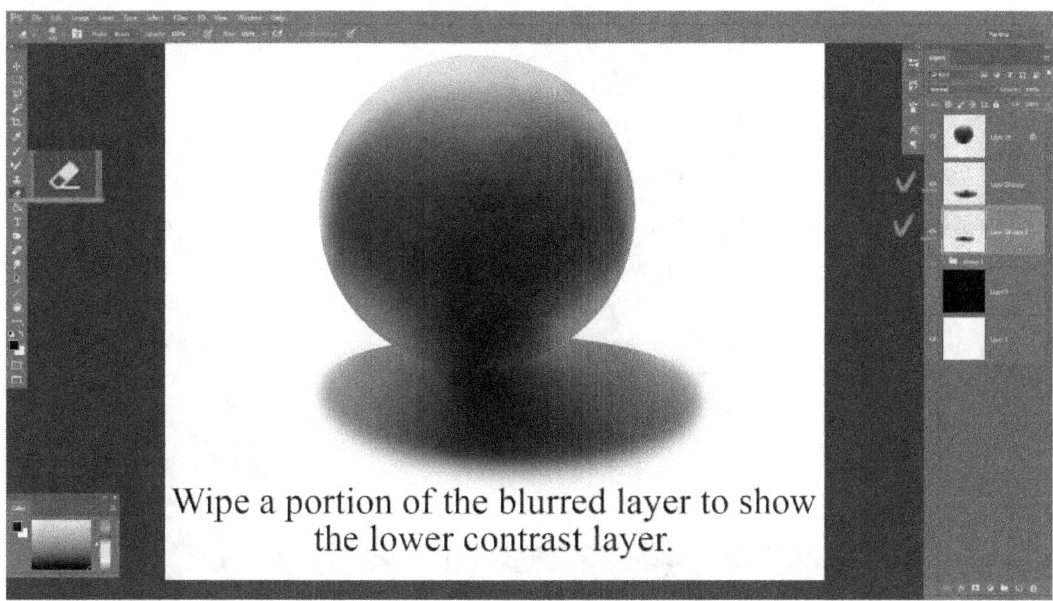

15. Merge the two layers of the shadow together.

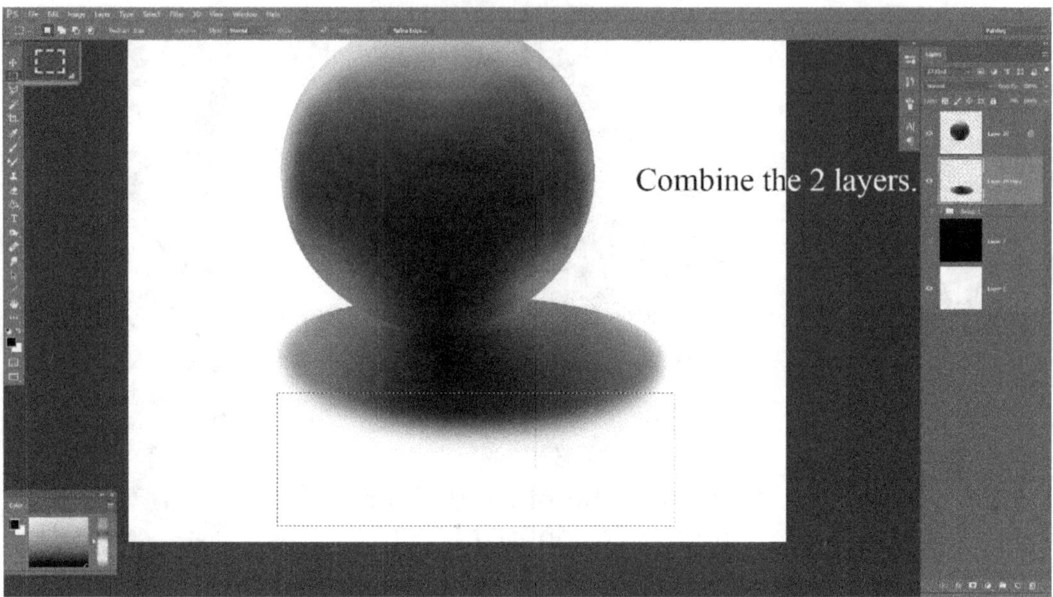

16. Select a portion of this new layer and transform it.

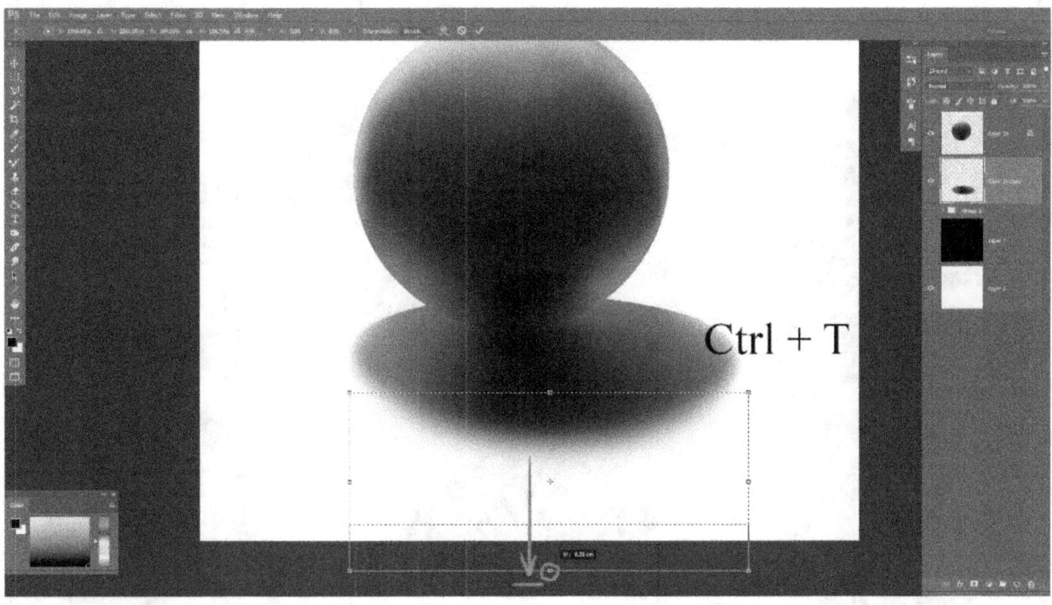

17. Press Ctrl+U to pull up the Hue/Saturation window for the shadow's layer. Decrease the value for saturation to the desired level. A value of -50 was used for this image.

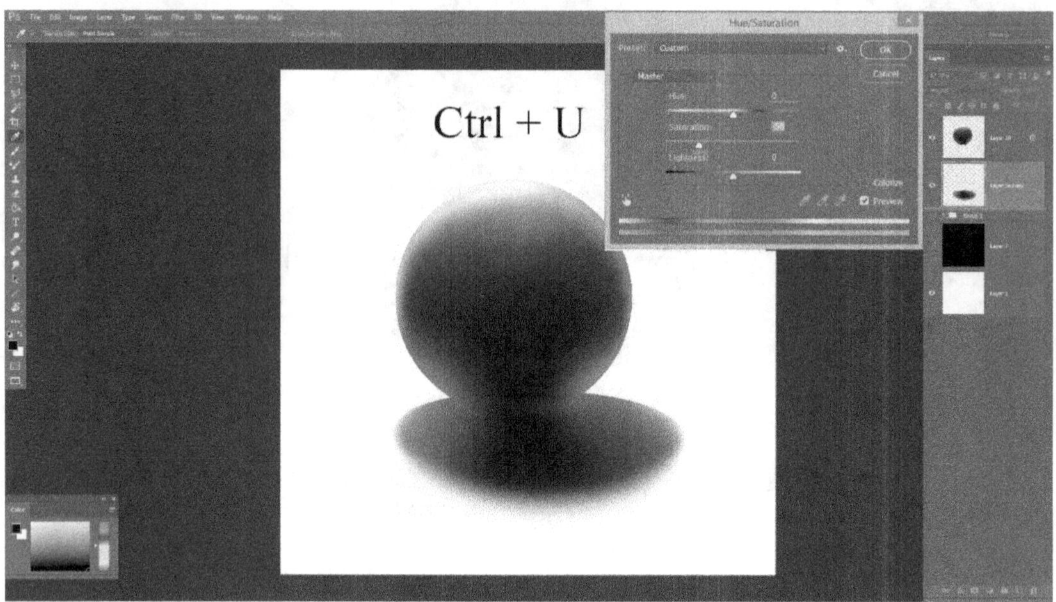

Rectangle

1. On a new layer, mark a square using the Rectangular Marquee Tool. Hold the Shift key to make a perfect square.

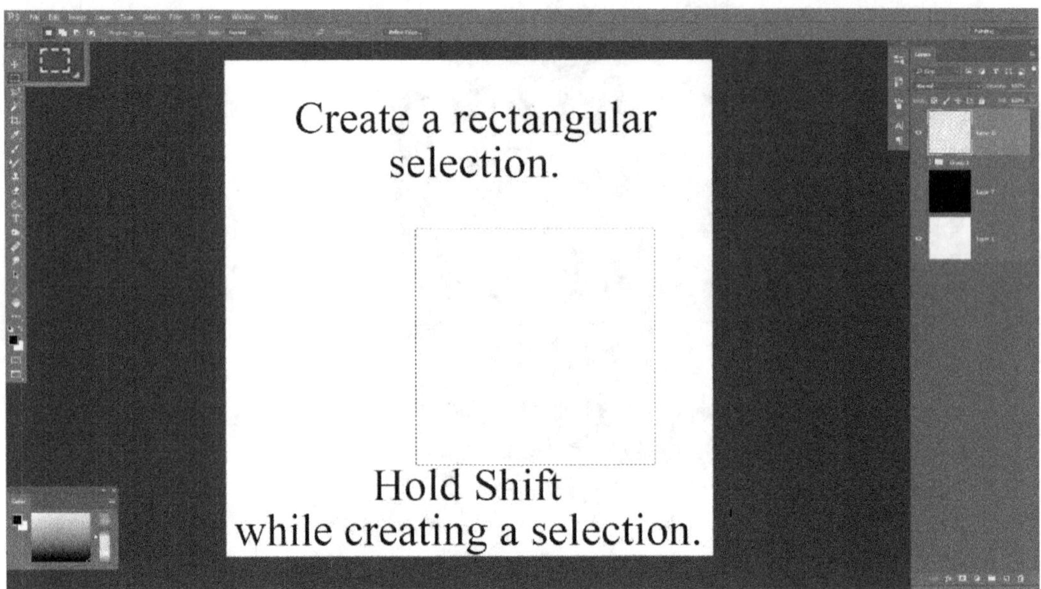

2. Fill the square with any color with the Paint Bucket tool.

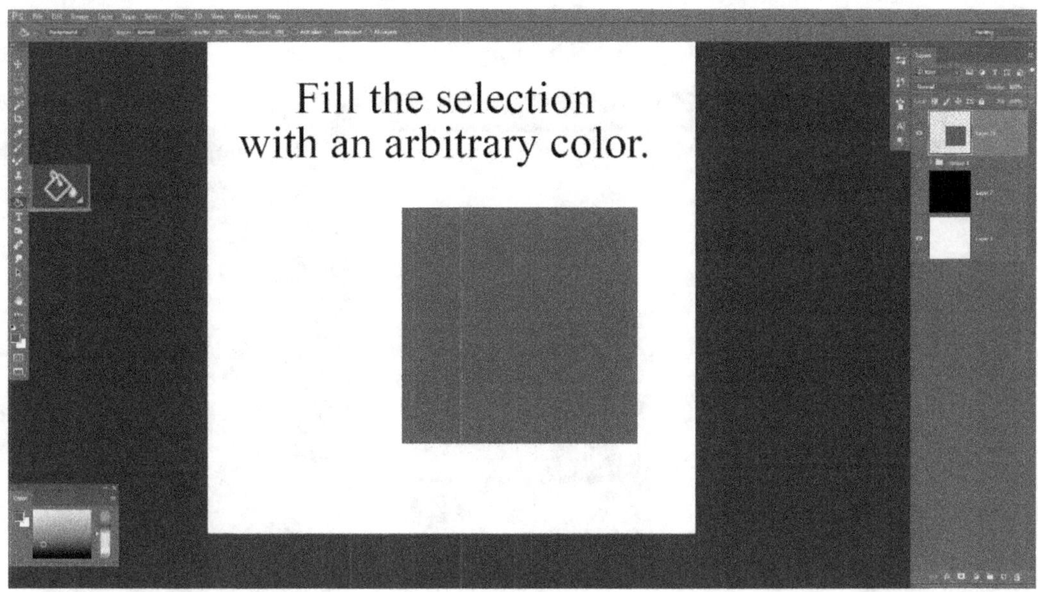

3. Press Ctrl+T and transform the square into a trapezoid. To drag individual points of the transformation area, hold the Ctrl key while dragging the point.

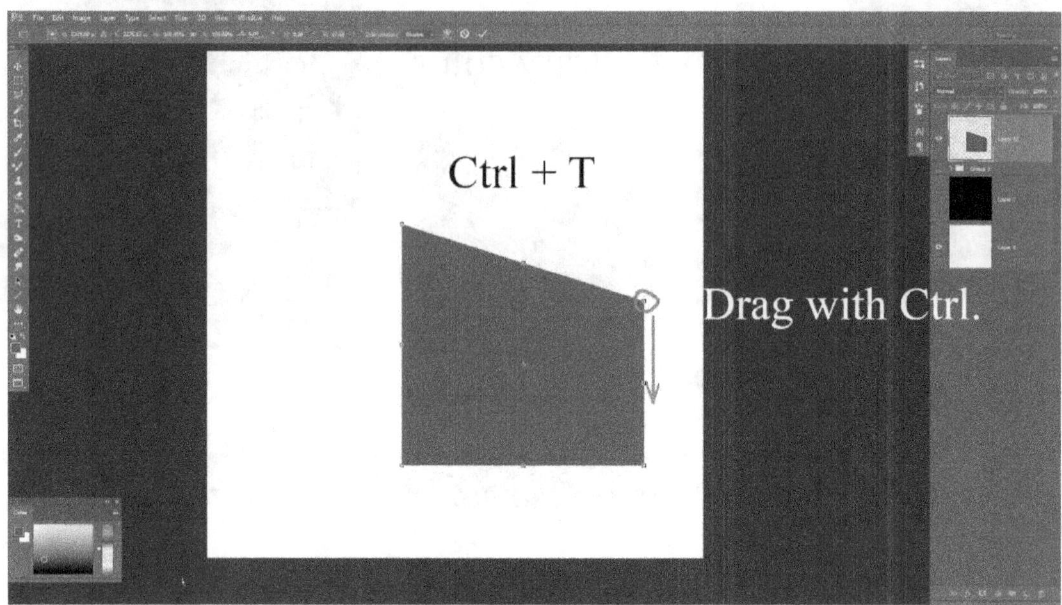

4. Make the trapezoid narrower by dragging the middle node of the transformation area.

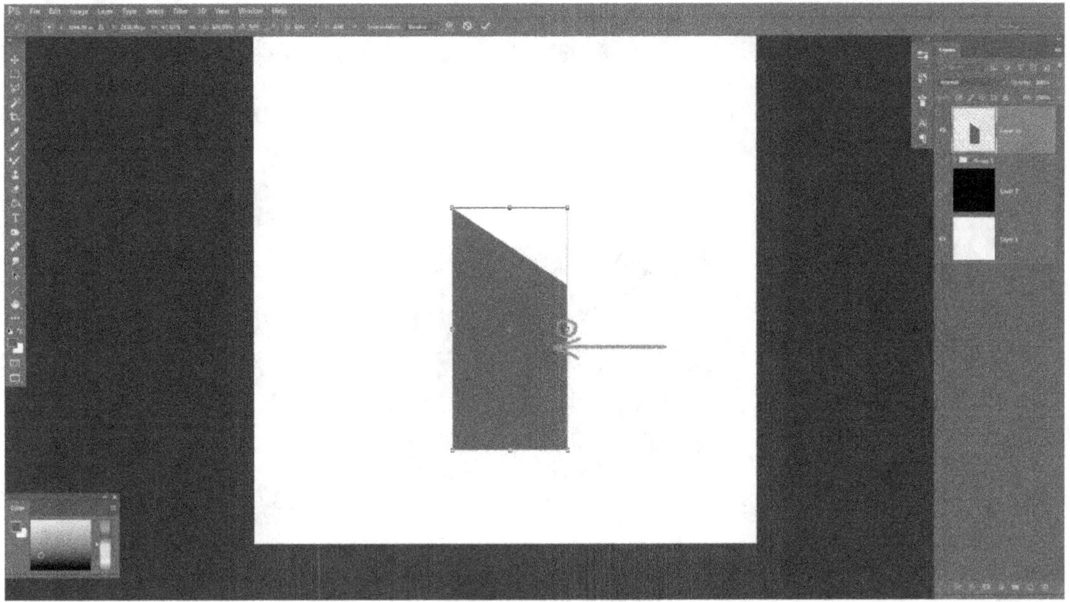

5. Draw another square on a different layer. Transform this square into a trapezoid as well.

6. Move one of the shapes and place it next to the other.

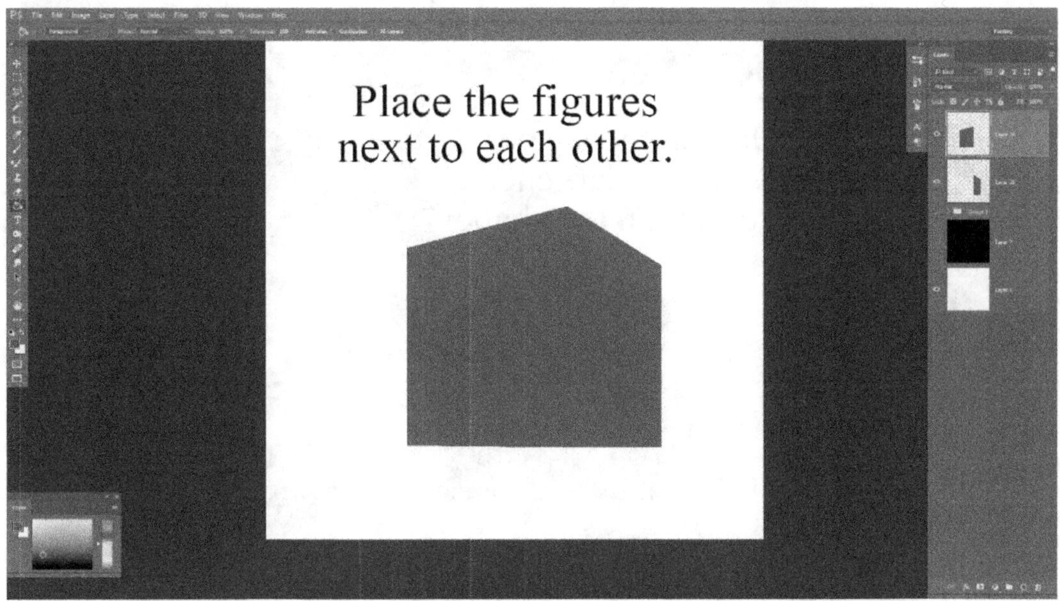

7. Darken one of the shapes by adjusting its levels. The Levels window can be accessed by pressing Ctrl+L, while the shape is selected.

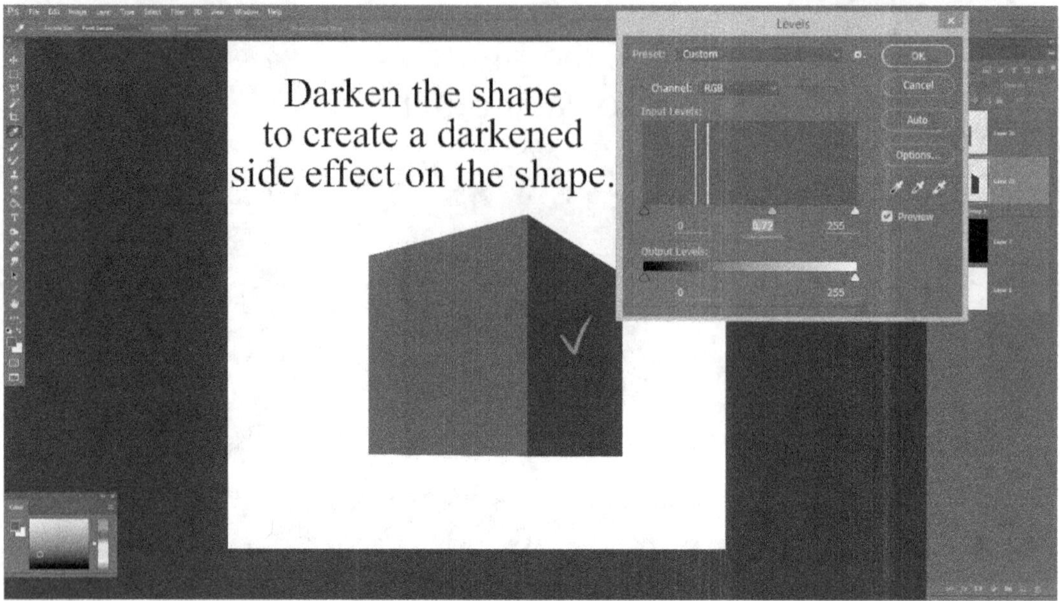

8. Drag the lower corner of the darkened shape down.

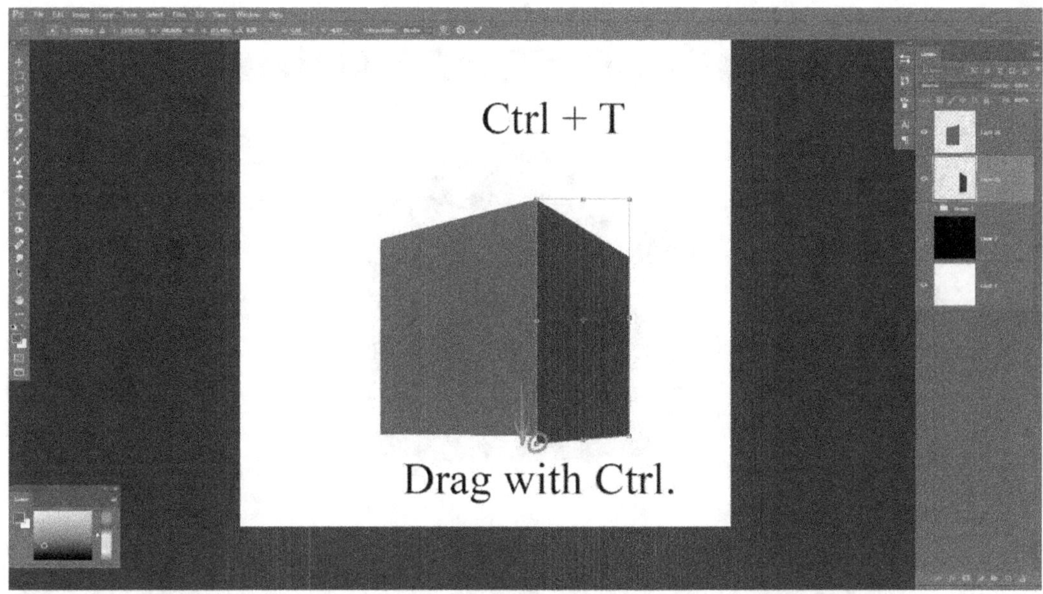

9. On the other shape, drag the corner adjacent to the previously adjusted one and lower it to the same point or level.

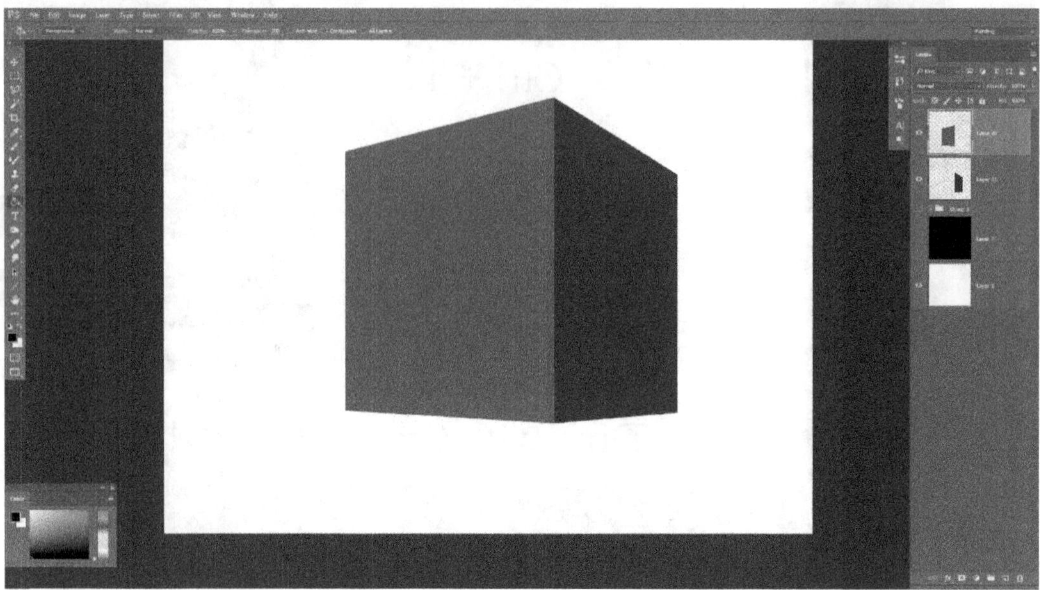

10. Select the two layers, and then press Ctrl+T. Hold the Shift, Ctrl and Alt keys simultaneously and drag one of the top corner points.

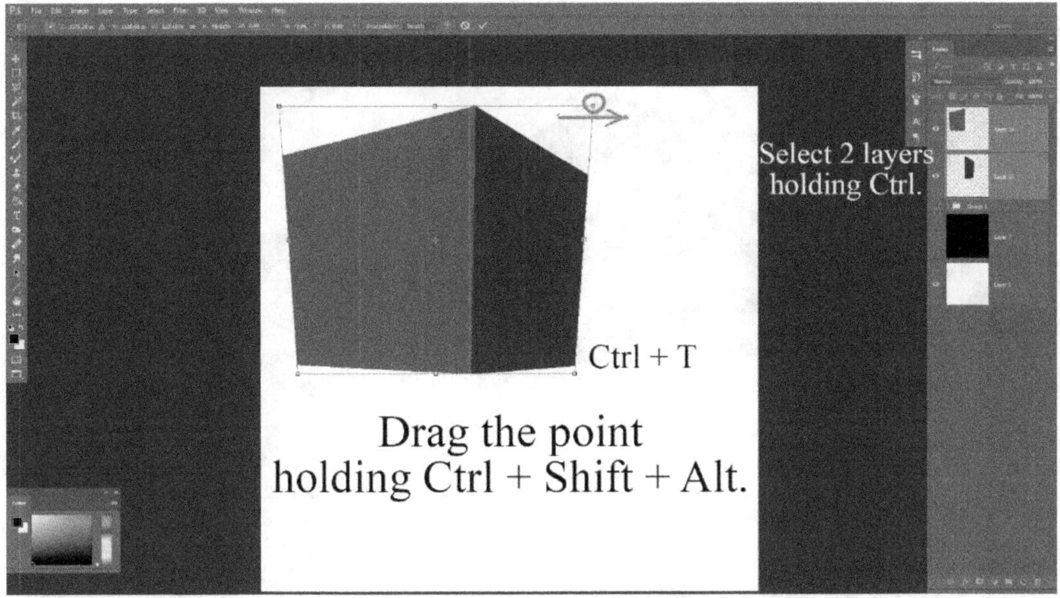

11. Merge the two layers by clicking the Right Mouse Button on the selected layers and choosing "Merge Layers" on the popup menu.

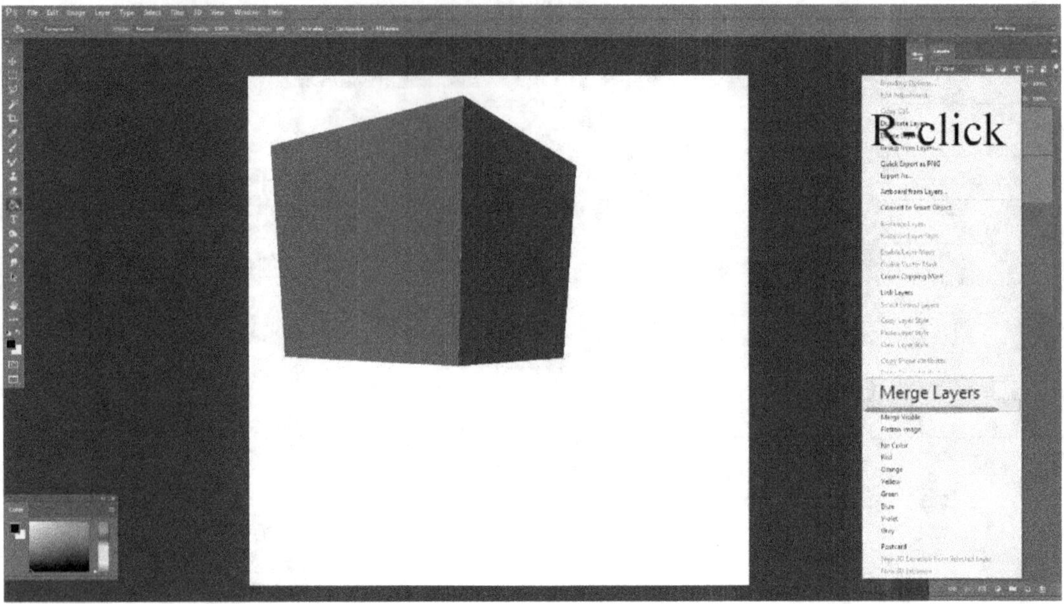

12. Copy the layer and press Ctrl+T again to pull up the transformation area. While holding Ctrl, drag one of the top points down as shown.

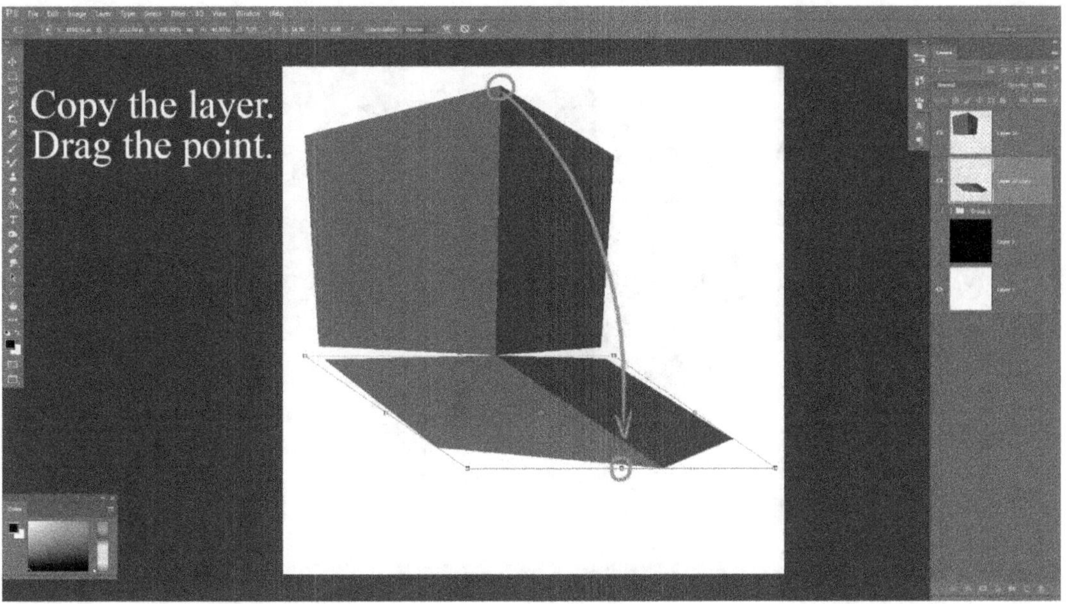

13. While it is still selected, press Ctrl+L to pull up the Levels window and adjust the Output levels all the way down to 0.

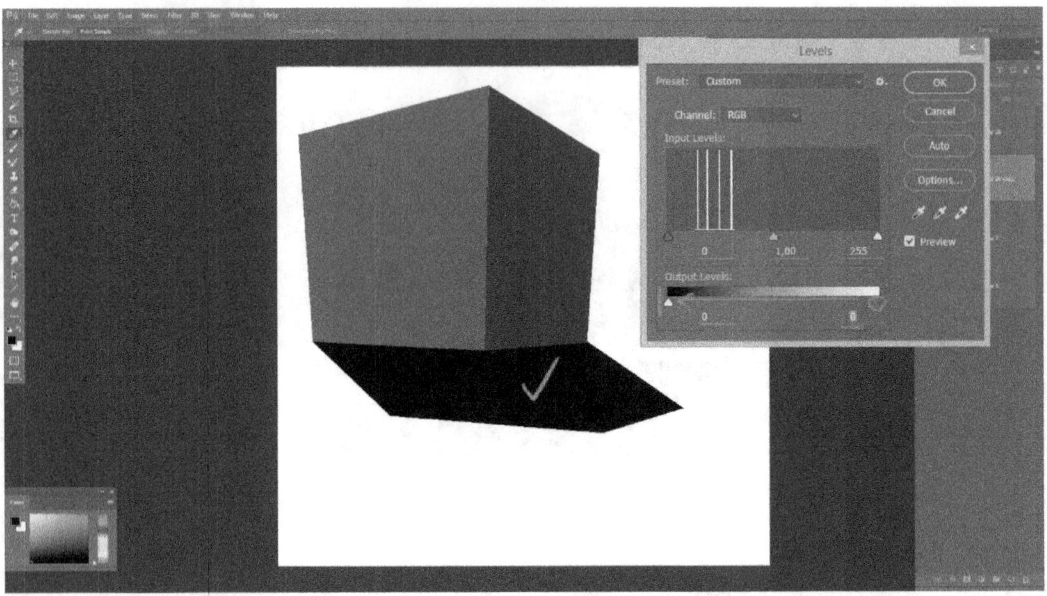

14. Select the lower portion of this figure and right click on it. Choose Feather on the popup menu.

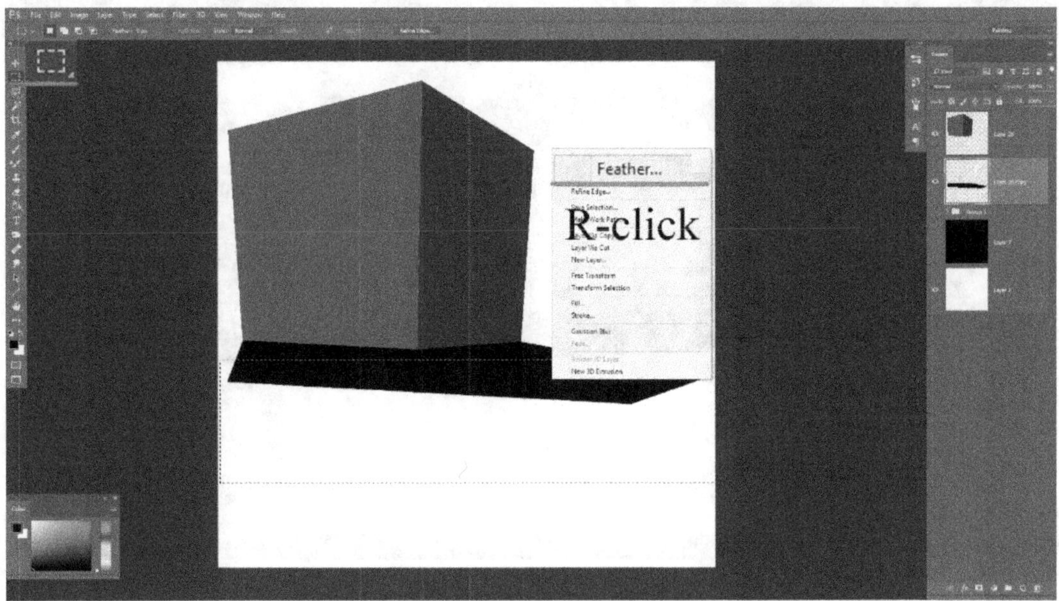

15. Adjust the Feather Radius to 70.

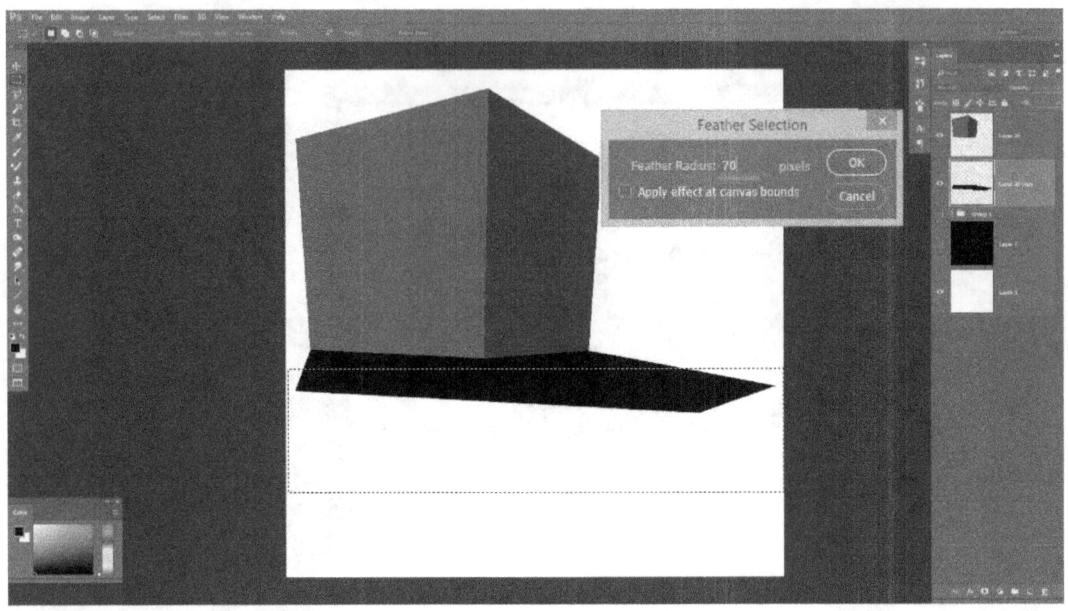

16. On the same selected figure, apply the Gaussian Blur. This can be found in Filters > Blur > Gaussian Blur. Set the radius to 31.8.

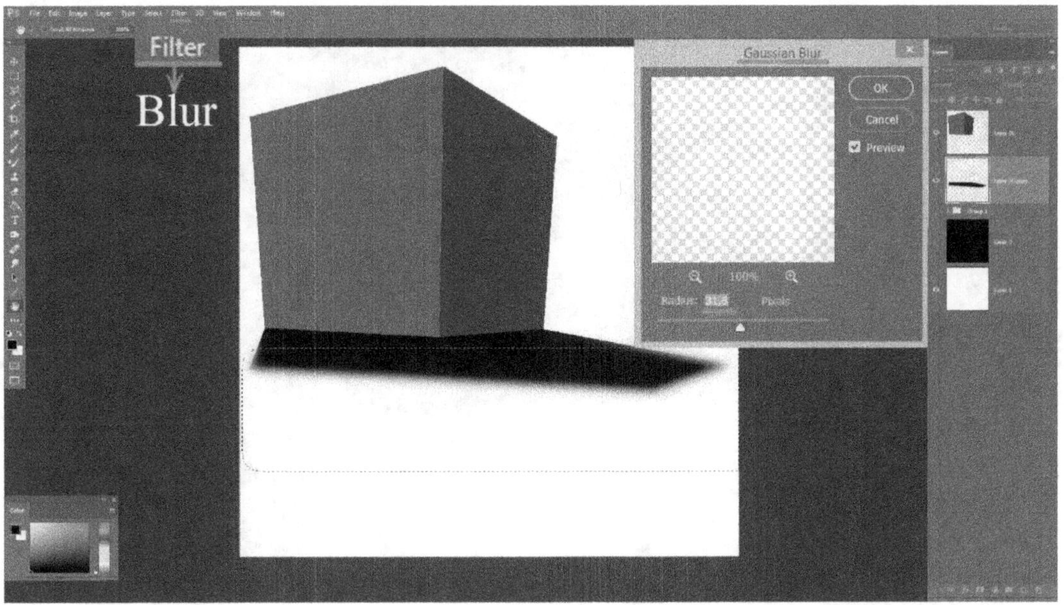

17. Adjust the levels for the entire layer by setting the lower limit of the output levels to 57.

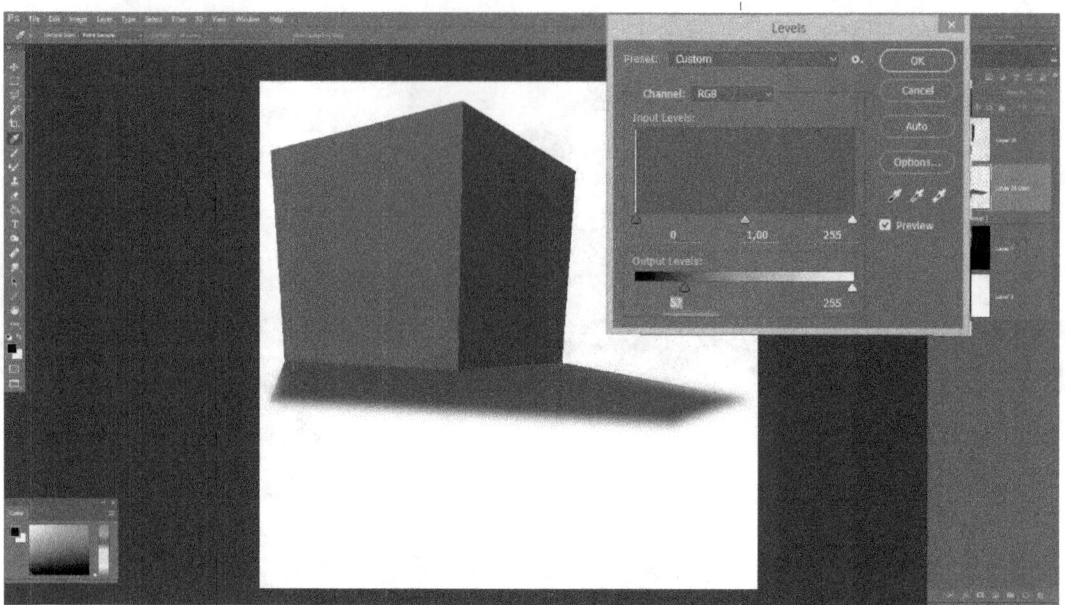

18. Using the Burn Tool, darken the apparent corner of the shape and its intersection with the shadow.

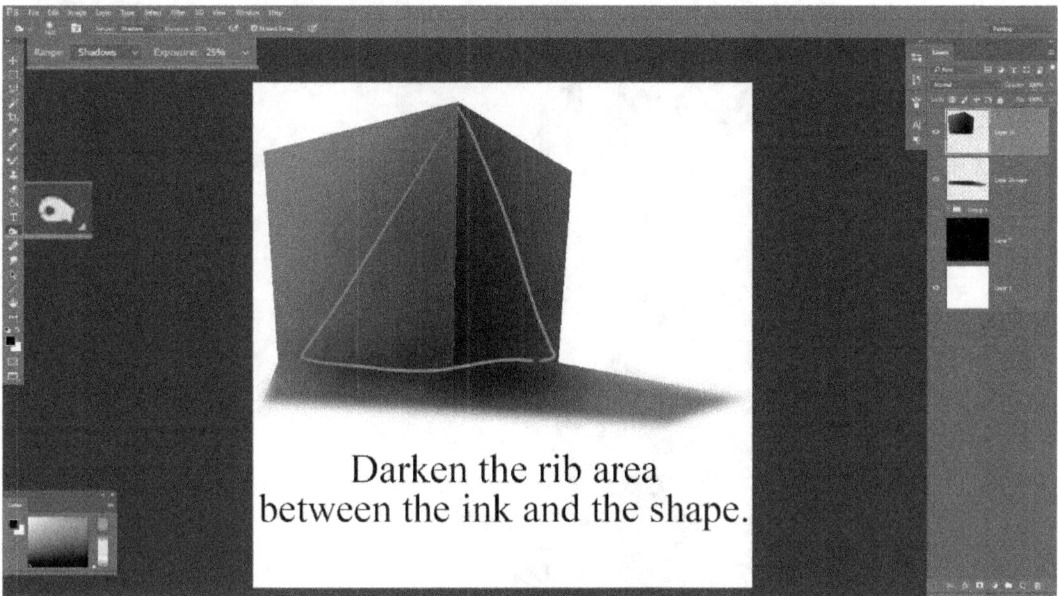

Cylinder

1. Make a new Layer. After that, make a vertical rectangle using the Rectangular Marquee Tool.

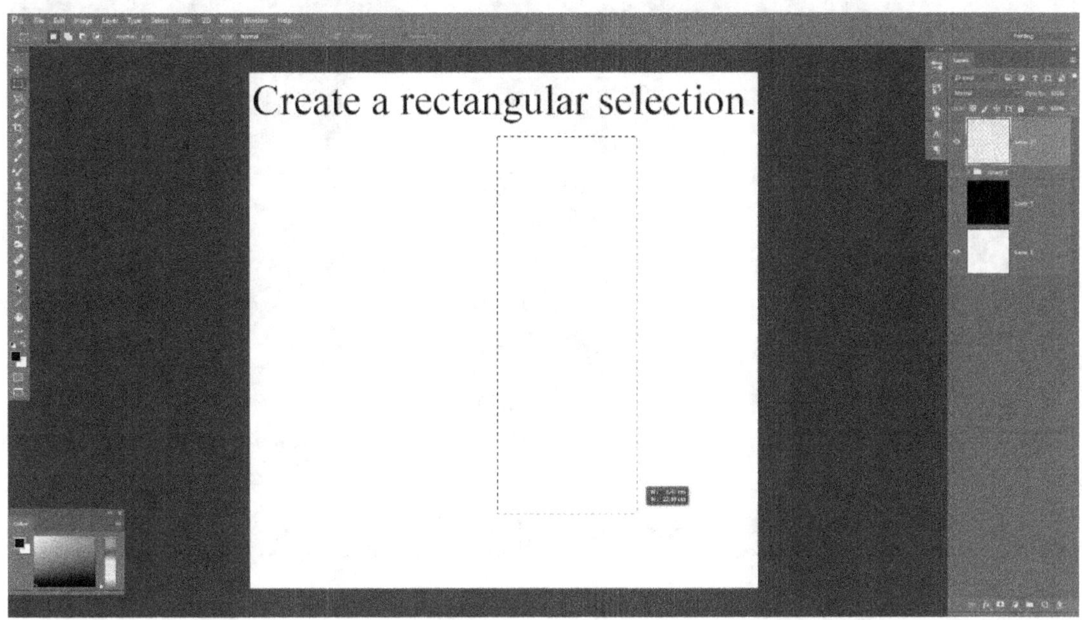

2. Fill the rectangle with any color.

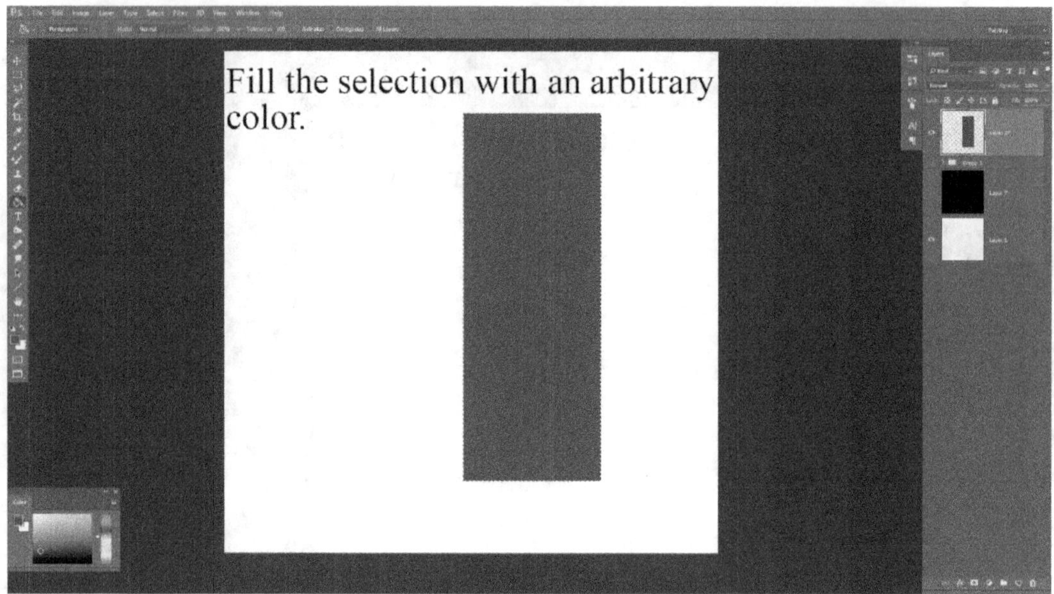

3. Press Ctrl +T and widen the rectangle.

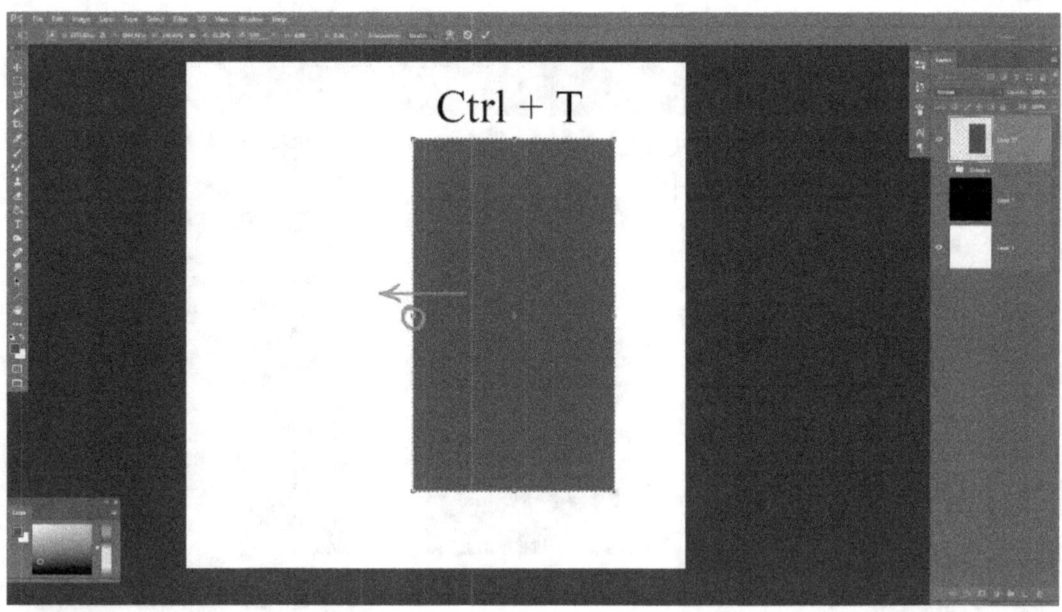

4. On another layer, make a long horizontal oval shape with the Elliptical Marquee Tool.

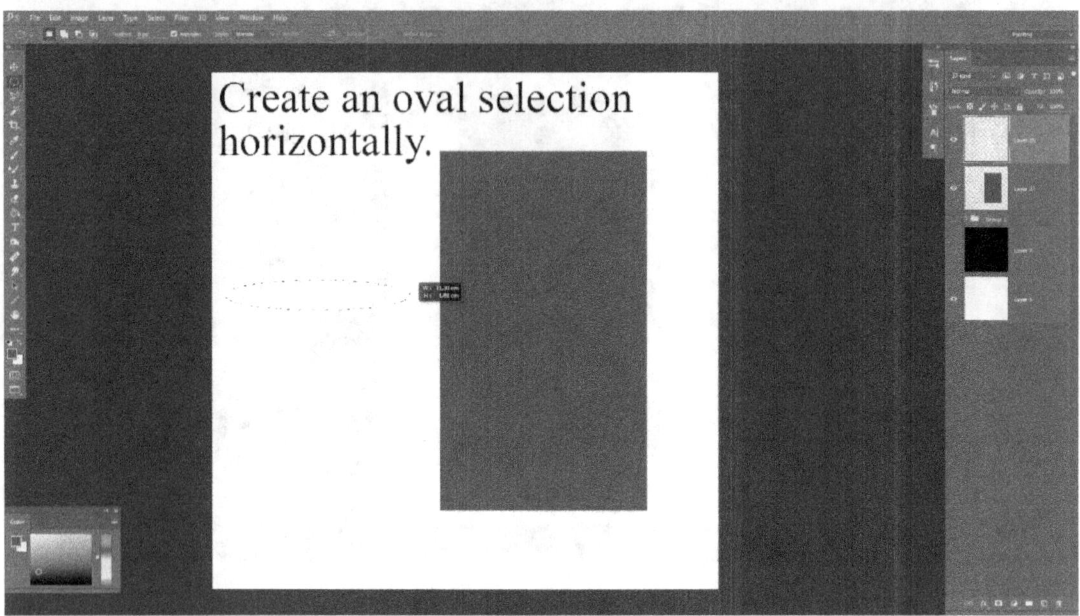

5. Fill this ellipse with the same color as the rectangle. Press Ctrl+L to adjust its levels. Adjust the middle input level to 0.70.

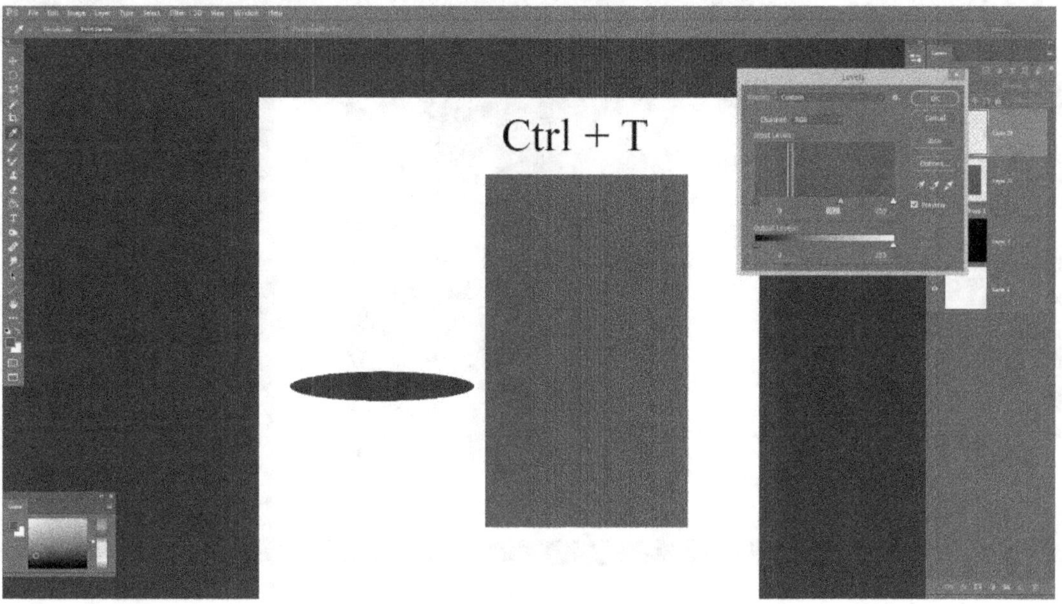

6. Press Ctrl+T and move the ellipse under the rectangle.

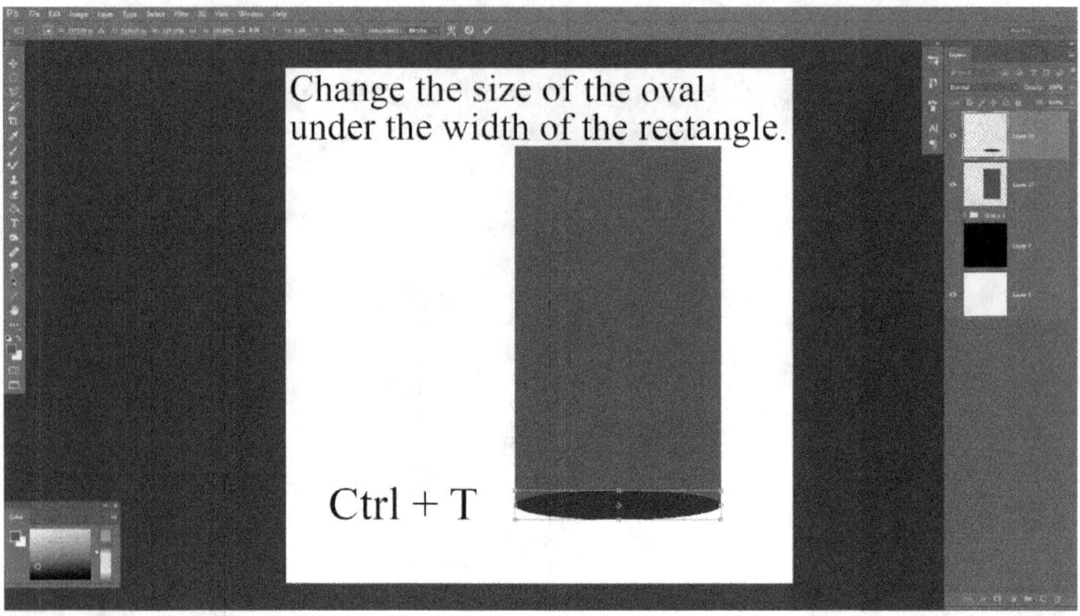

7. Copy the layer of the ellipse. Move the ellipse to the top of the rectangle.

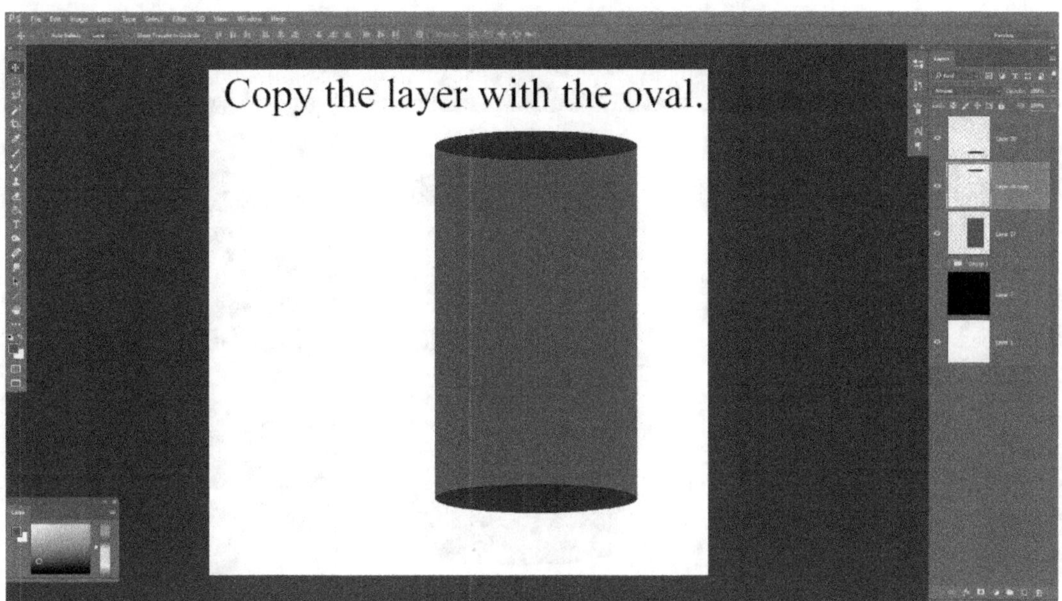

8. While on the copied layer, press Ctrl+T and adjust the height of the ellipse a little bit. Remember to realign the ellipse with the rectangle.

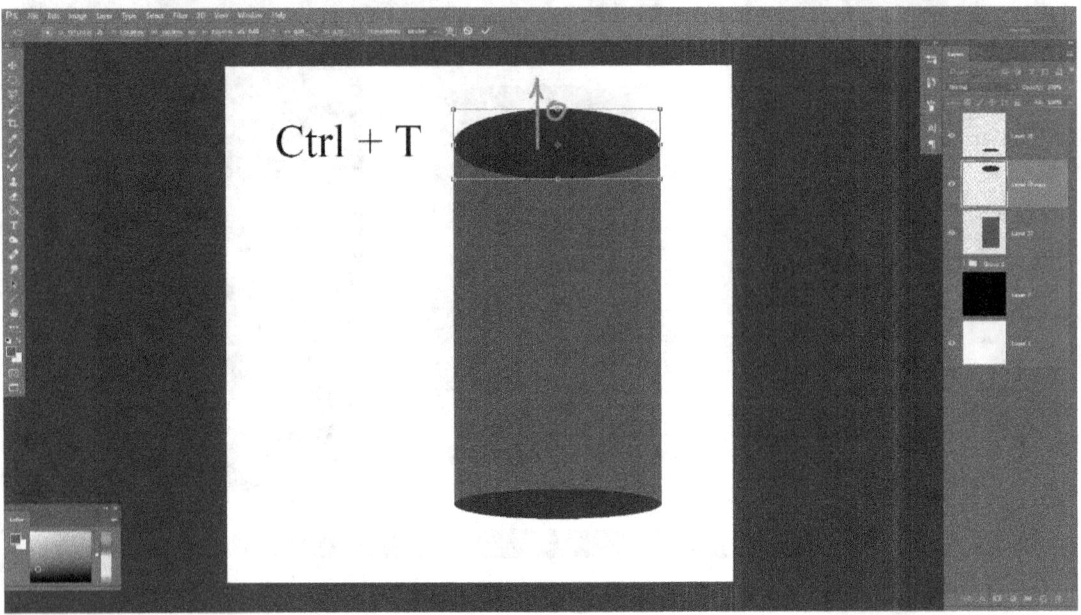

9. Click on the Paint bucket tool. Hold the Alt key over the rectangle and click it to copy its color.

10. Apply this color to the lower ellipse.

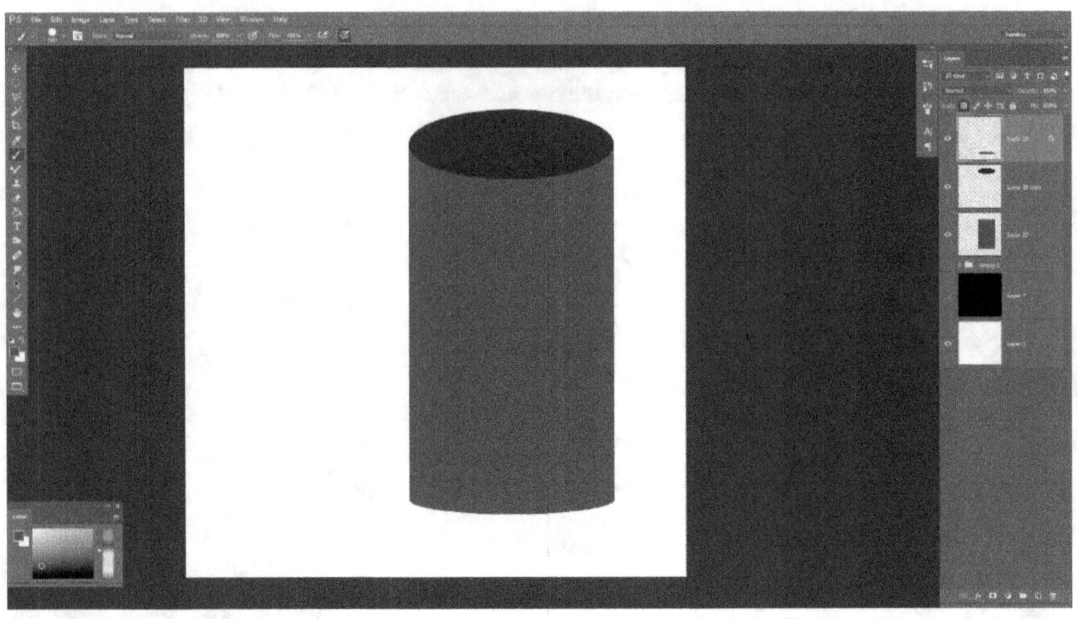

11. Press Ctrl+T and adjust the ellipse's height to the same as that of the upper one. Merge the layers of the rectangle and the lower ellipse by clicking both layers while holding down the Ctrl key. Click the Right Mouse button. Select Merge Layers from the popup menu.

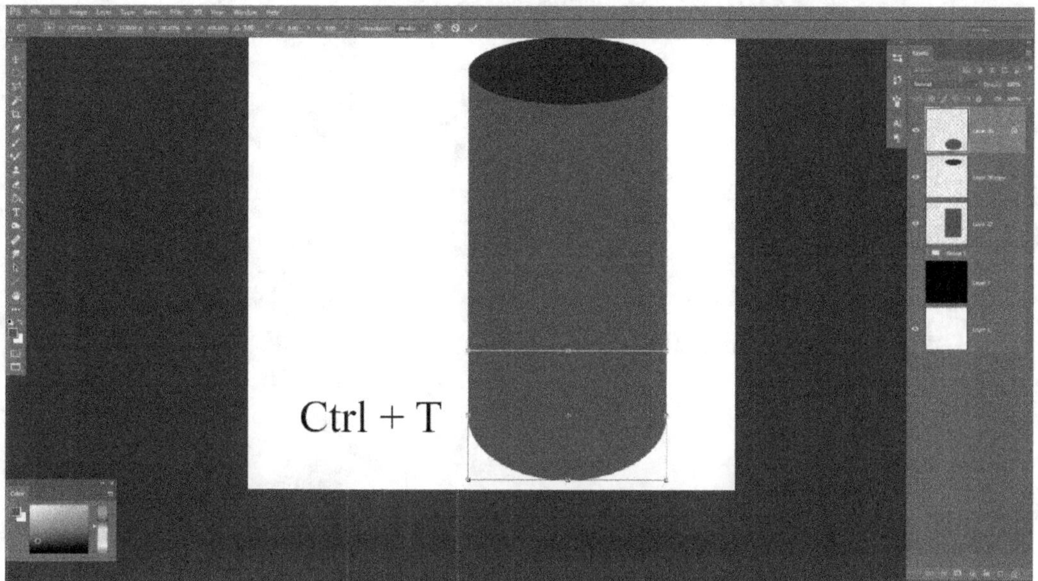

12. Select the Dodge Tool and adjust its parameters for Range and Exposure to Midtones and 100%, respectively. While holding the Shift key down, drag the mouse downwards on the merged rectangle and ellipse figures.

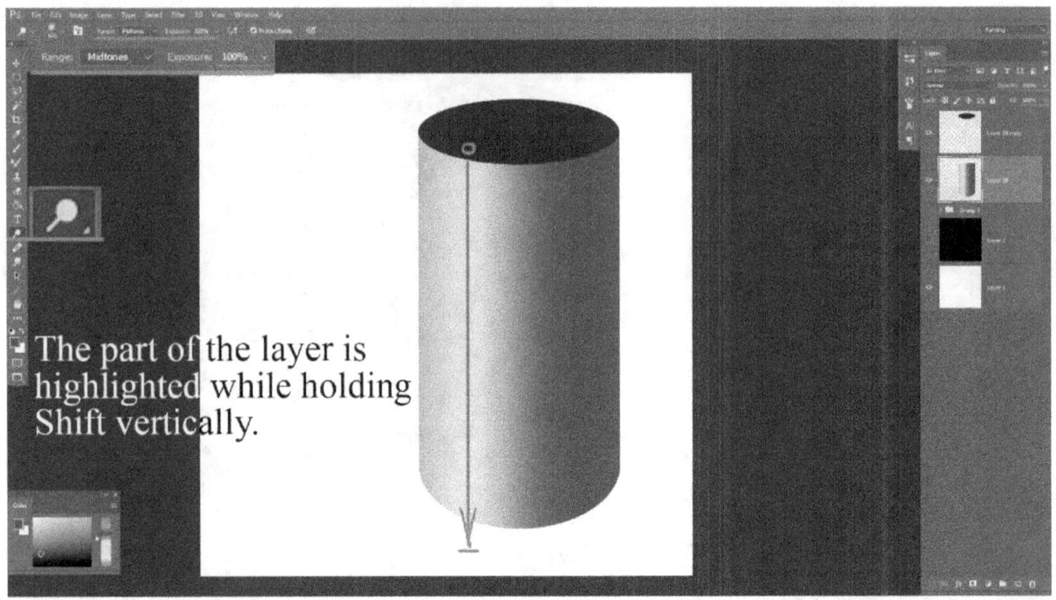

13. Do the same on the figure's right side to draw the highlight of the reflex.

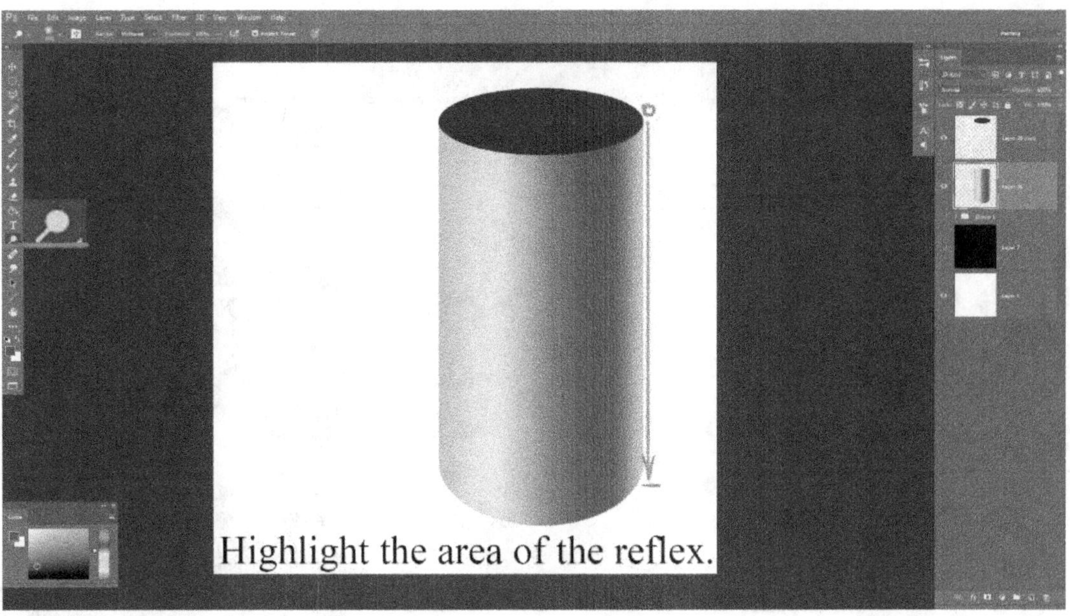

14. Using the Burn Tool and holding the Shift key, drag the mouse downwards between the areas you highlighted earlier.

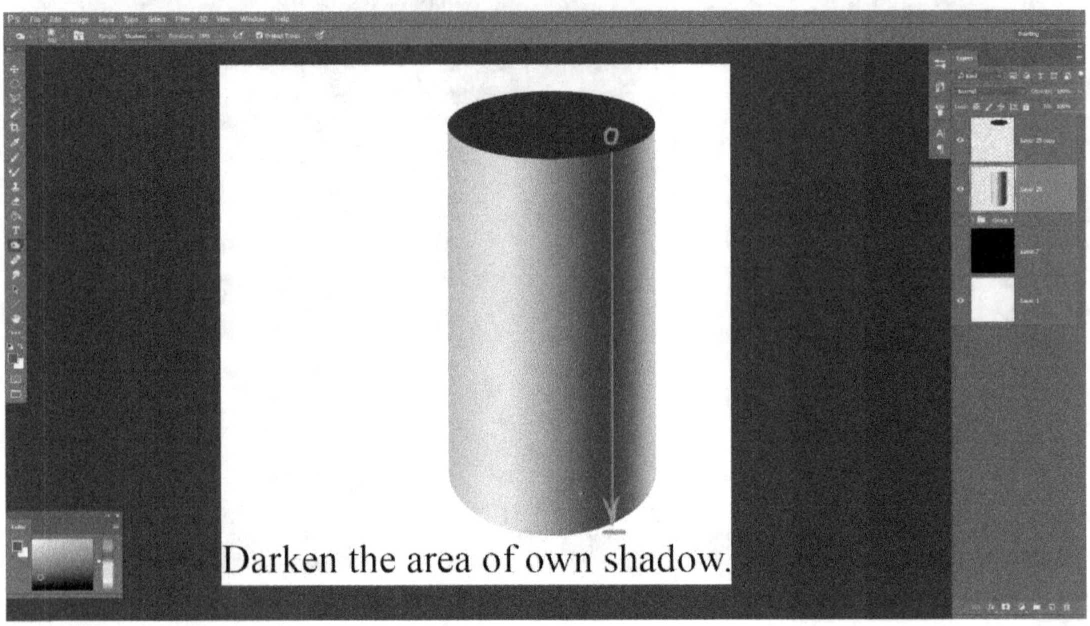

15. Select the layer for the upper ellipse and press Ctrl+L. Adjust the middle Input Level to 2.93.

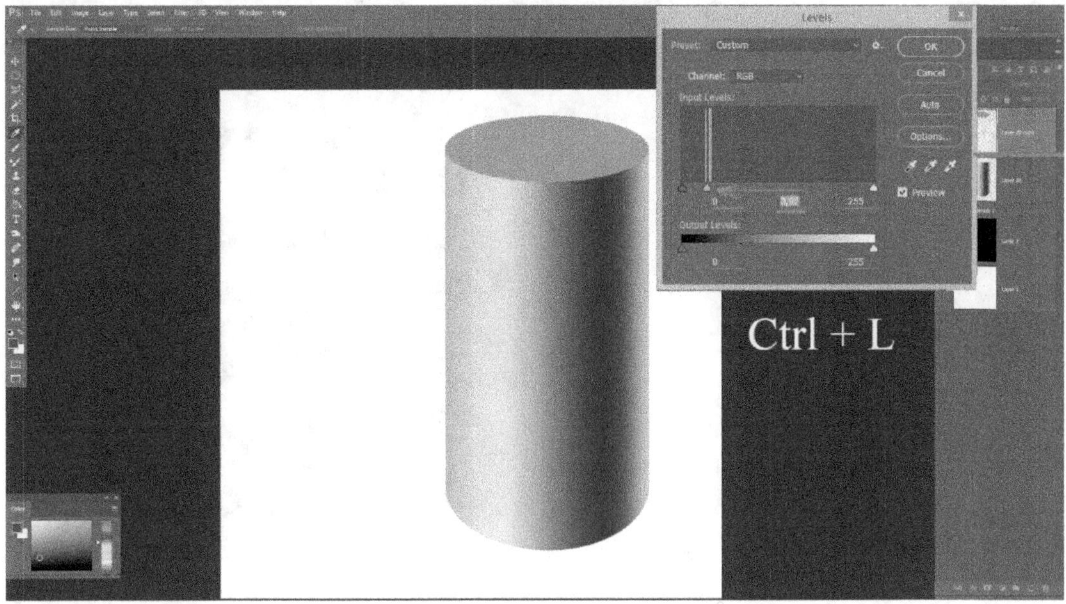

16. Press Ctrl+U and change the value for Saturation to 69.

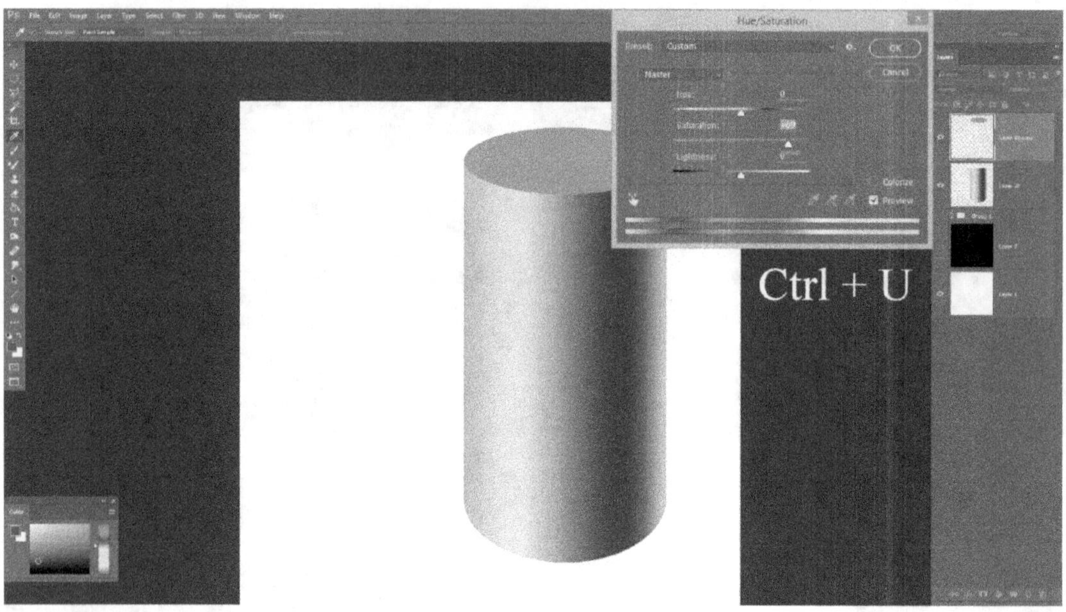

17. Merge all the layers for the figure together and press Ctrl+T. Hold down the Ctrl key and drag the middle left node upwards a little bit to skew the figure.

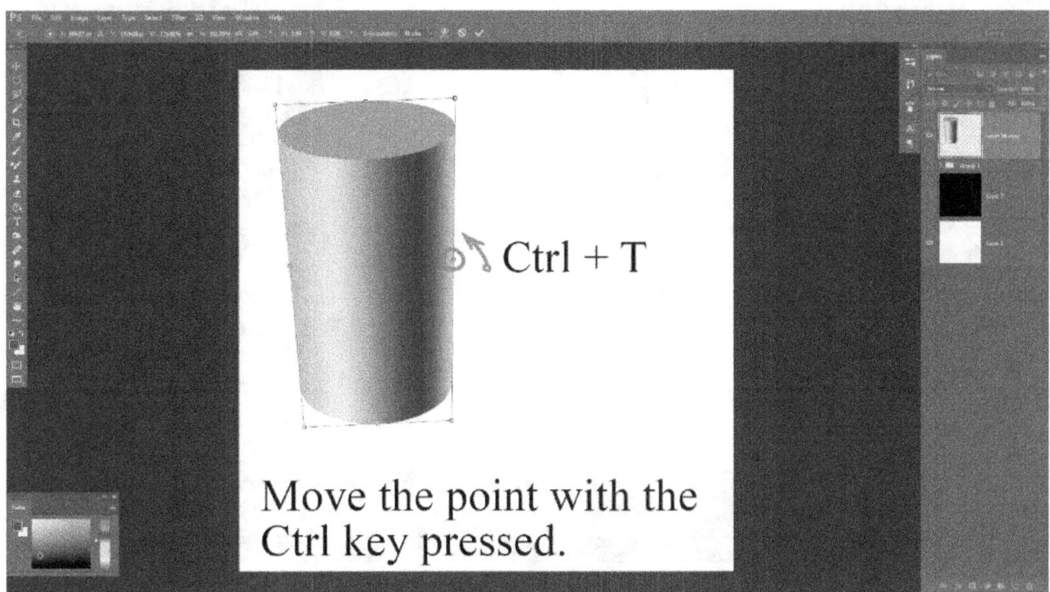

18. Copy the layer and distort the image to make it appear as if it were on a flat surface.

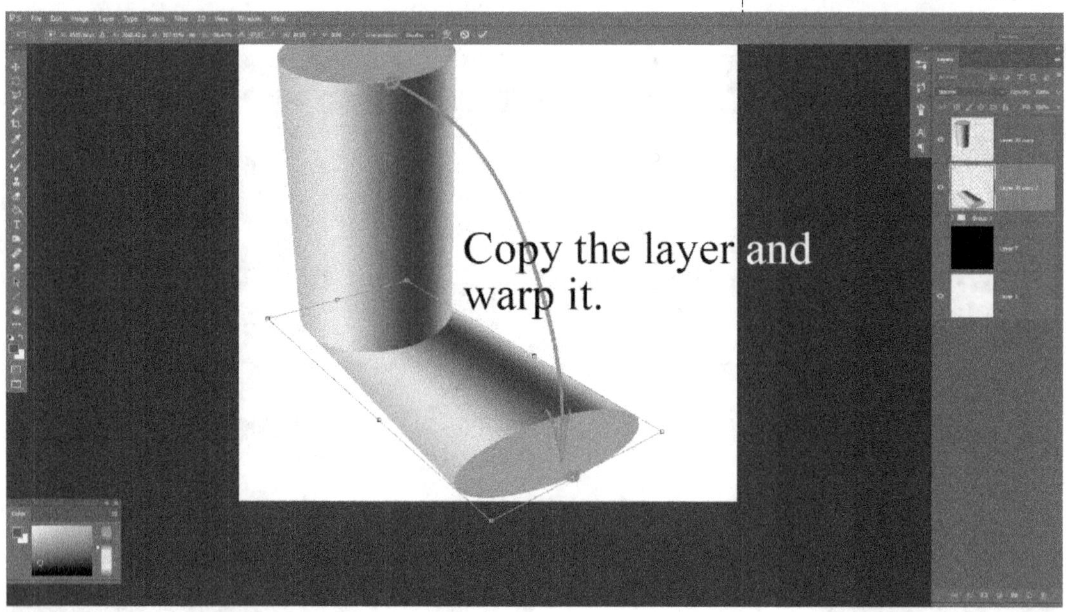

19. Lock the layer. To do this, click the lock icon beside the layer and fill the selected shape with a dark color with the Brush Tool.

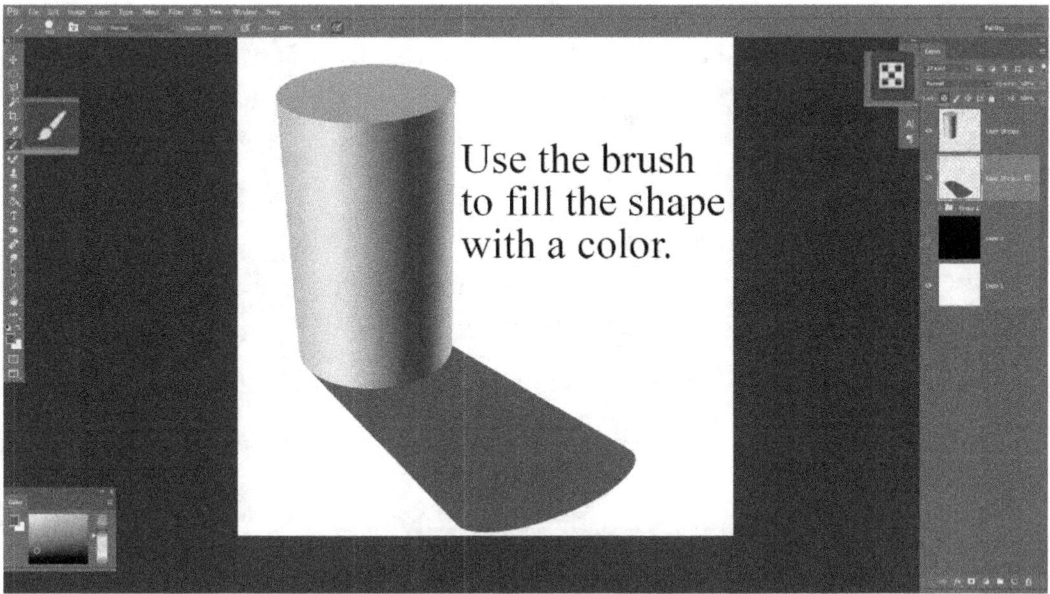

20. Make another layer. With the Gradient Tool draw a gradient along the line of the shadow.

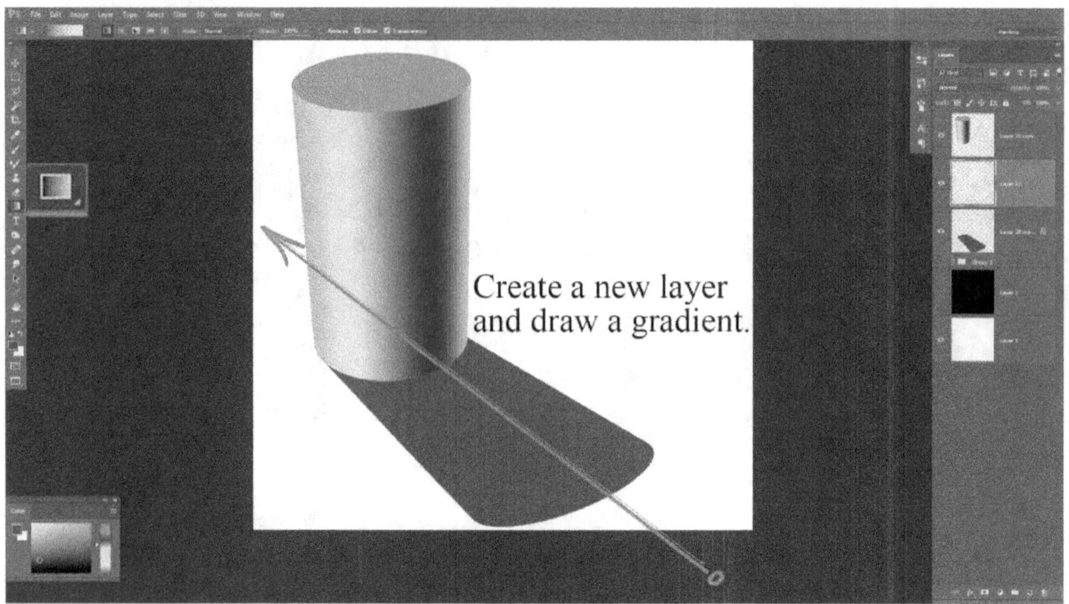

21. Click the icon for the layer while the Ctrl key is pressed.

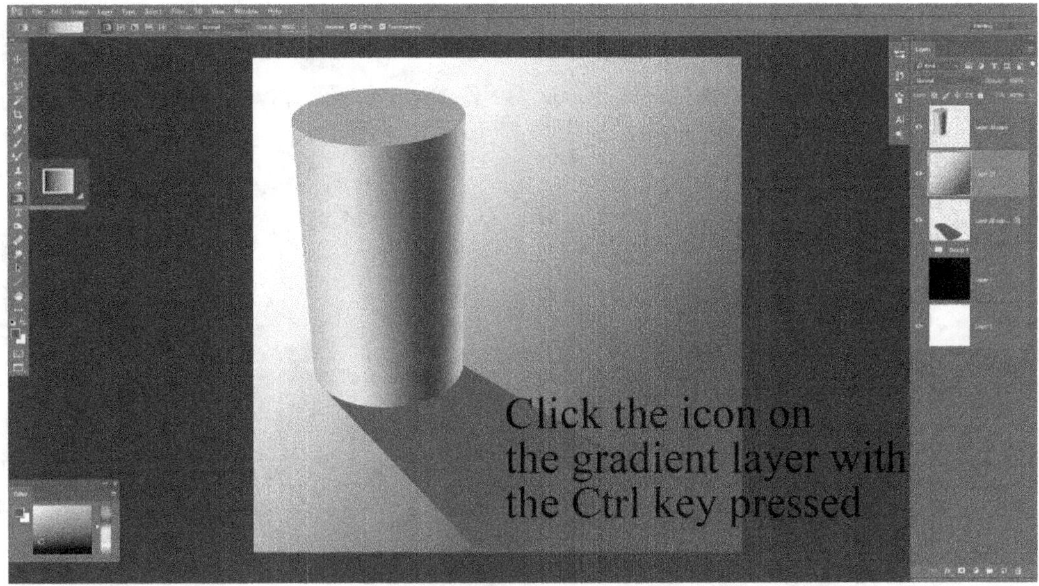

22. Click the layer for the Shadow

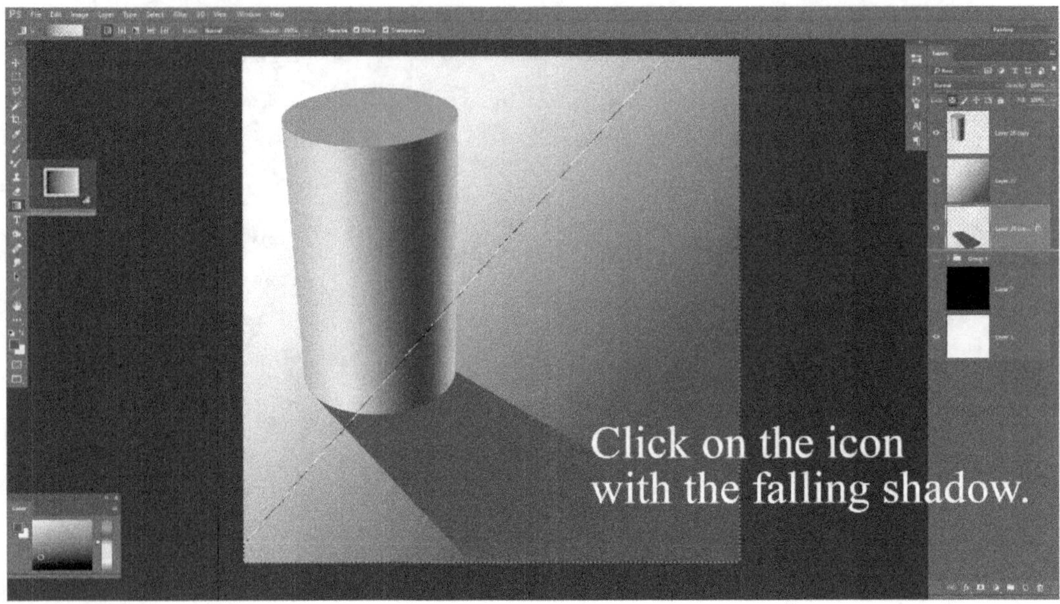

23. Unlock the layer of the shadow. Then apply the Gaussian Blur by selecting Filter > Blur > Gaussian Blur.

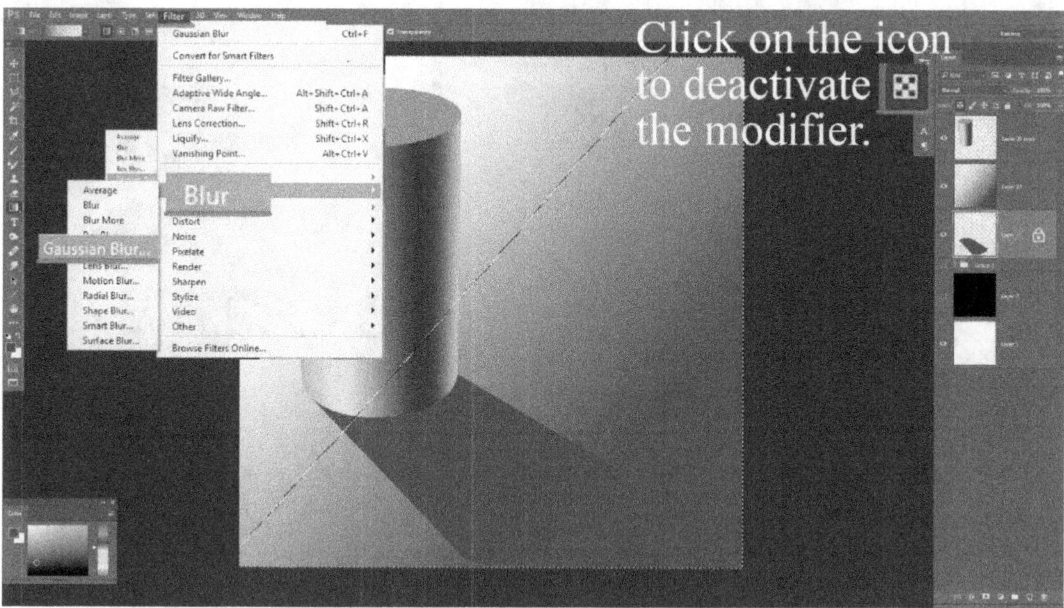

24. Adjust the radius of the Gaussian Blur to 30.4.

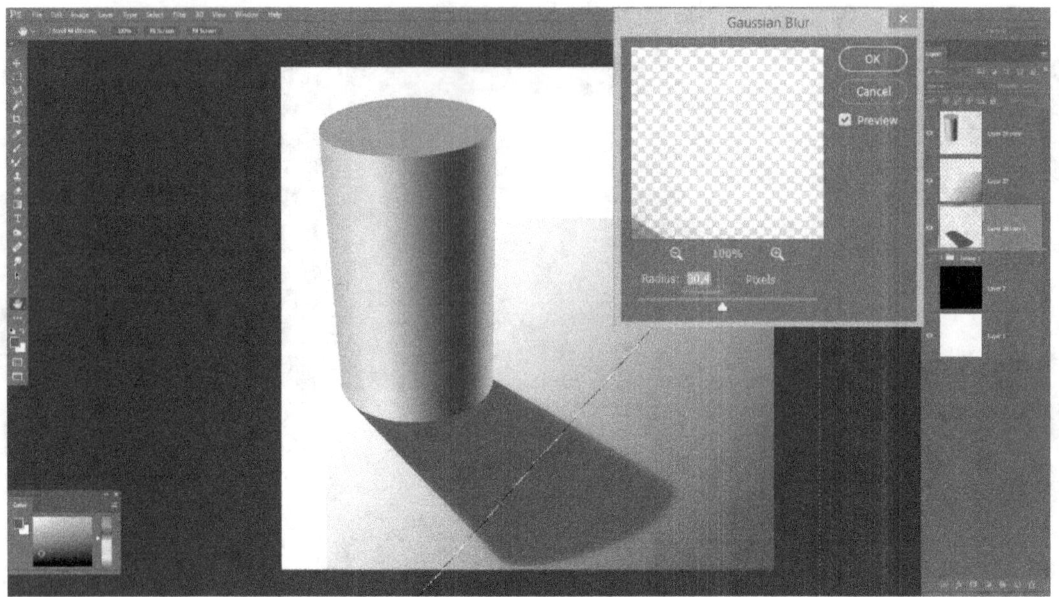

25. Delete the layer for the Gradient. Click the burn tool and adjust its parameters for Range and Exposure to Shadows and 25%, respectively. Darken some parts of the shadow, especially the parts directly under the cylinder and the middle of the shadow.

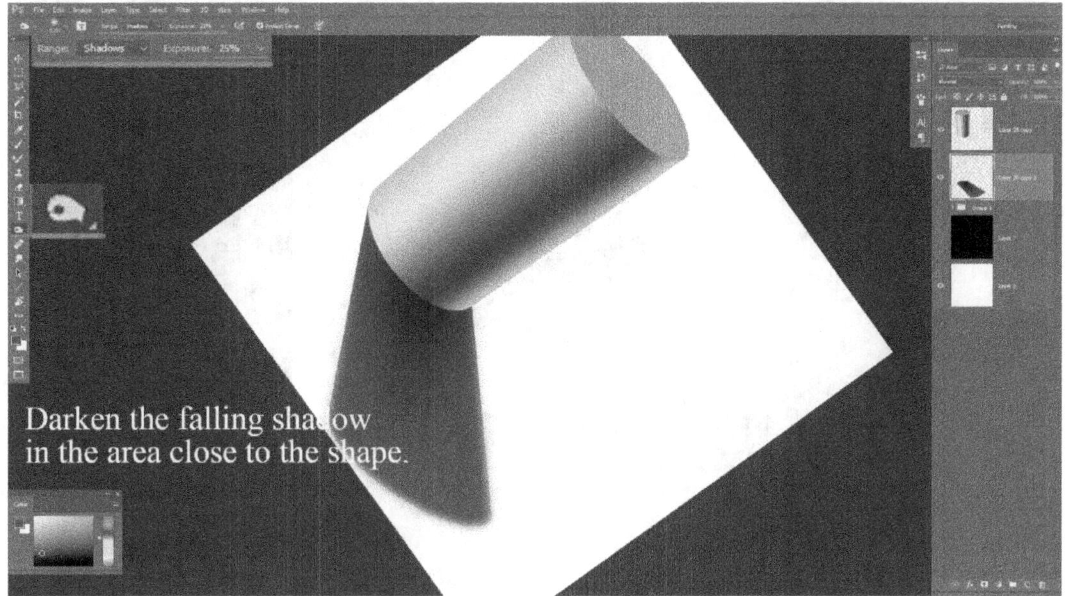

26. Erase some of the edges and the far side of the shadow.

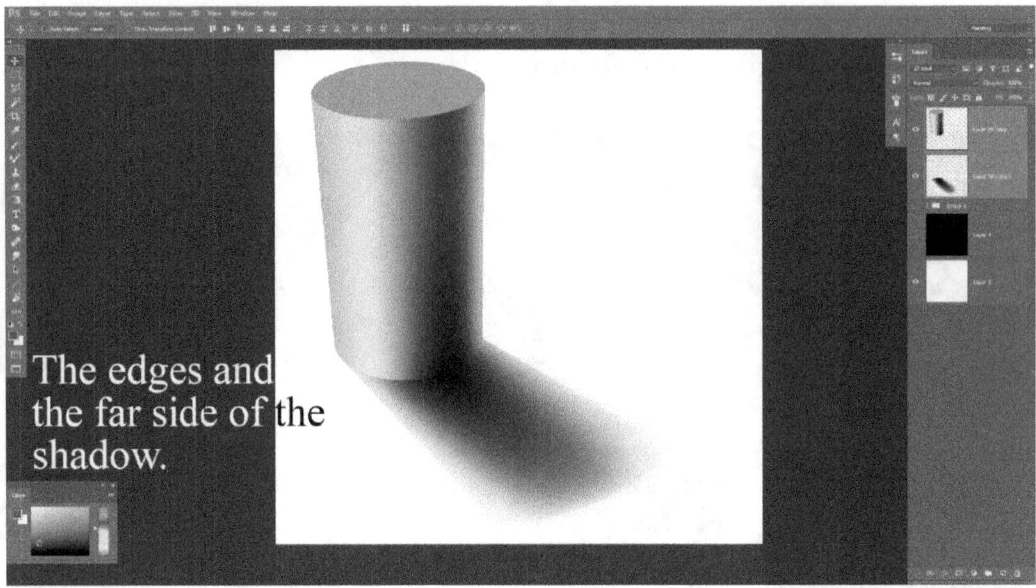

27. Press Ctrl+U and open the Hue/Saturation window. Adjust the shadow's Saturation value to -65.

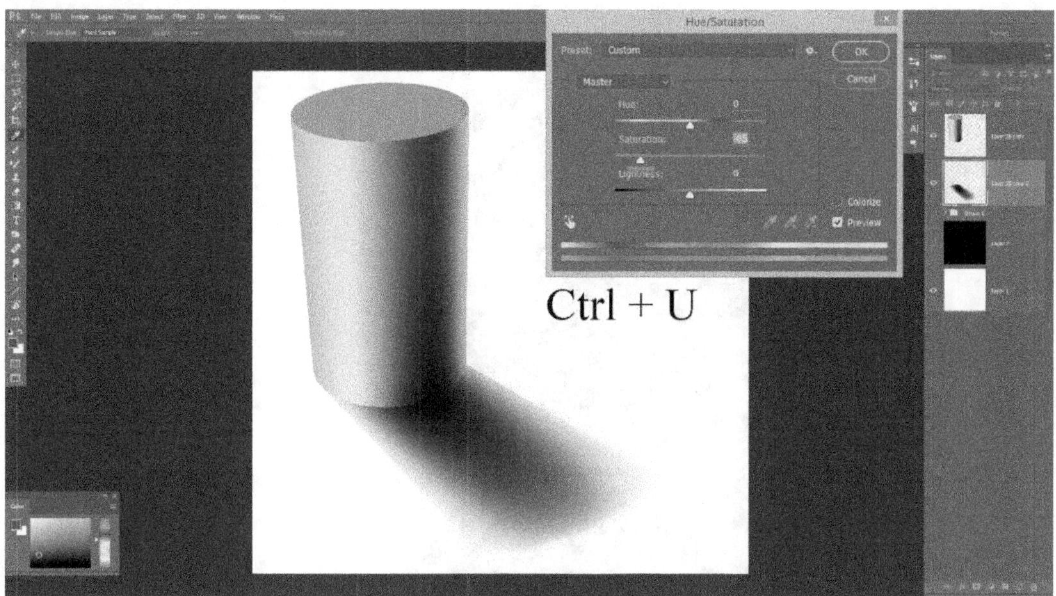

Hexagon

1. Make a new layer. Use the Rectangular Marquee Tool to mark out a vertical rectangle.

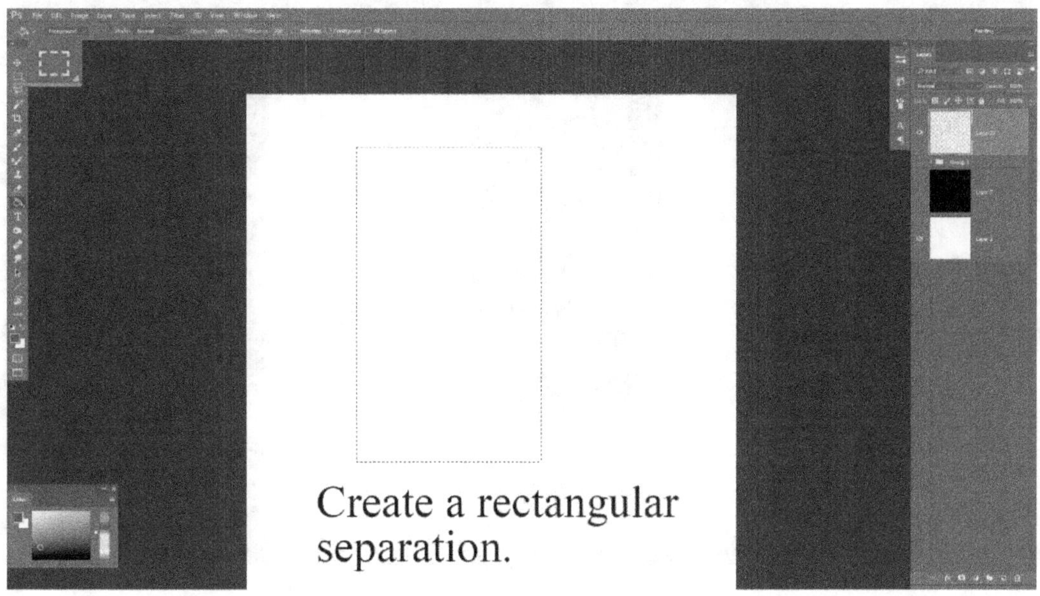

Create a rectangular
separation.

2. Fill this rectangle with any color.

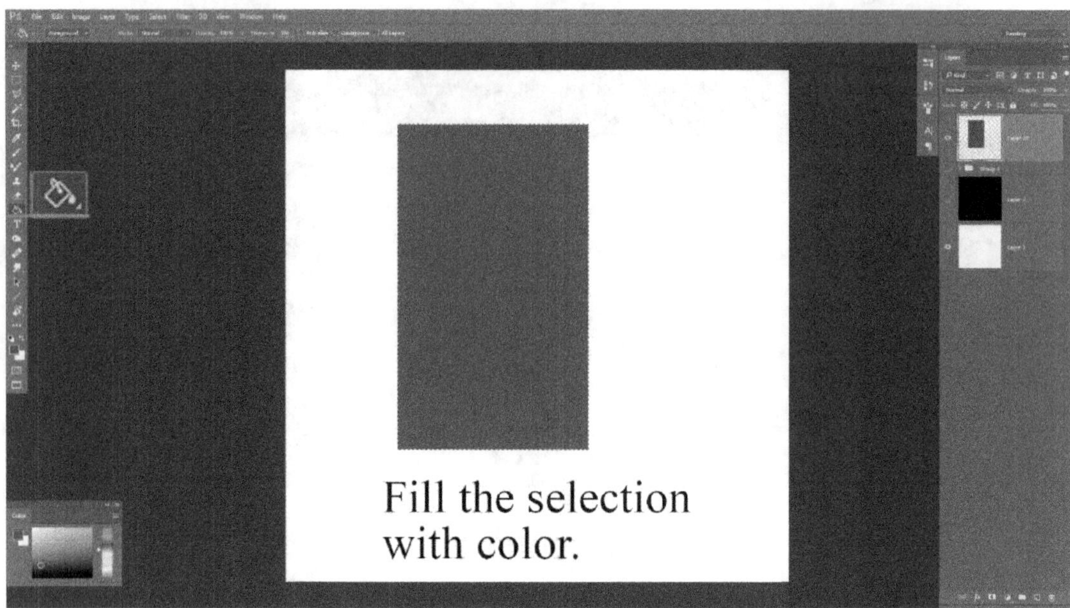

3. Create another new layer. Click the Polygon Tool. Set the Stroke to 5px and the Sides to 6 to create a hexagon.

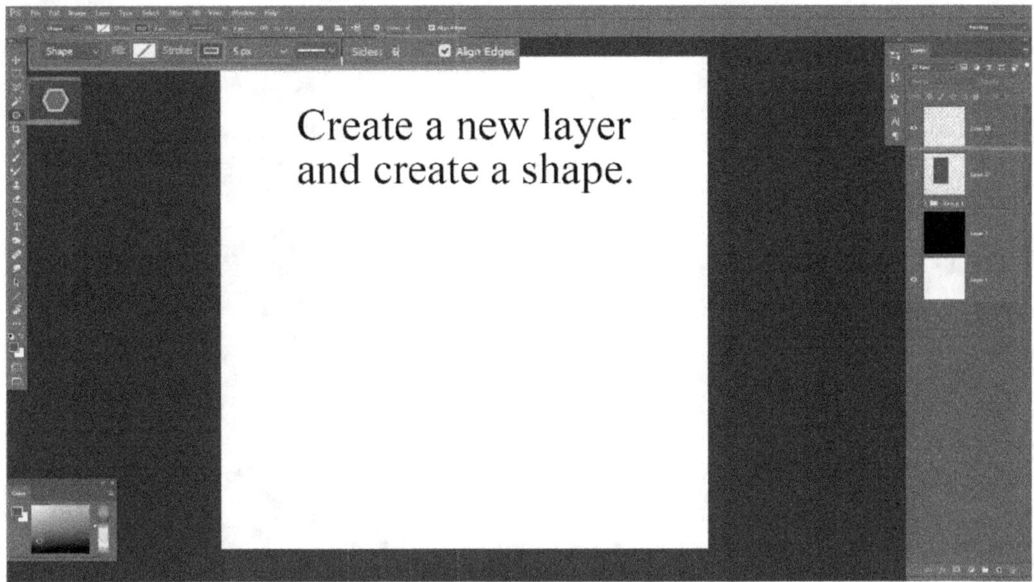

4. Draw the hexagon while pressing down on the Shift key to create a regular one.

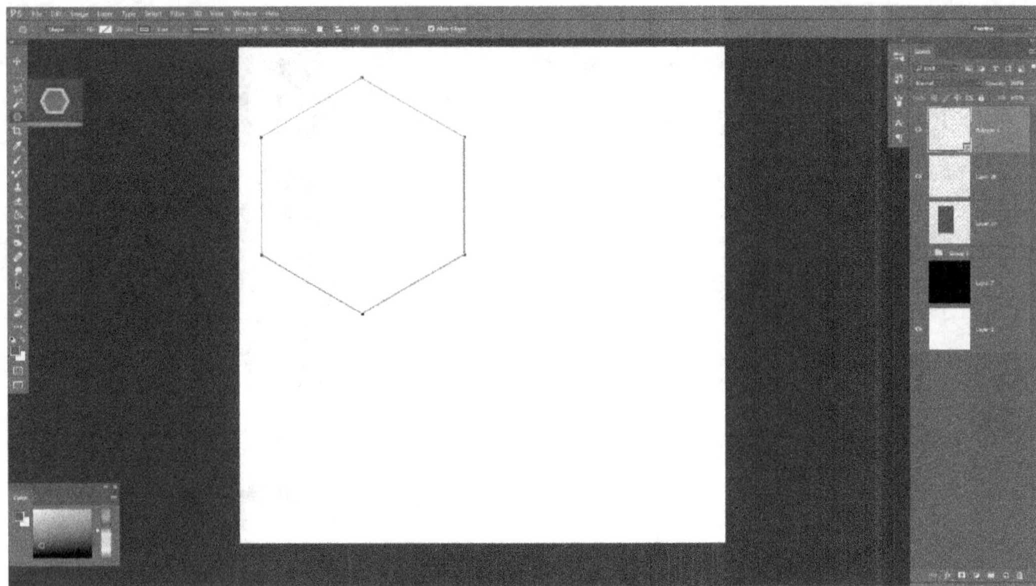

5. Use the Brush Tool fill the hexagon with the color.

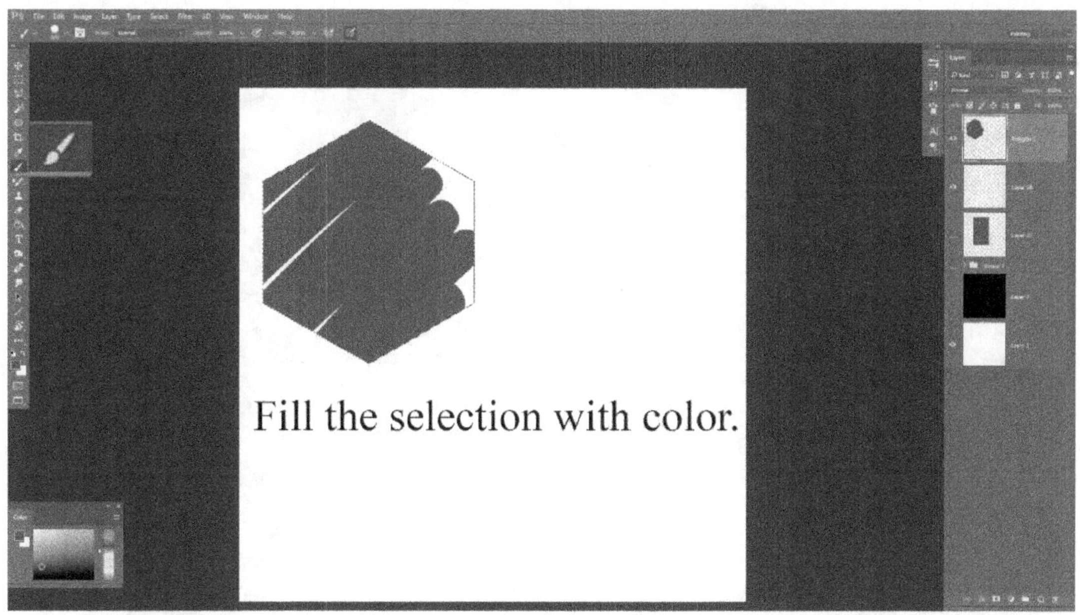

6. Press Ctrl+L and adjust the levels of the hexagon. Set the middle Input Level to 1.37.

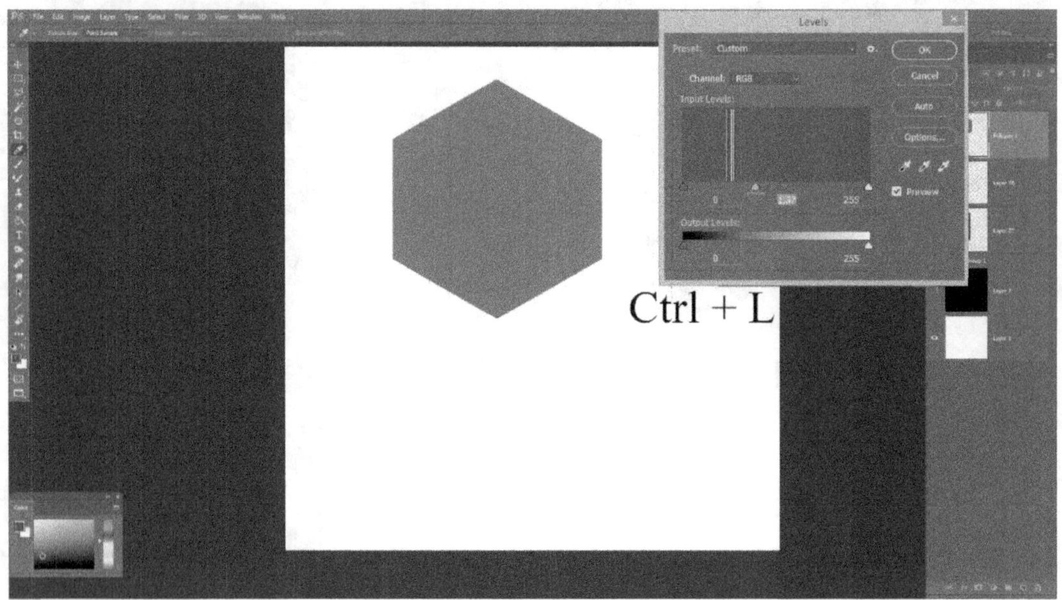

7. Press Ctrl+T and deform the hexagon. Adjust its height and direction to make it look as if it were a horizontal surface.

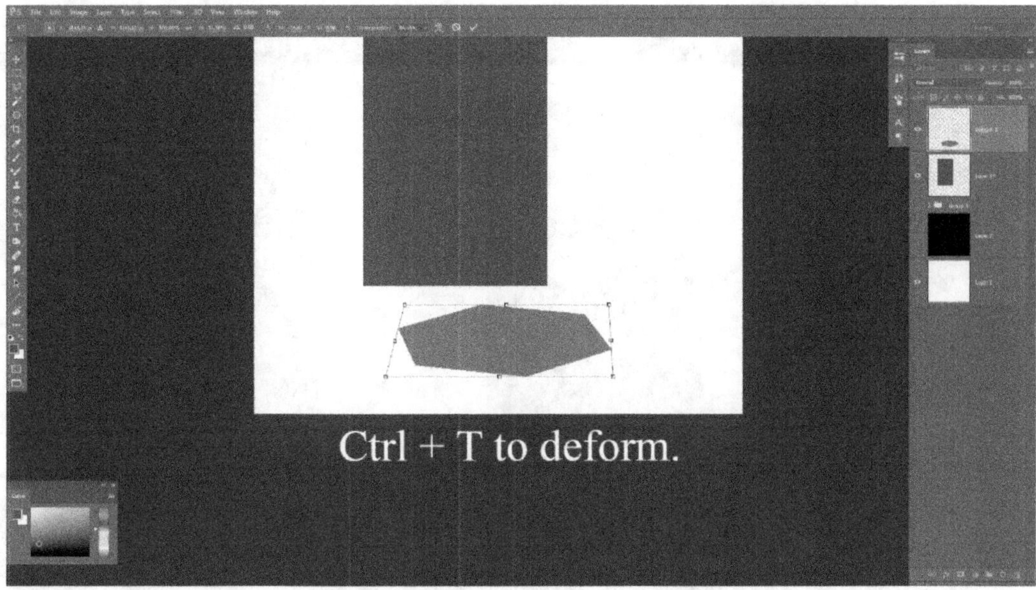

8. Select the layer of the rectangle and press Ctrl+T. Adjust its width to be the same as that of the hexagon.

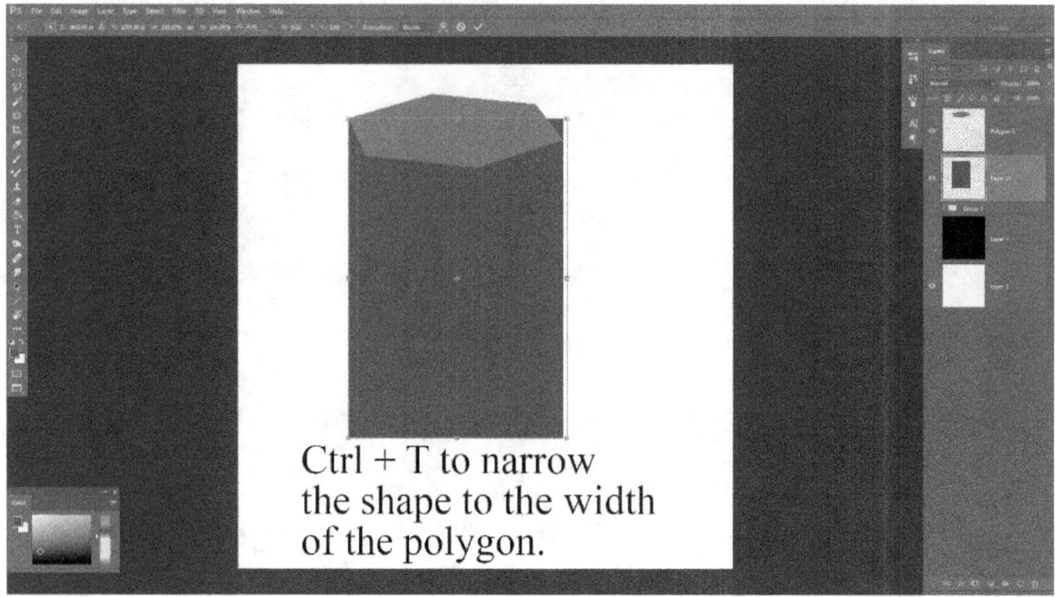

9. Copy the layer of the rectangle and press Ctrl+T. Deform the shape of the rectangle to follow the shape of the edge of the hexagon.

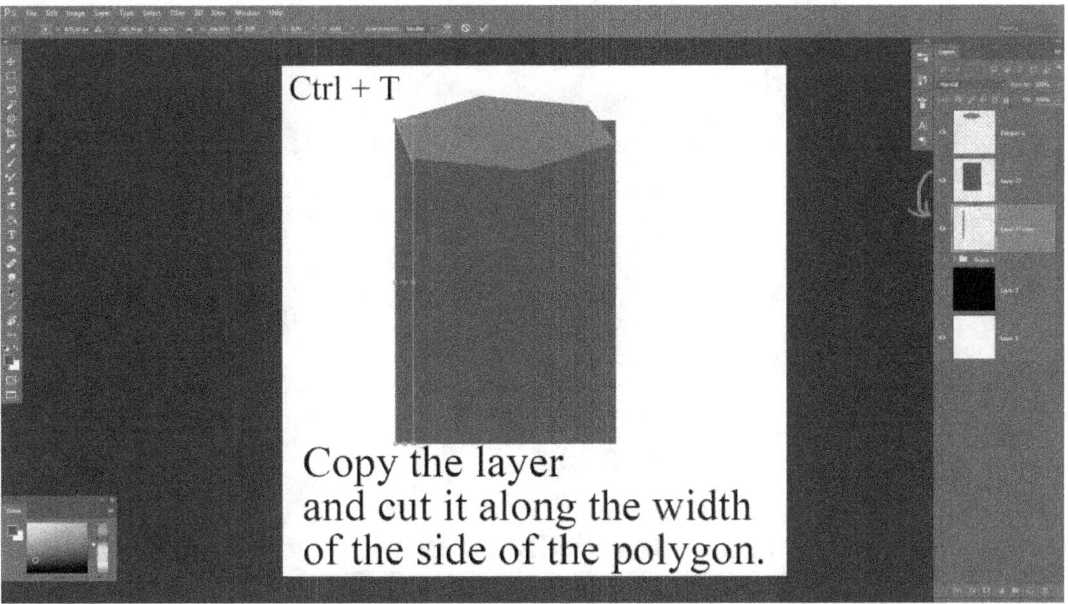

10. Copy the layer again and adjust the shape to match the next side of the hexagon.

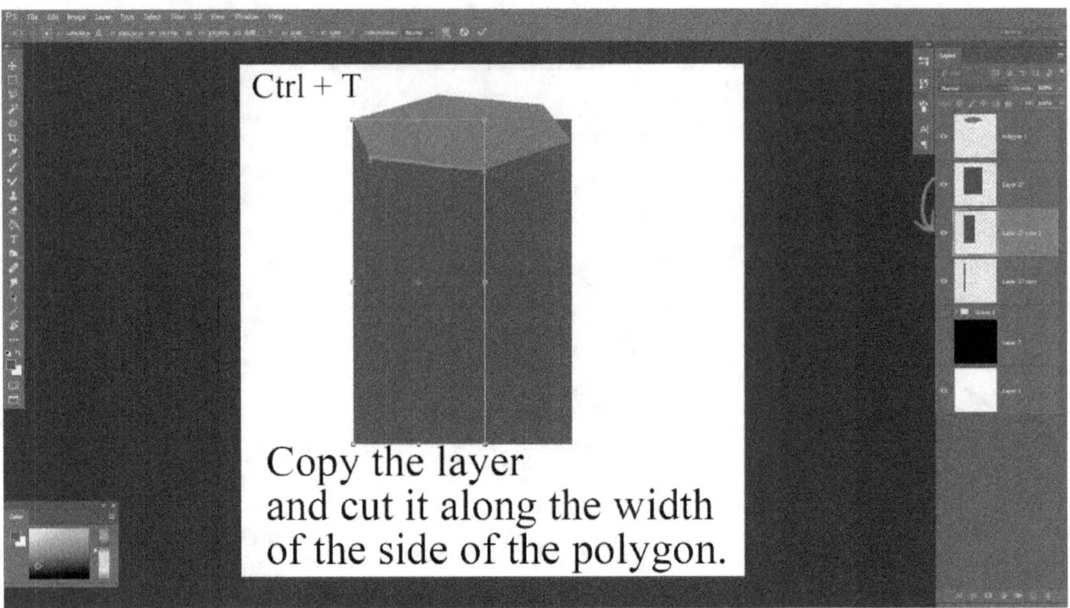

11. Copy the layer of the hexagon and move it to the bottom of the rectangle.

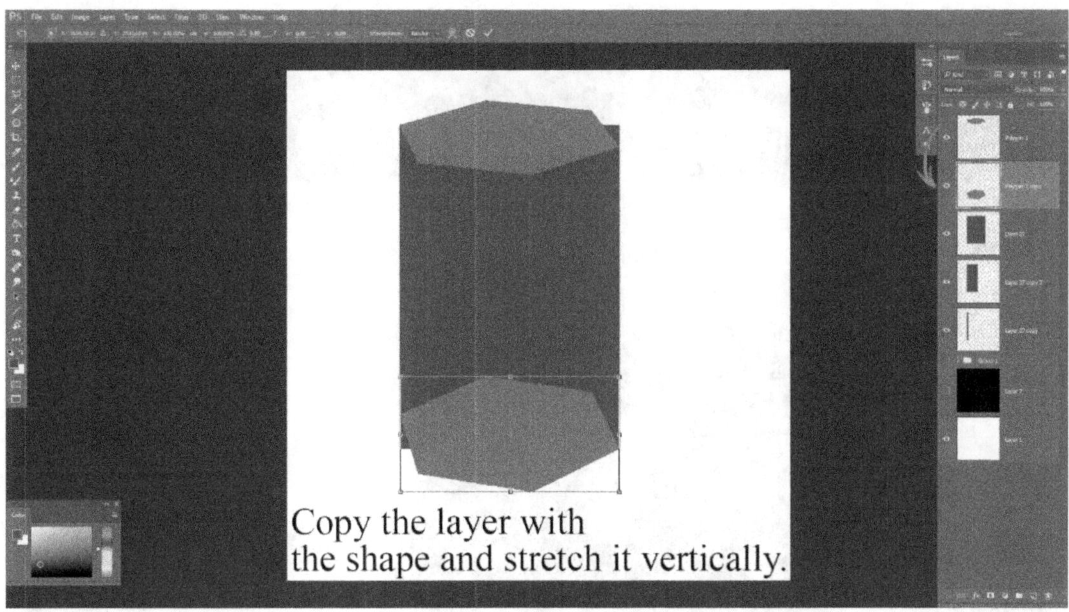

12. Remove any parts of the rectangle that are exposed under the hexagon with the Eraser Tool.

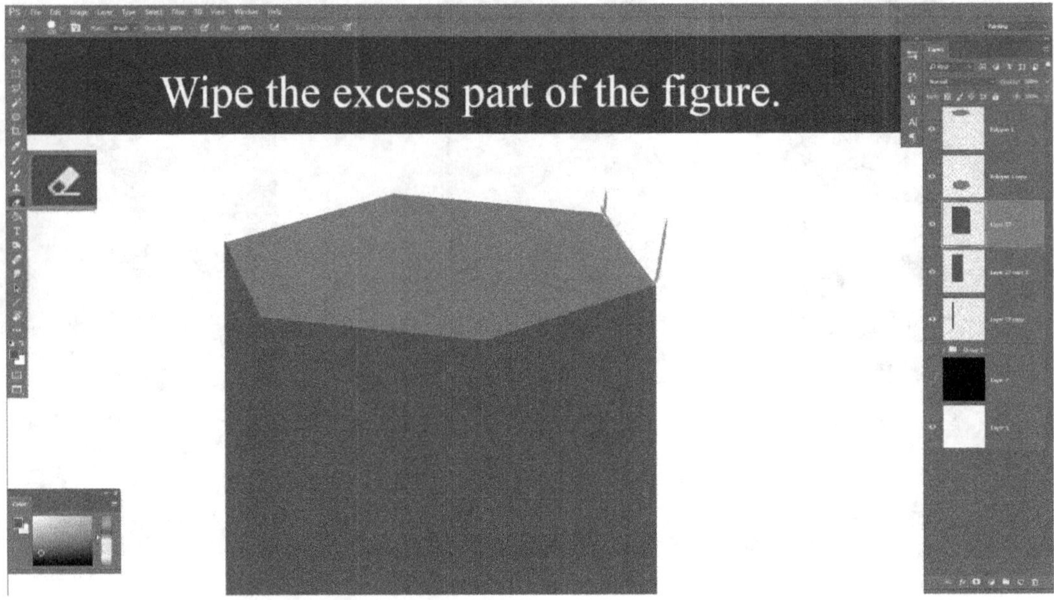

13. You should end up with this figure.

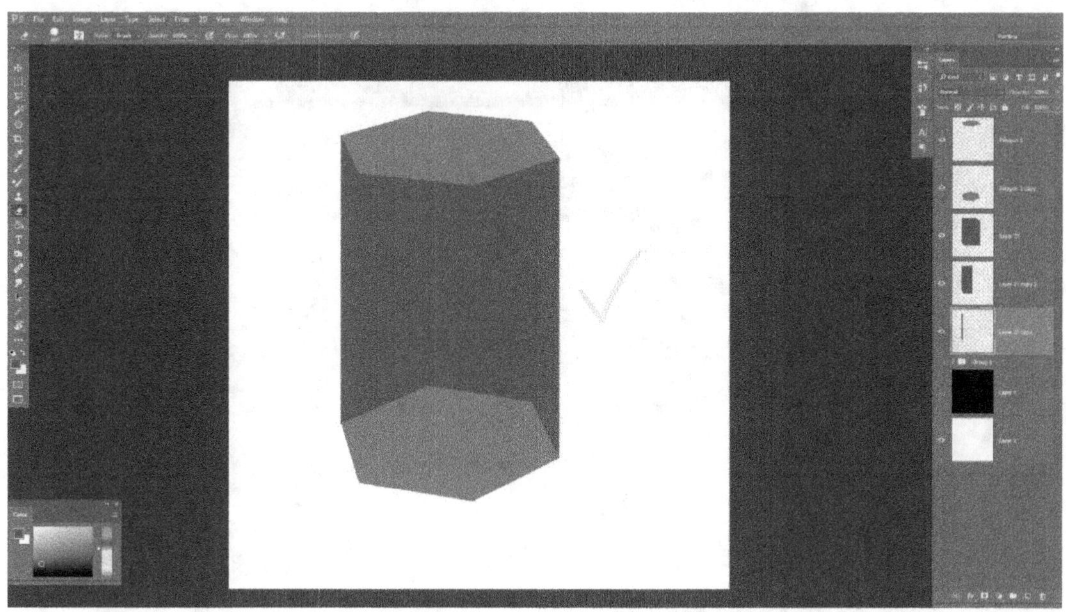

14. Click on the layer of the lower hexagon. Fill the shape with the same color as the rectangle using the Brush Tool.

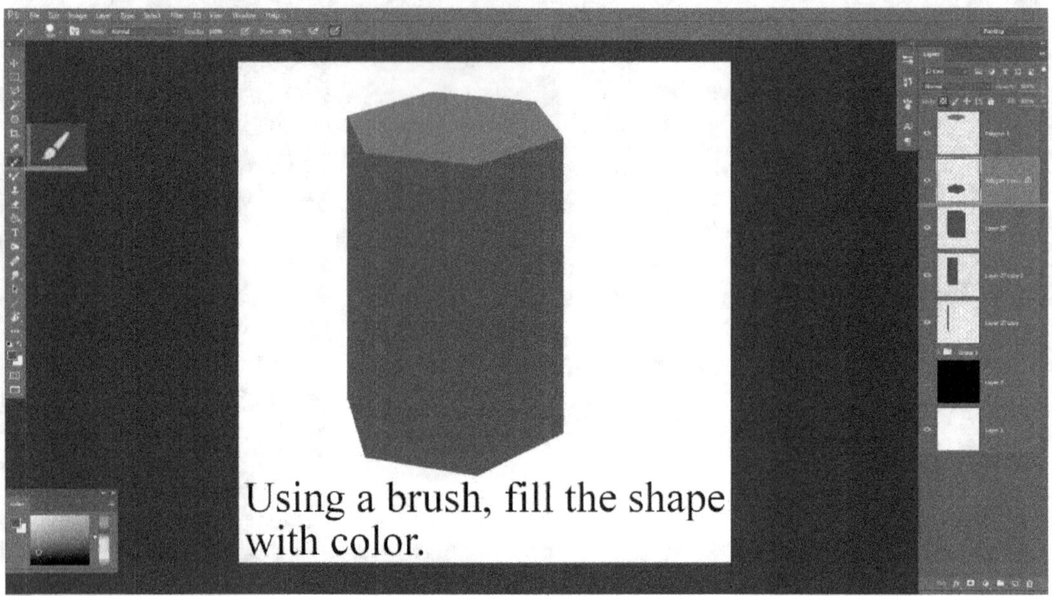

15. Select the layer for the leftmost transformed triangle and press Ctrl+L. Adjust the middle Input Level to 2.58.

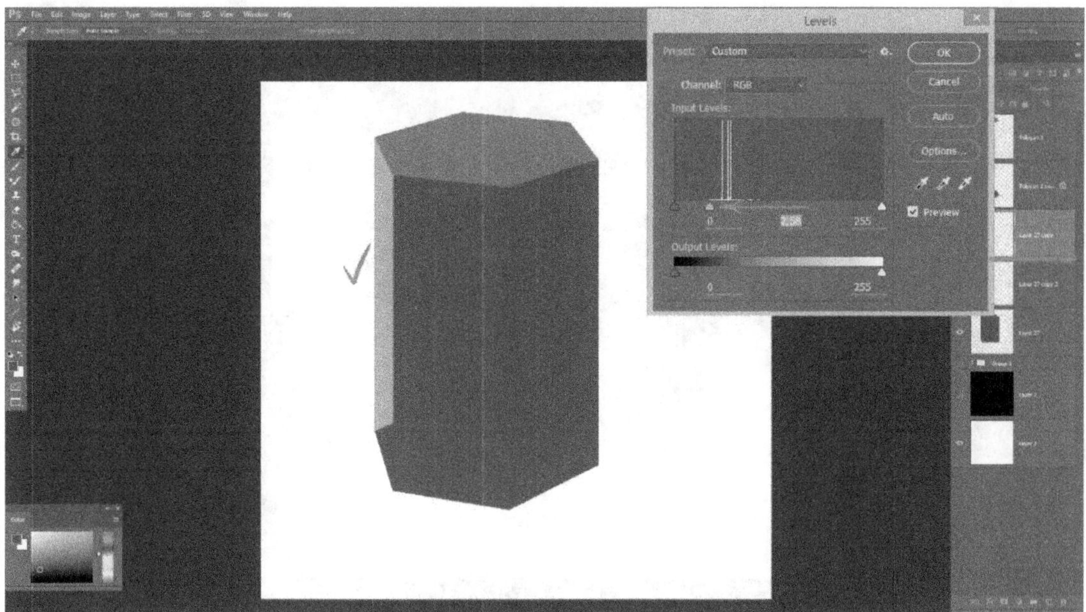

16. Select the layer for the original rectangle and press Ctrl+L. Adjust the middle Input Level to 0.75.

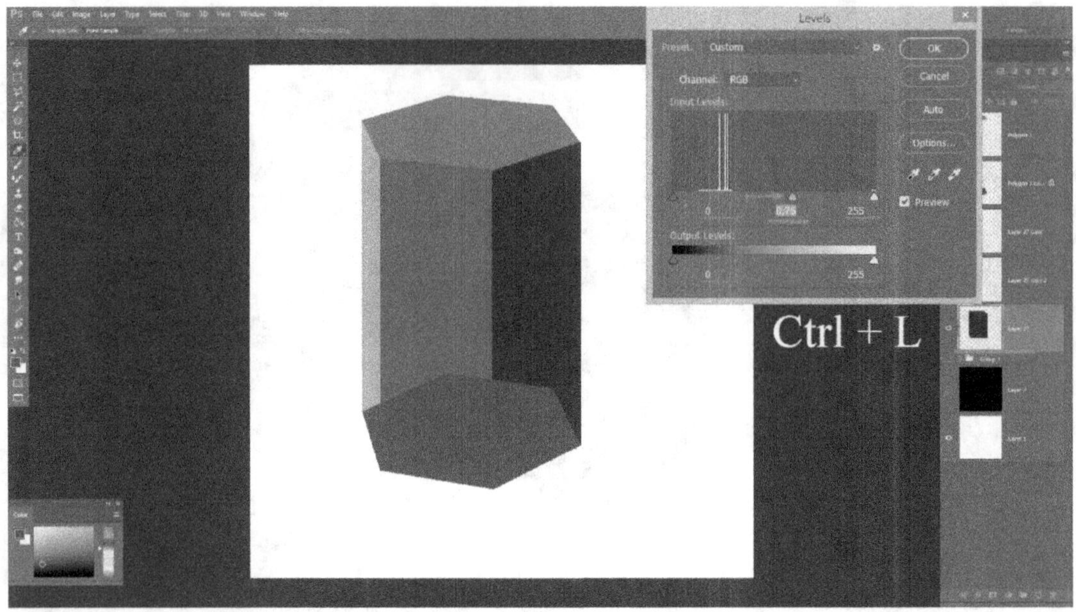

17. Move the layer of the lower hexagon below the layers with the rectangles. Press Ctrl+T and adjust the leftmost rectangle's shape to match the edge of the lower hexagon.

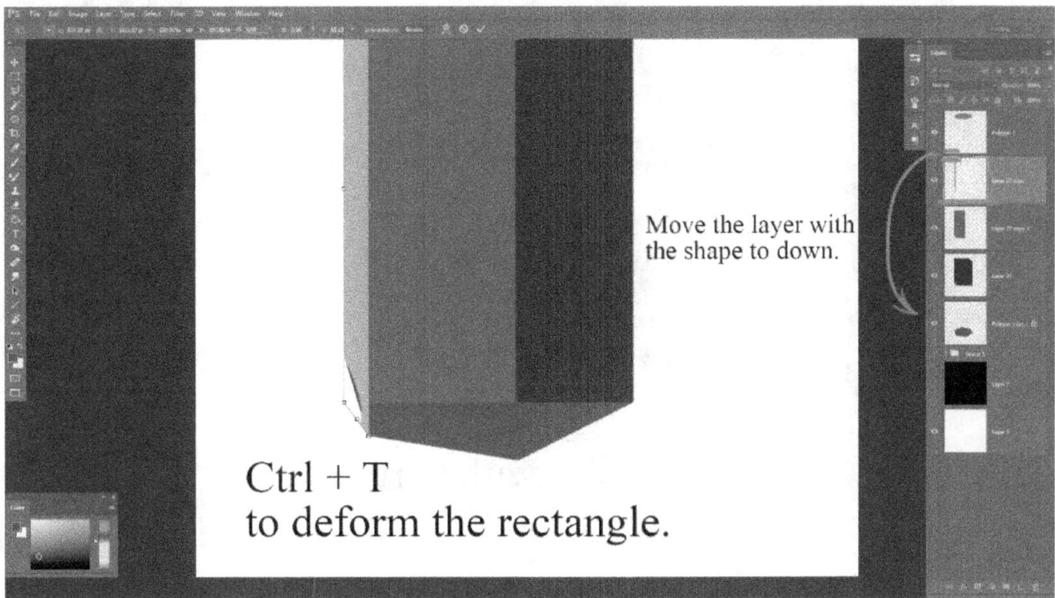

18. Deform the next rectangle and match it to the next side.

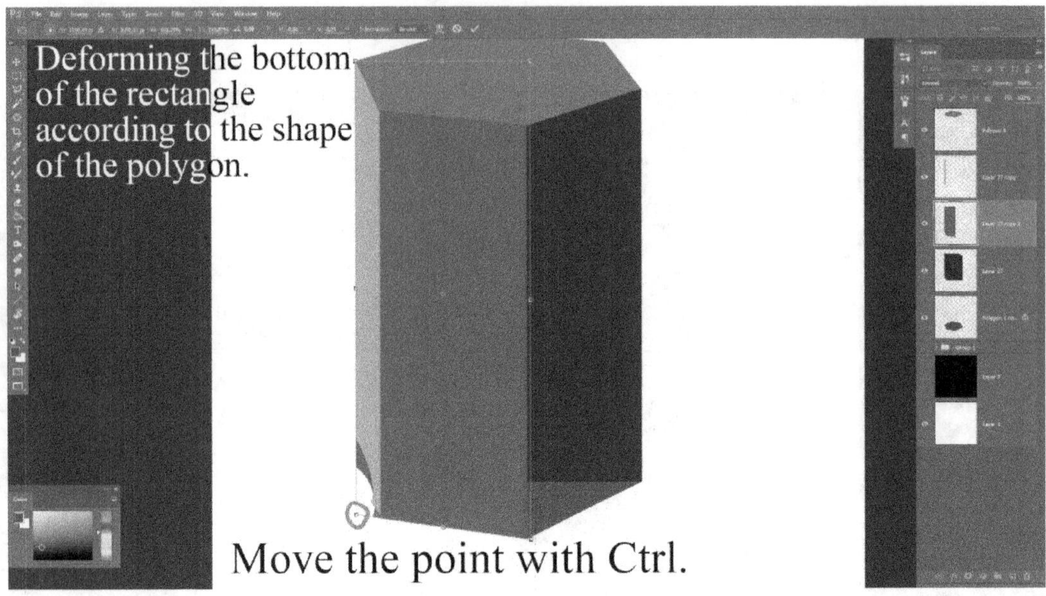

19. Do the same for all three rectangles.

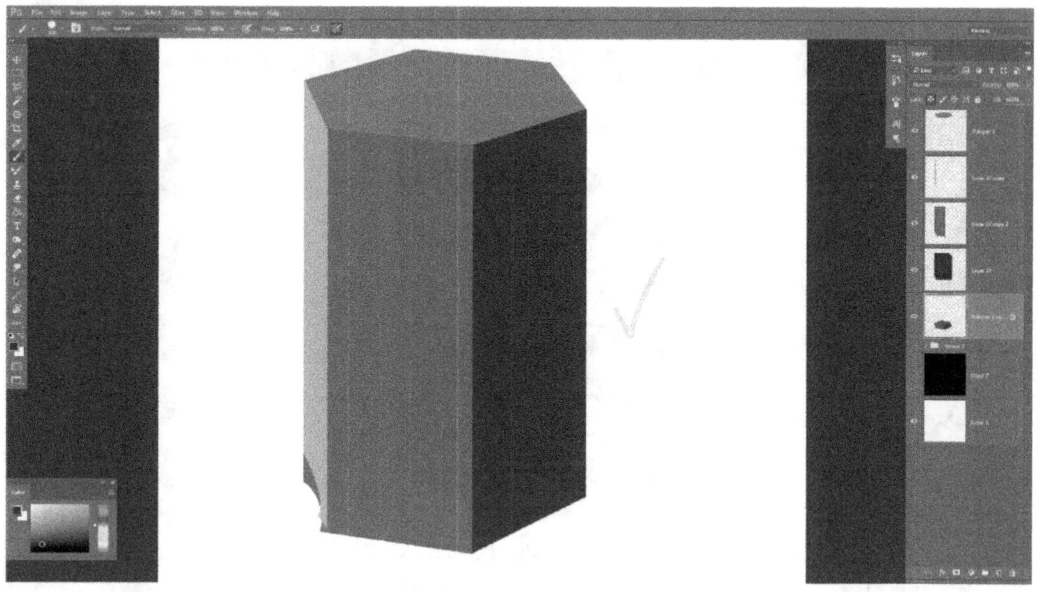

20. Select the icon of the layer with the lower hexagon. Press Ctrl+Shift+I to select those outside the shape.

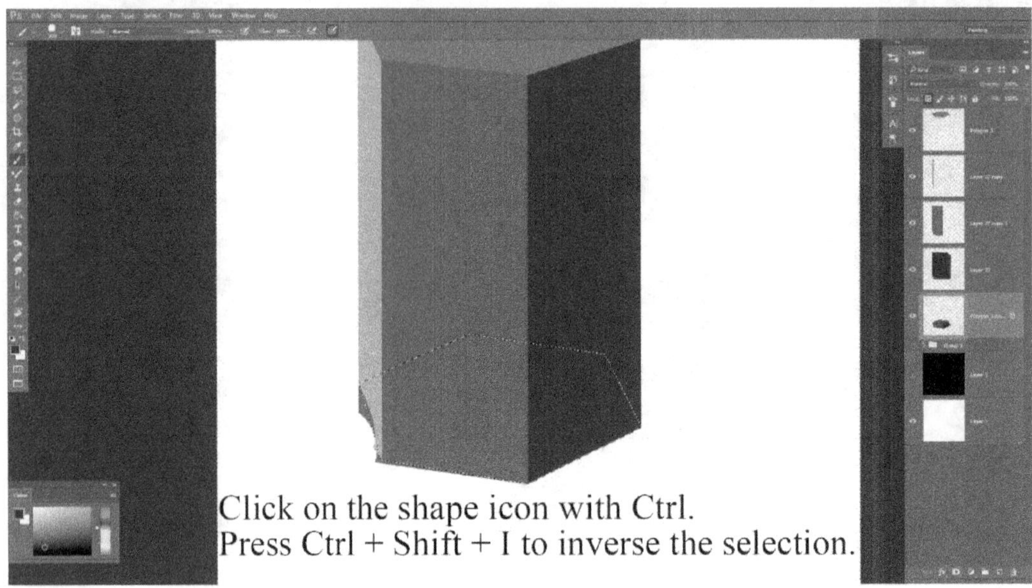

21. Erase any parts of the rectangles that overlap the hexagon.

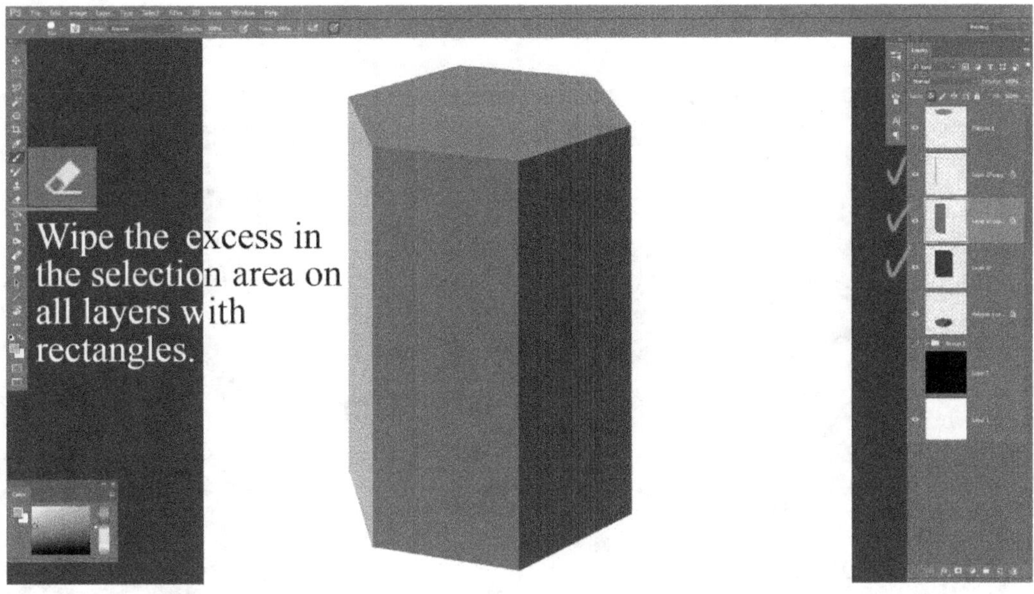

22. Merge all the shape layers. Create a perspective effect by pressing Ctrl+T and moving the corners of the Transformation Area while the Ctrl Key is being held down.

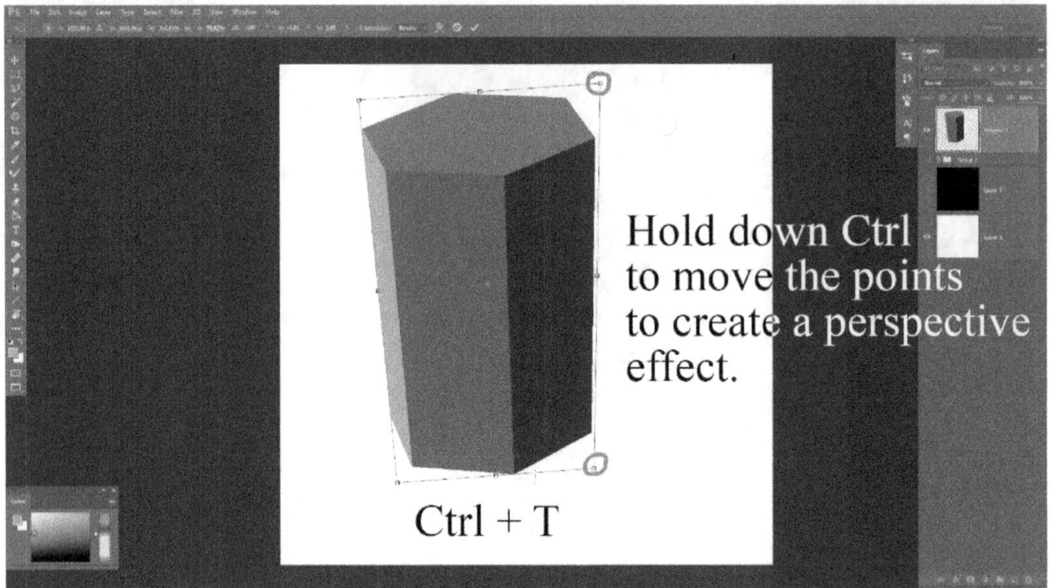

23. Copy the layer and move the copied shape. Press Ctrl+T and the press the Right Mouse button. From the menu, choose Flip Horizontal.

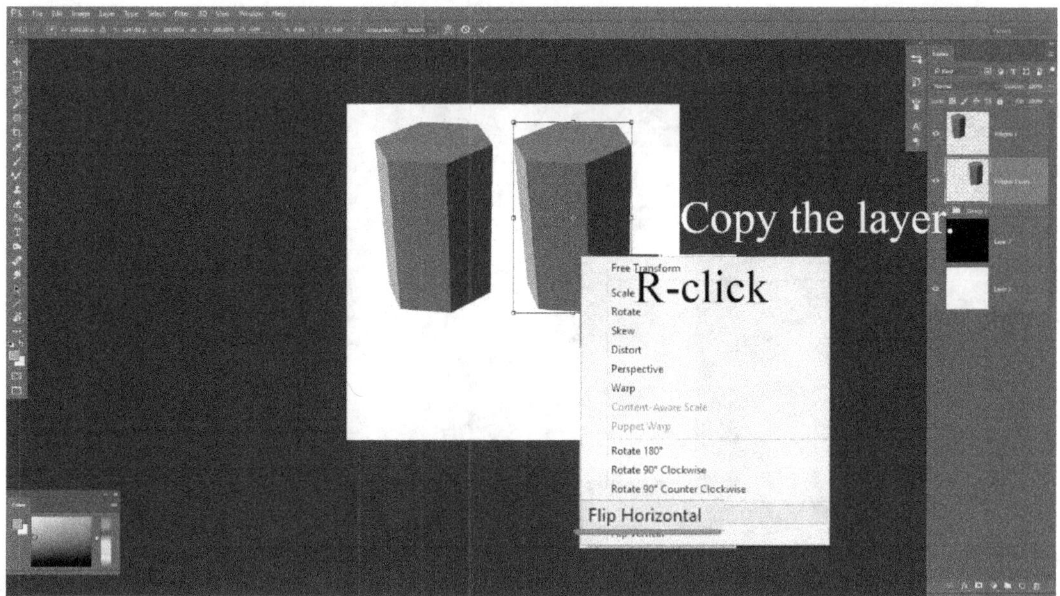

24. Press Ctrl while moving the middle node of the top of the shape downwards.

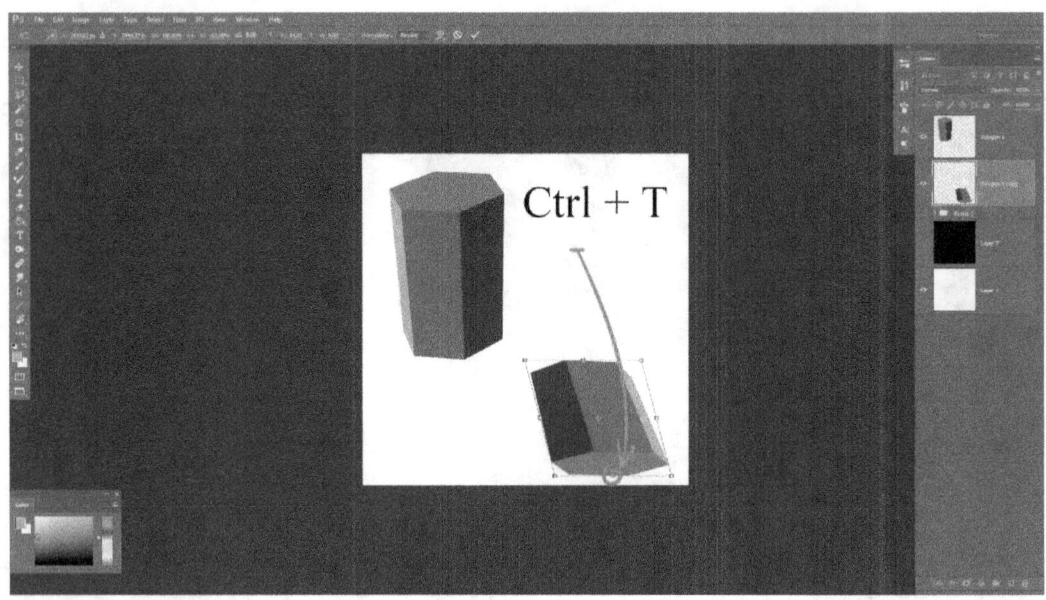

25. Widen the shape a little bit and move it under the original one.

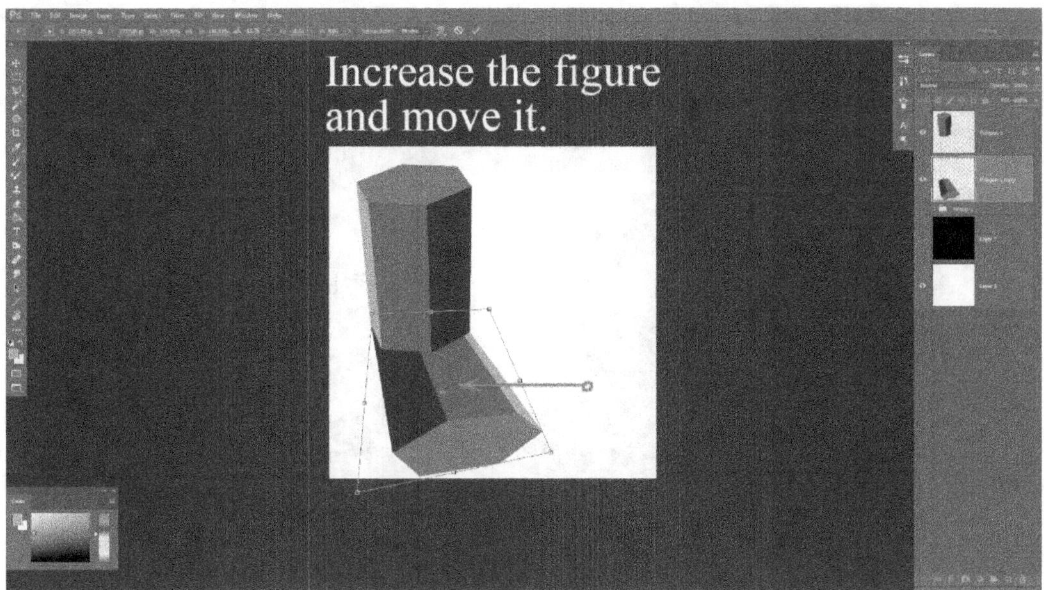

26. Fill the shape with a darker color with the Brush Tool.

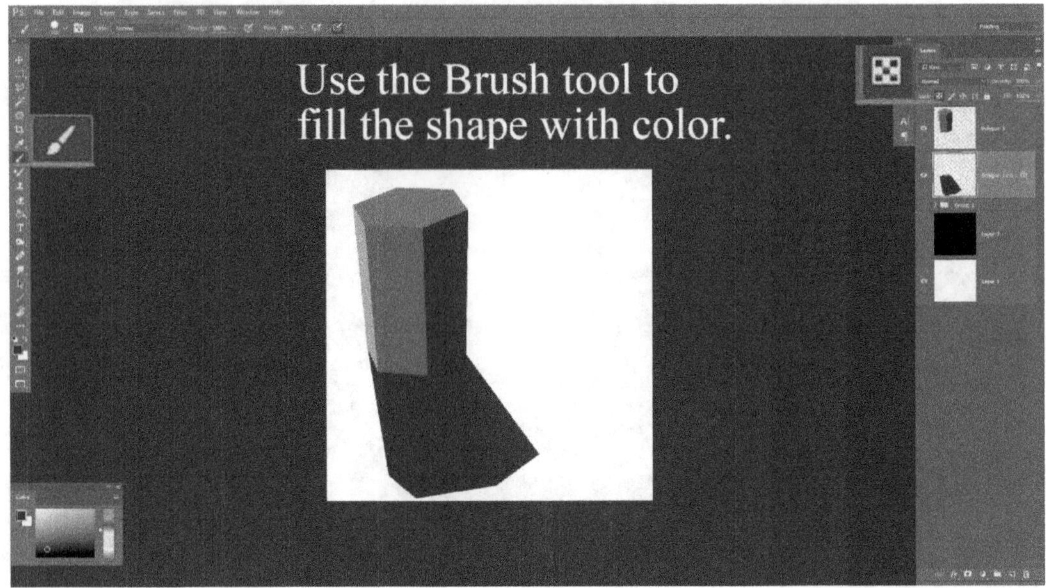

27. Click on the Dodge Tool and change the value of Exposure to 100%. Lighten the edges of the shadow.

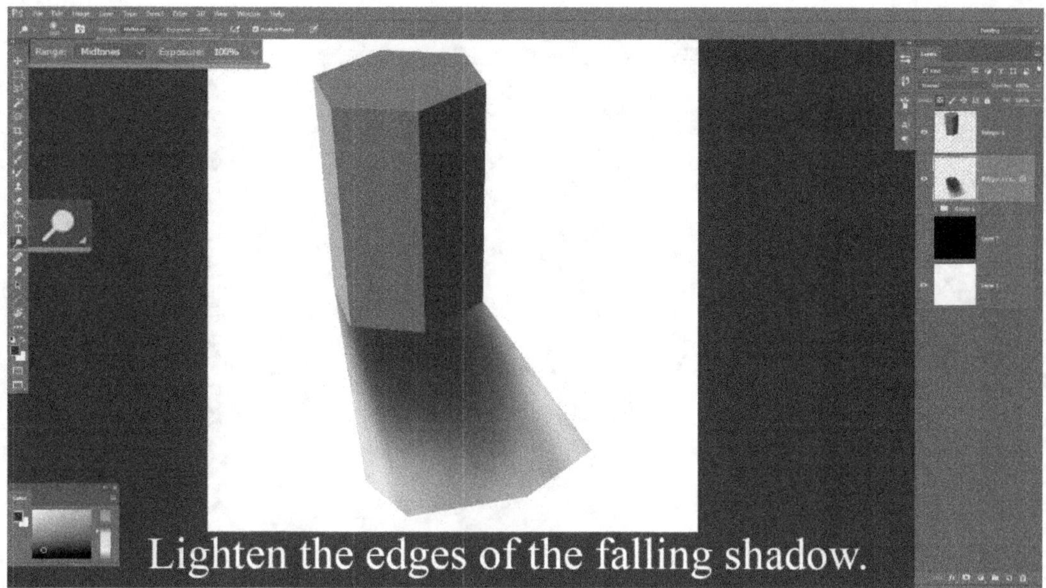

28. Bring up the Hue/Saturation Window by pressing Ctrl+U. Change the value for Saturation to -69.

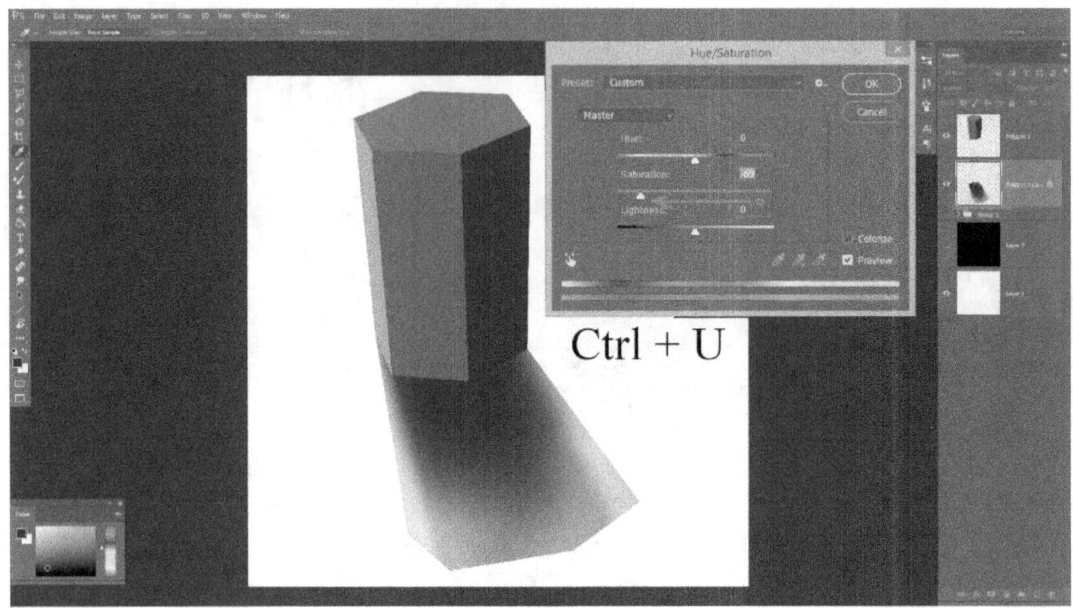

29. Make a new layer. Click on the Gradient Tool. Draw a gradient aligned with the shadow.

30. Select the shadow's layer. Mark a rectangle on the shadow with the Rectangular Marquee Tool. Apply the Gaussian Blur effect. Go to Filter > Blur > Gaussian Blur to apply.

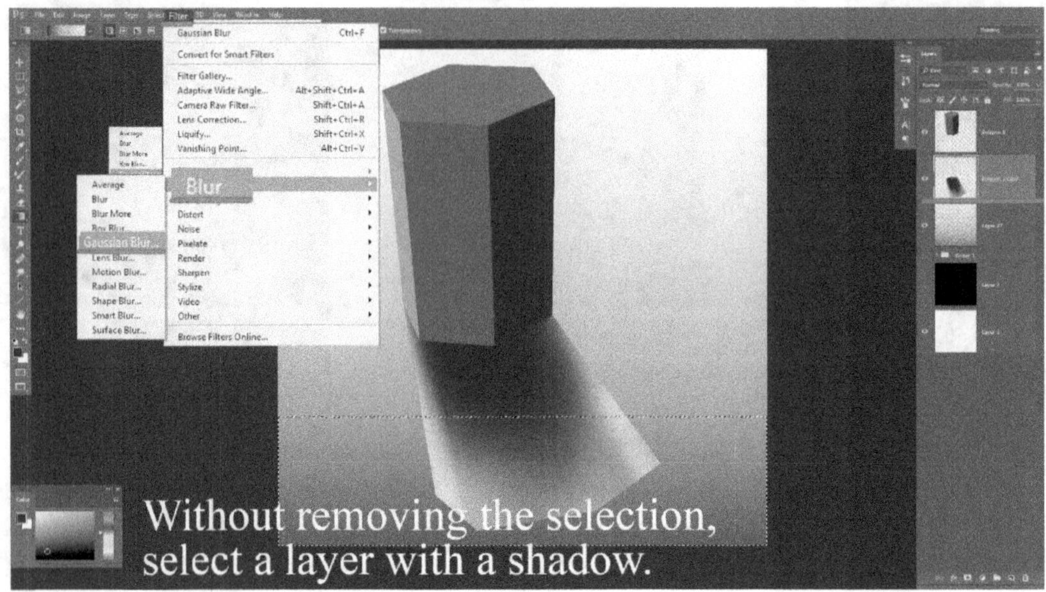

31. The image you create should be similar to this one.

32. Use the Burn Tool to darken the parts of the figure close to the shadow, especially the lower part.

33. Delete the layer of the Gradients and merge the remaining layers. Click the Magic Wand tool and select the hexagon.

34. Press Ctrl+L to pull up the Levels window. Change the value for the middle Input Level to 2.80.

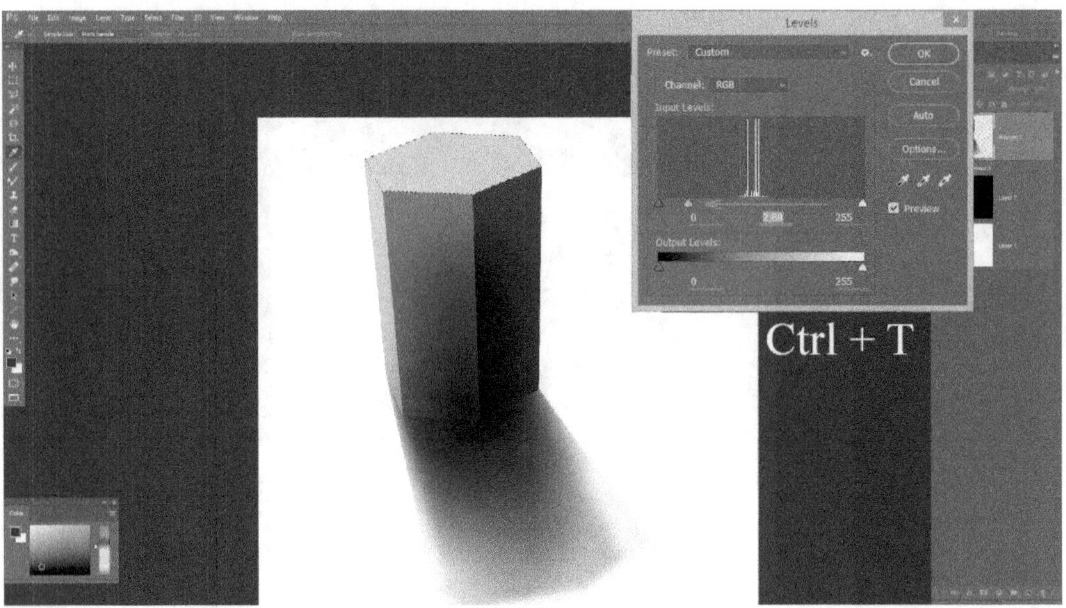

Simple Shading Tricks

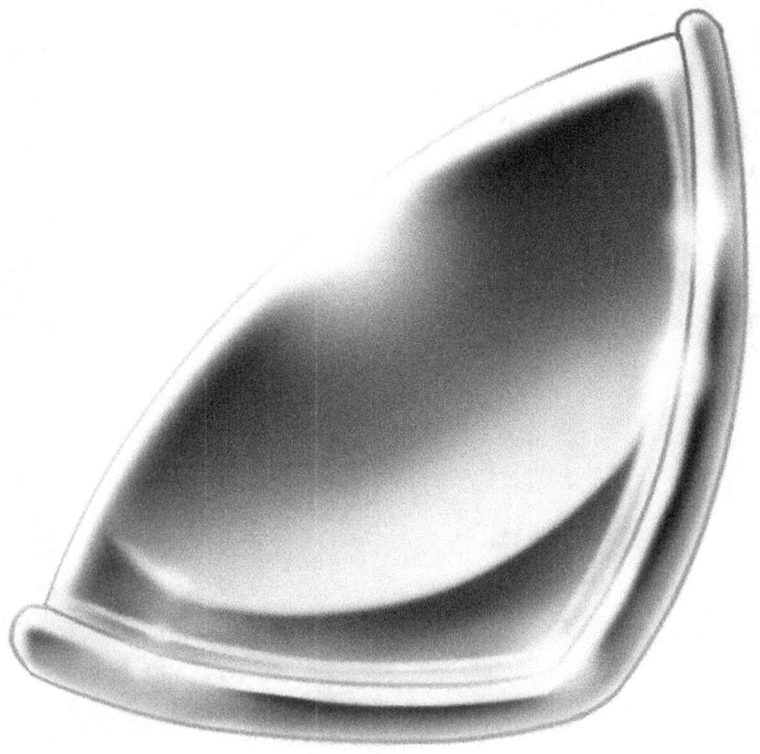

1. Make a new layer. Draw a shape or a sketch.

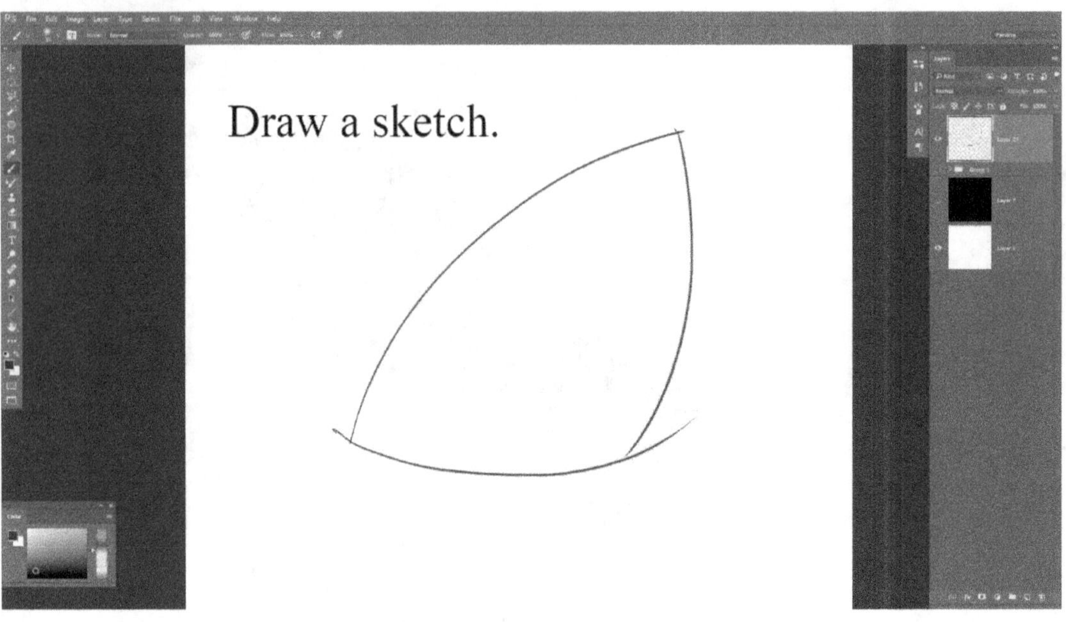

2. Add more details to the drawing.

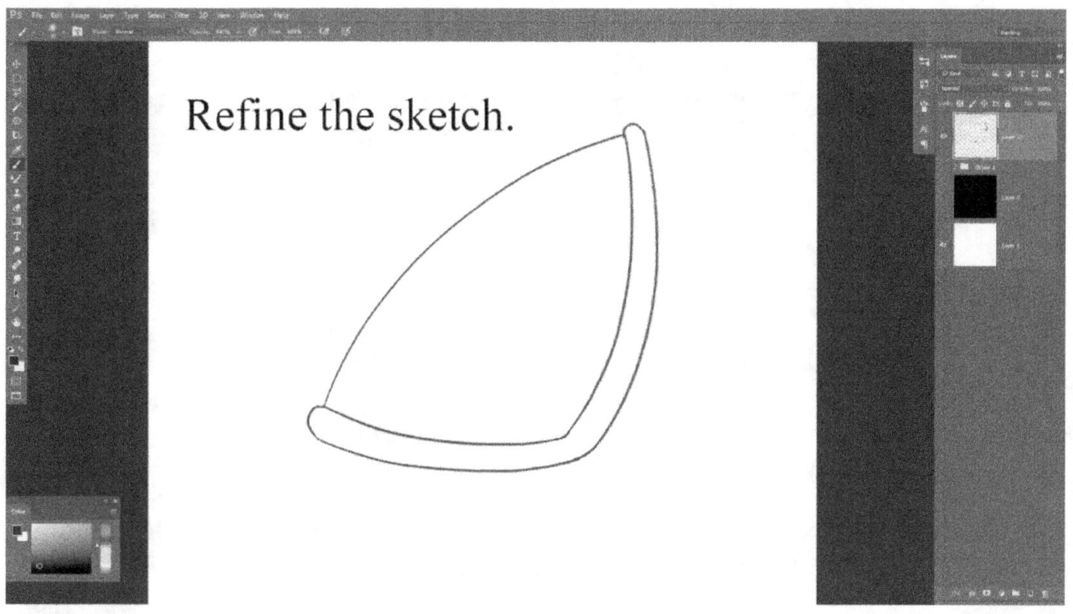

3. Make a new layer. This time, instead of using the keyboard shortcut click the "New Layer" icon on the lower right corner of the workspace. Then Draw a line of the "own shadow" or the dark parts of the figure.

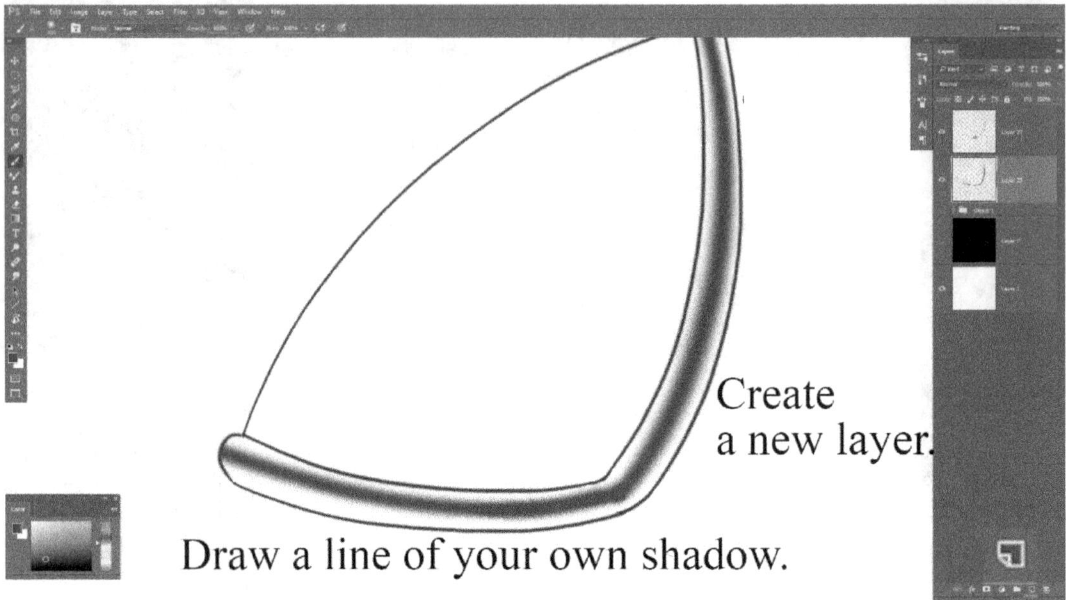

4. Color the area behind and below the "own shadow" with respect to the light source.

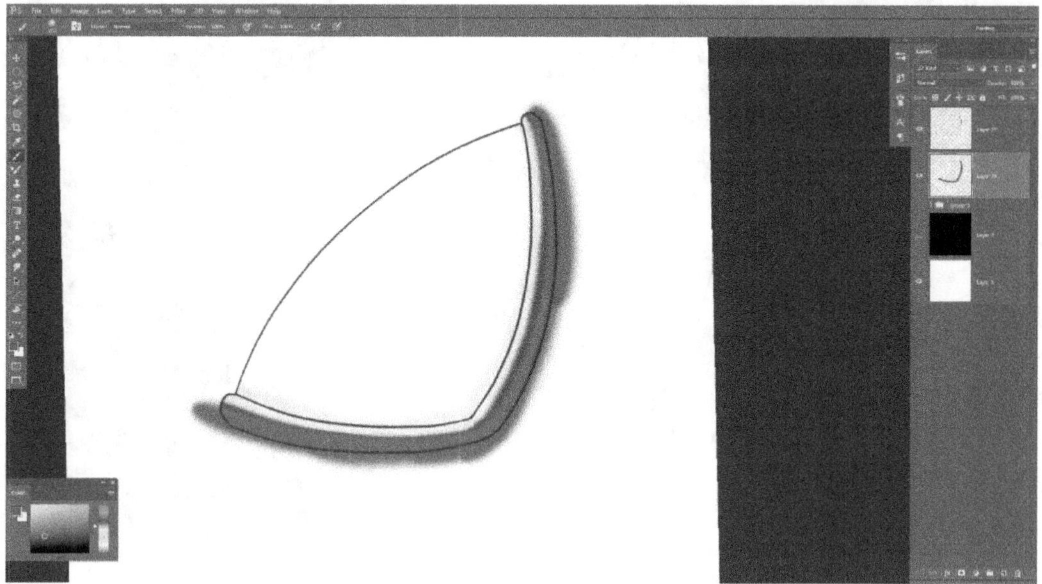

5. On another layer, add the own shadow to another part of the drawing.

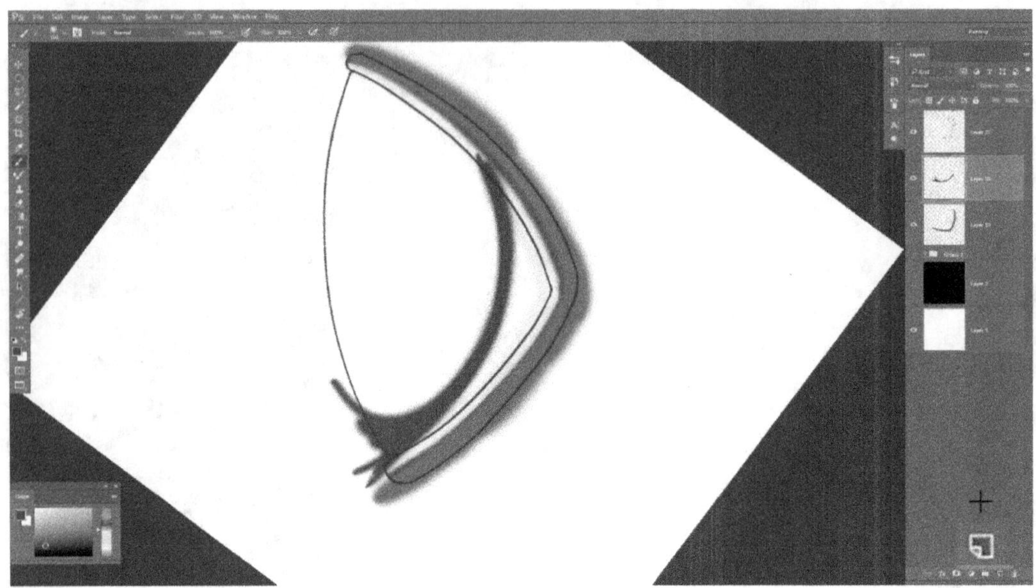

6. Color the areas below the own shadow of the new layer.

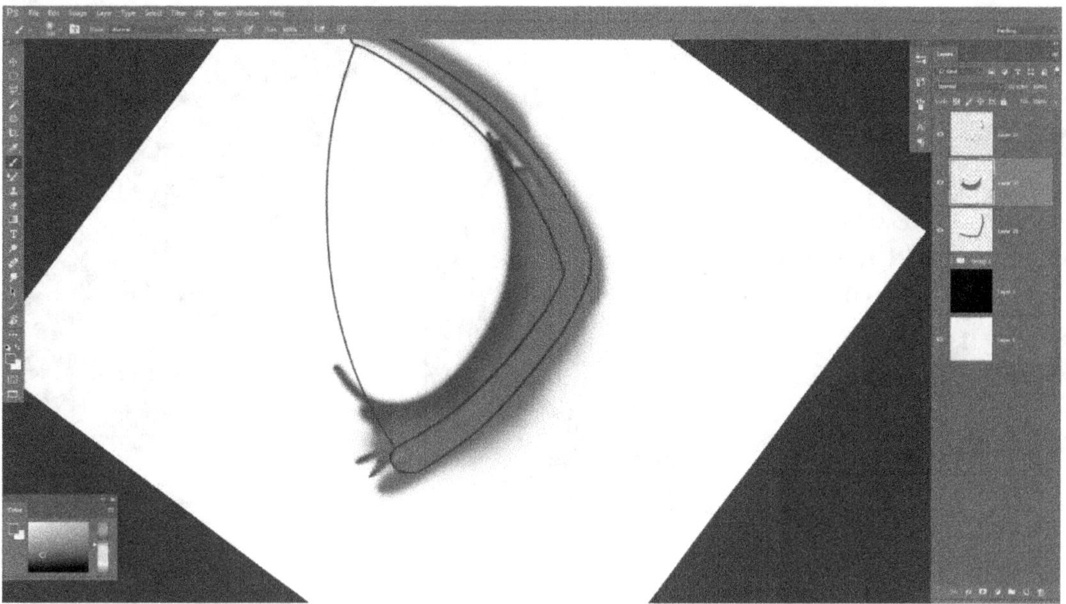

7. Click on the Eraser Tool and erase any strokes projecting over the layer.

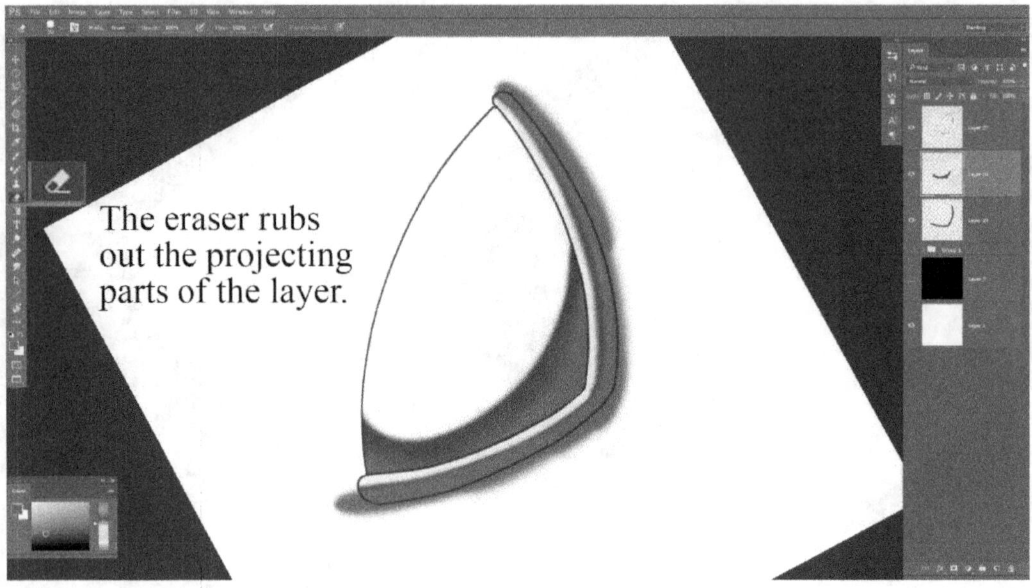

8. Make a new layer and increase the size of the Brush. Color the area above and in front of the own shadow.

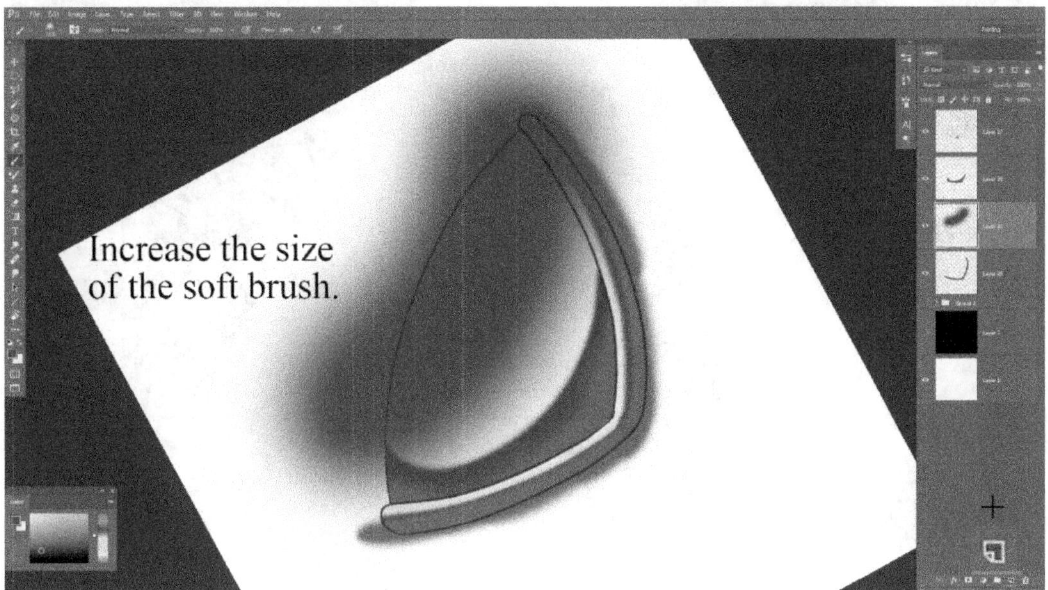

9. Use the Eraser Tool to erase any excess strokes.

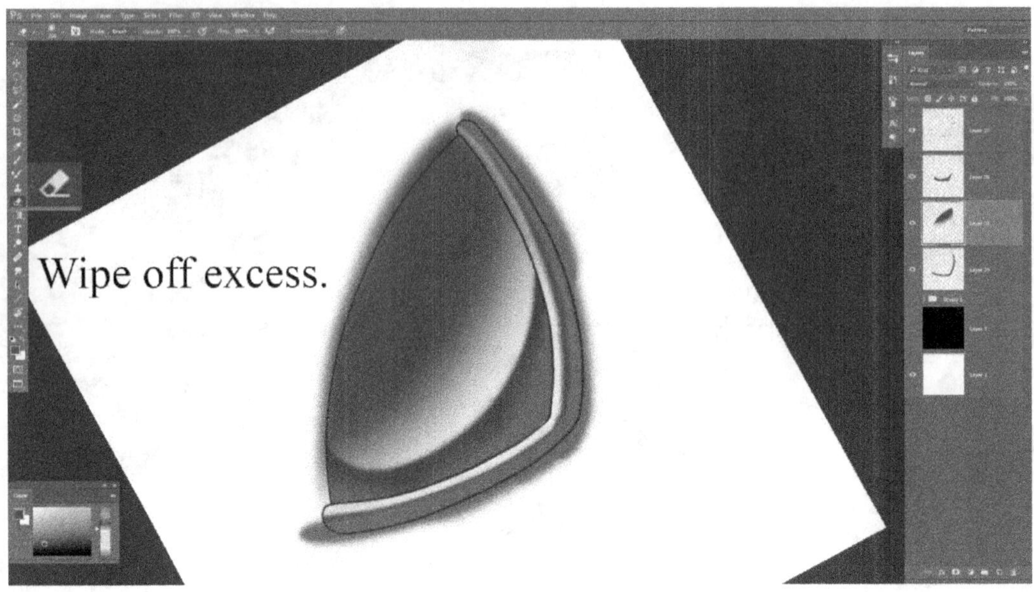

10. Add some gloss effect by erasing a part of the soft brush strokes.

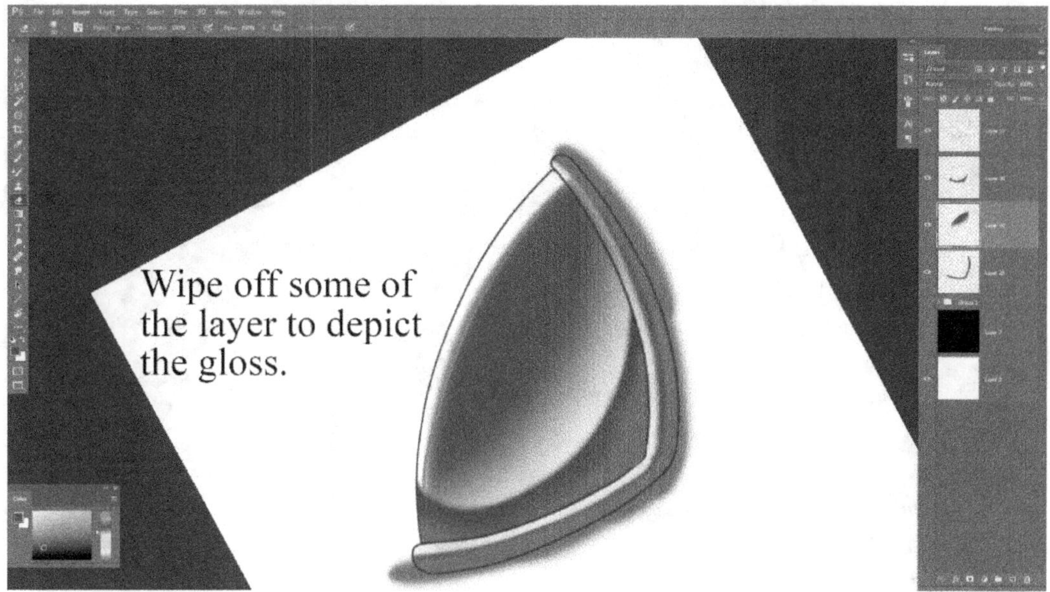

11. The eraser can also be used to add some glare to the object.

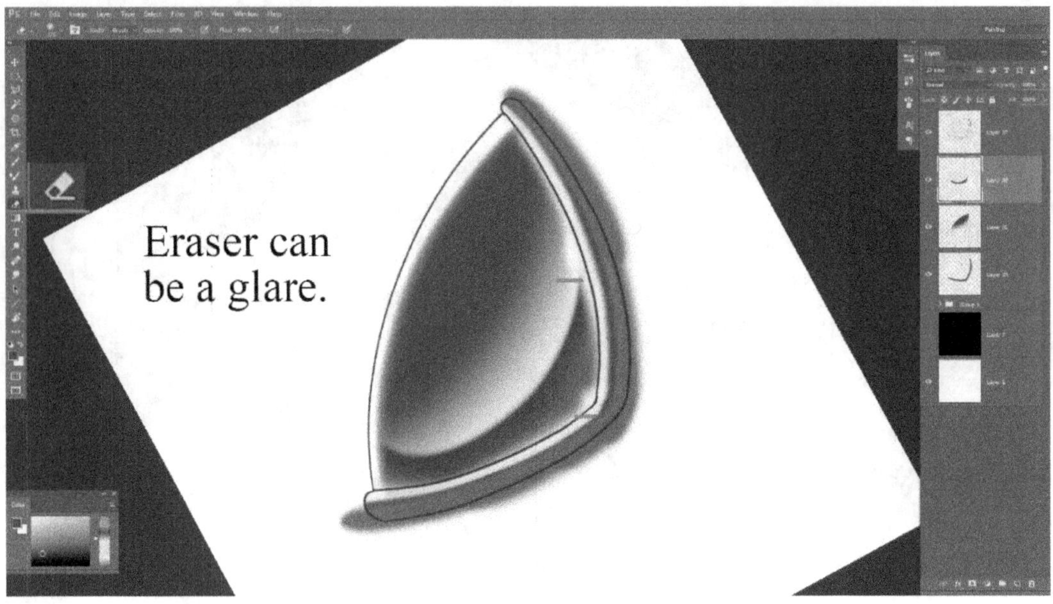

12. Add some highlights using the Eraser Tool.

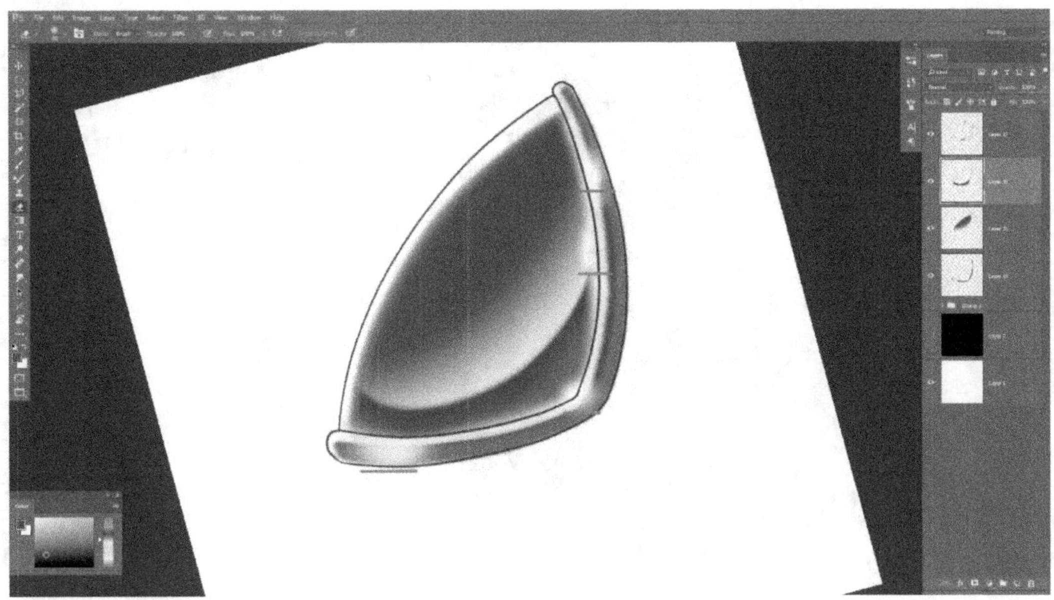

13. Merge all the layers for the color and shadows.

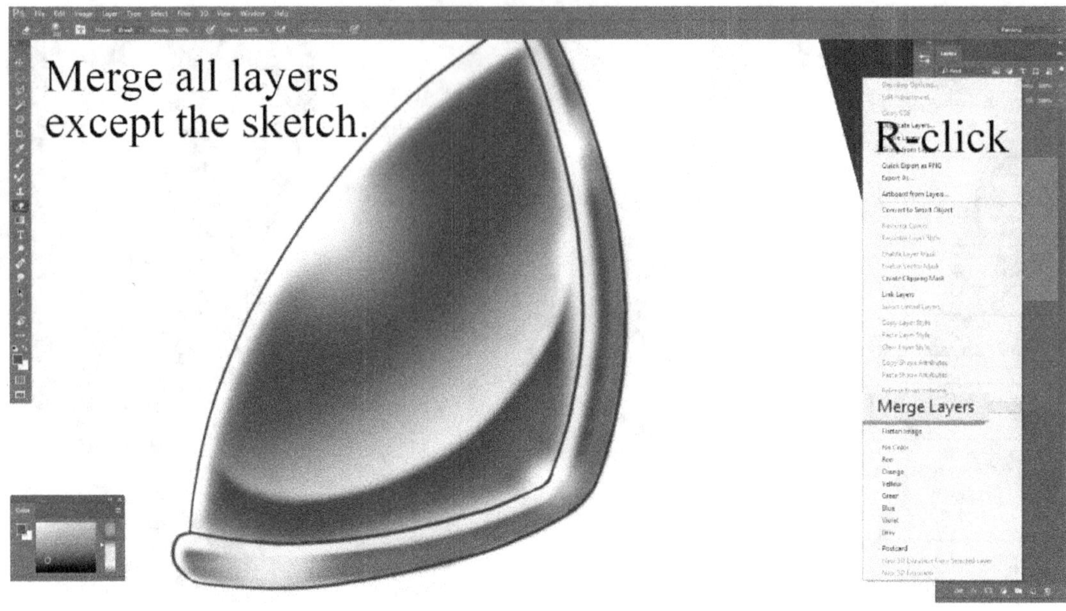

14. Click on the Burn Tool and darken areas behind and below the own shadow to add contrast to the object.

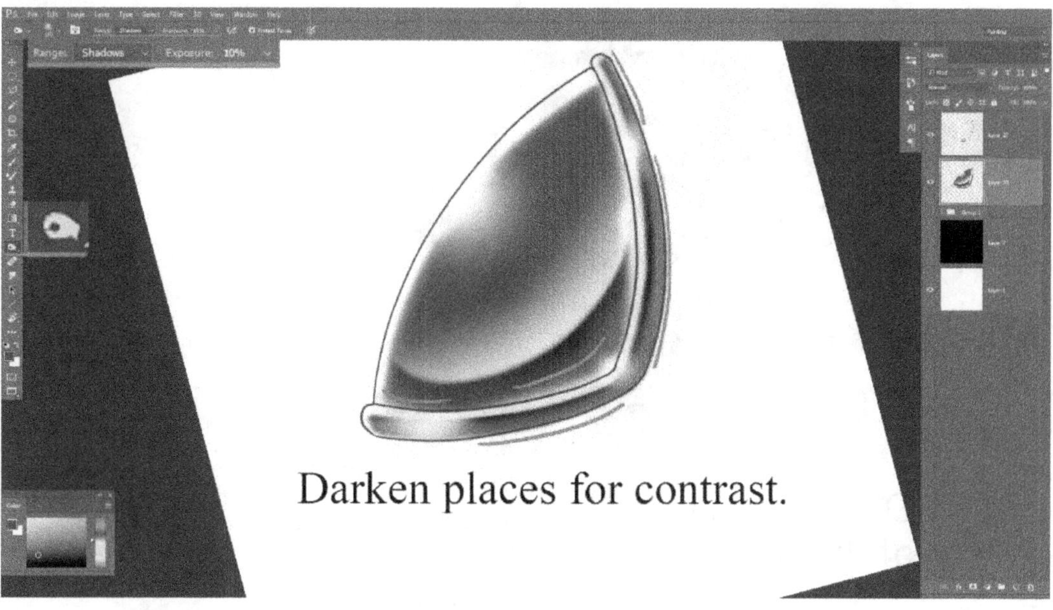

15. Add reflection to the surface of the object. Use the Brush Tool. Use a small radius Brush with 40% Opacity.

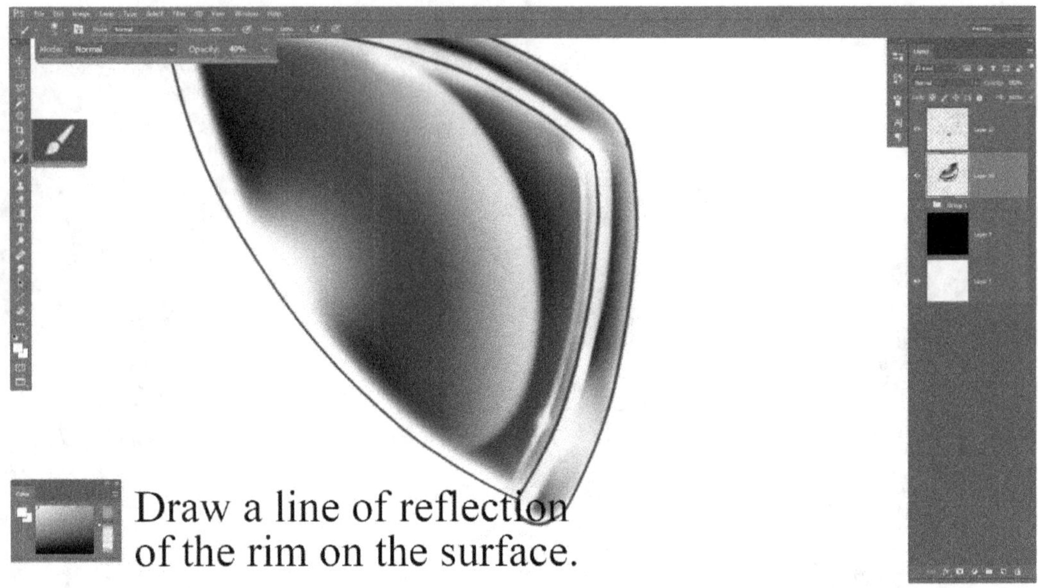

16. Add another reflection on the surface of the other part of the sketch with the Eraser Tool.

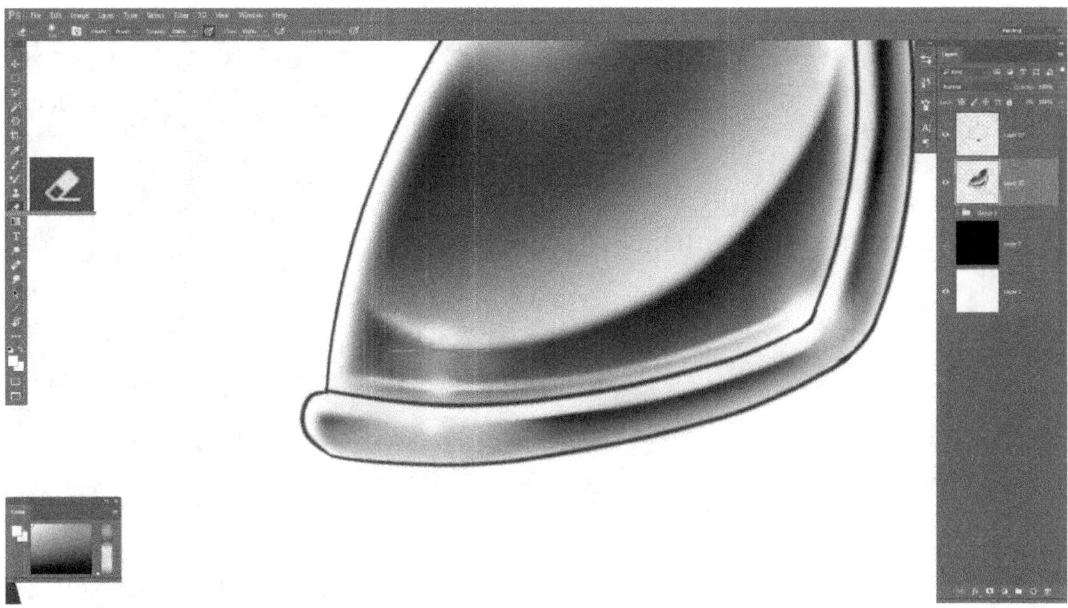

17. Lower the Opacity of the Brush Tool to 26%. Using the Brush Tool add some reflections to the other areas of the drawing.

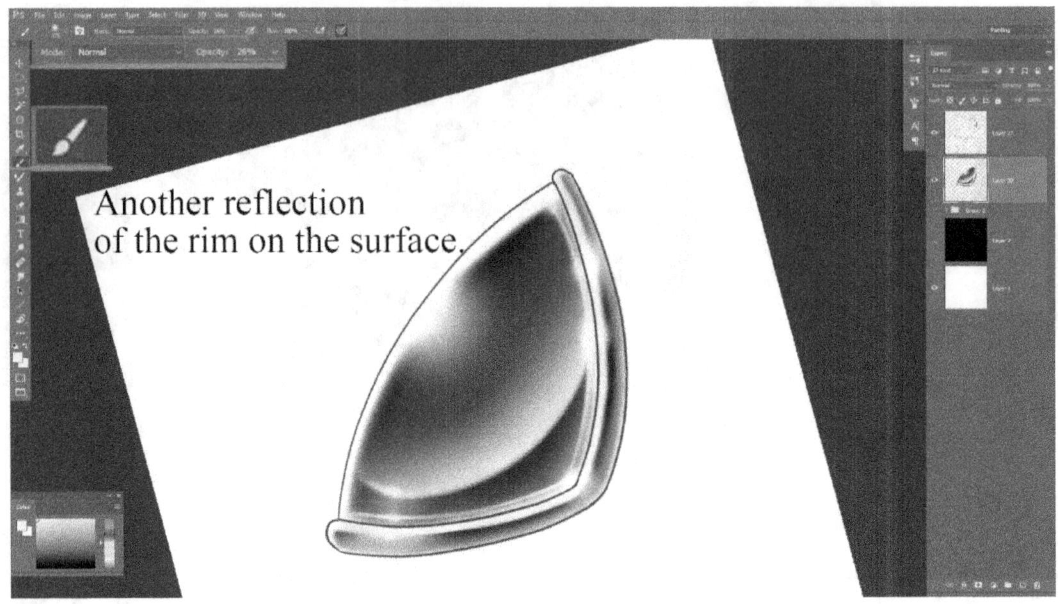

18. Lock the layer of the sketch and lower the Brush Tool's Opacity to 83%. Trace over the sketch to hide it a little bit.

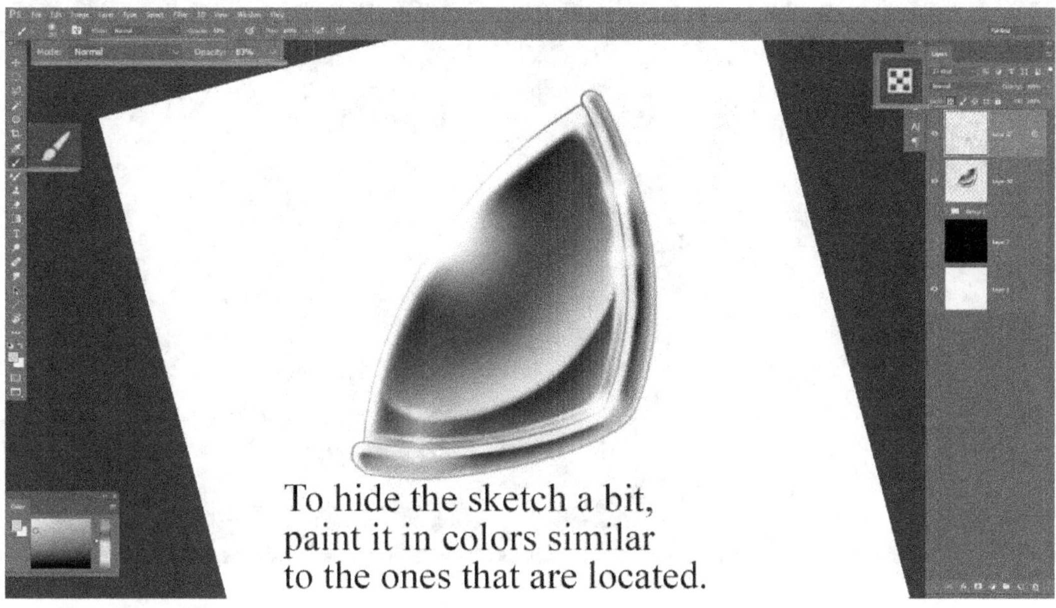

19. Make another layer. Fill it with black.

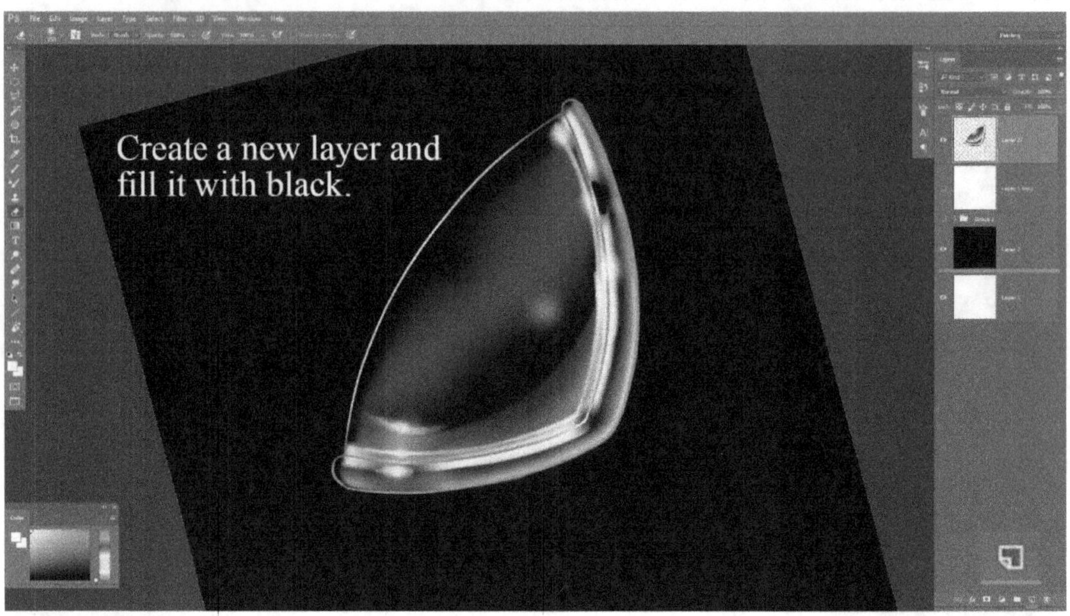

20. Click on the Brush Tool and change the mode to "Behind". Select the color white.

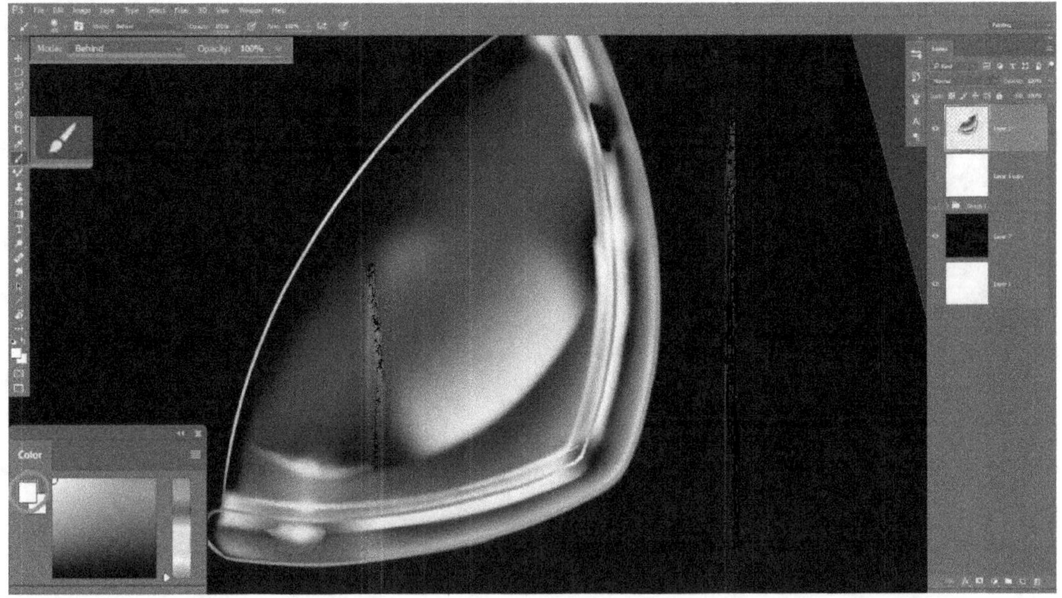

21. Select the Brush Tool and change the mode to "Behind". Select the color white.

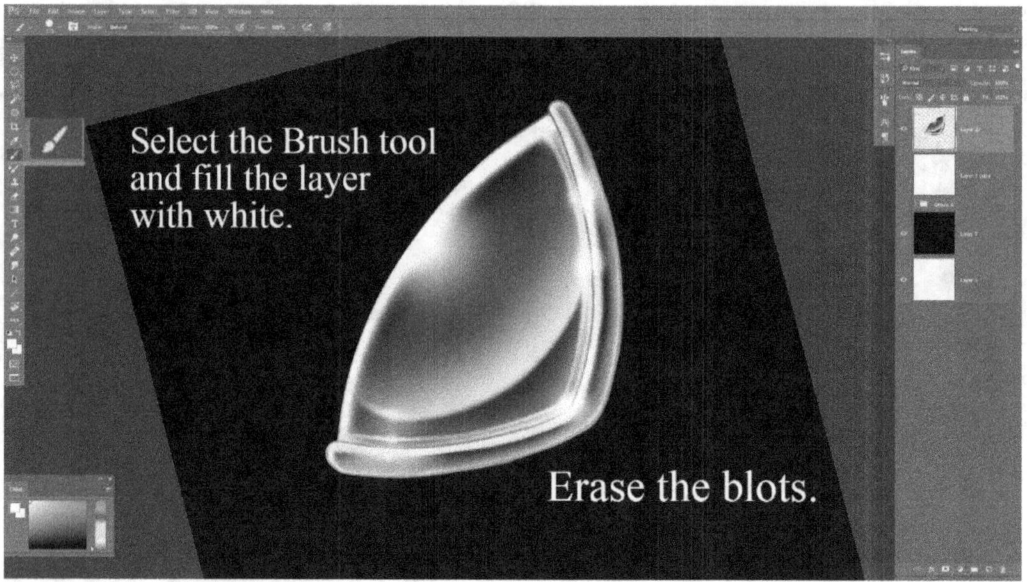

22. You should take note that the reflection on the surface is like a warped version of a two dimensional image. This is called the "Distorted Reflection."

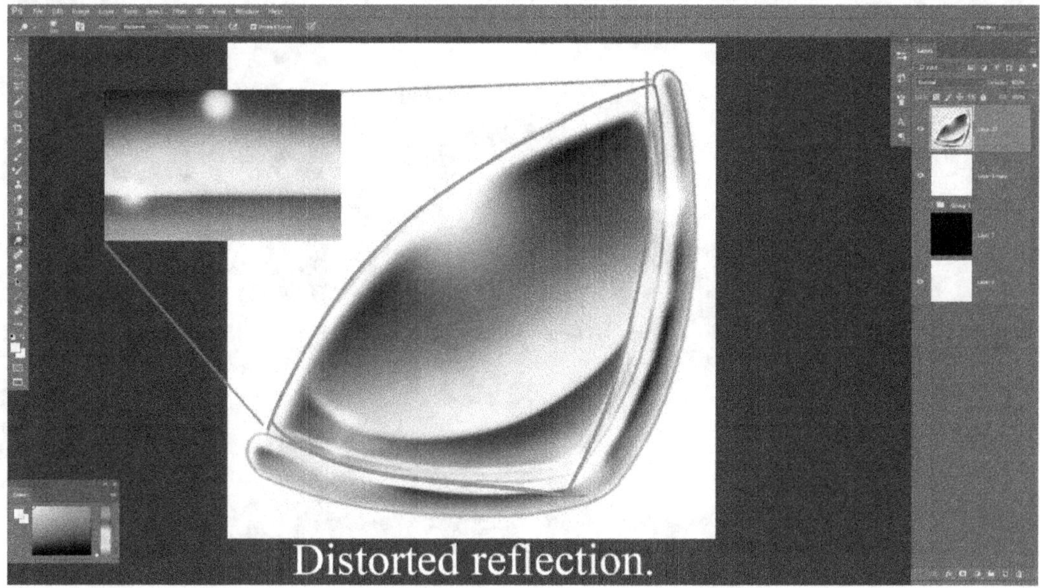

23. The finished image.

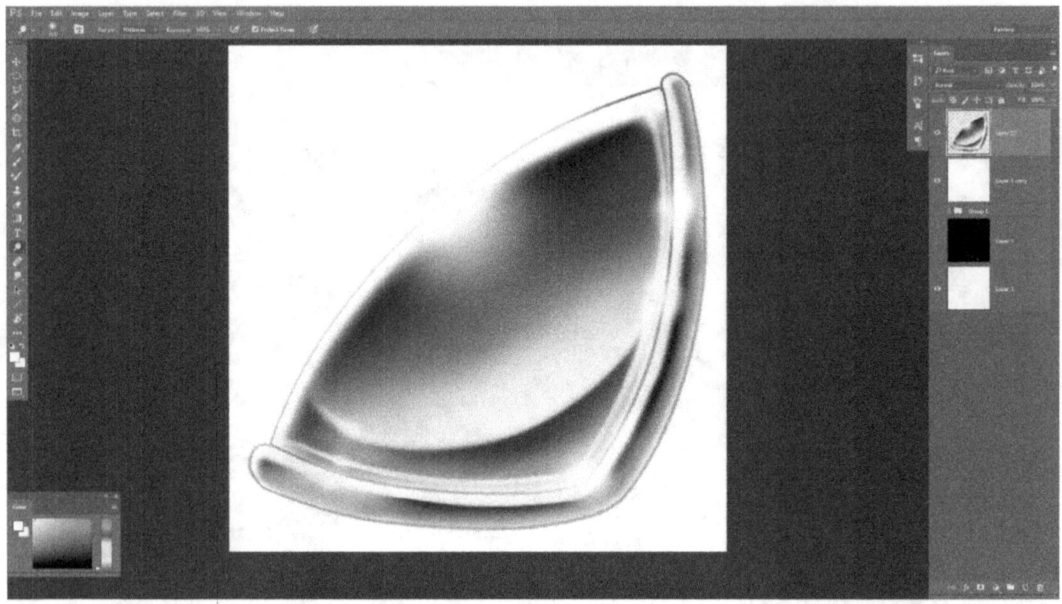

Creating Human Portrait using Adobe Photoshop

Learning to draw people is a bit difficult. We see humans every day and the struggle with drawing people is making them look more "human". This is because, excluding identical multiple siblings, every single person is unique. All the details for each person are different even though they have similarities. What we need to know about drawing humans is the proper, or ideal, proportions of the human body.

Now we will learn how to draw some examples of humans in a standing and sitting position.

Some Examples of Human Portrait

Standing man

1. Draw a vertical line with the Brush Tool to denote the drawing's standing height. Make 5 horizontal markings to denote the proportional sizes of the parts of the body.

The usual form of measurement for identifying the proportions of the body is the head. The total height of the figure is 7 heads. The torso, the distance from the hips to the knees, and the distance from the knees to the feet are 2 heads each.

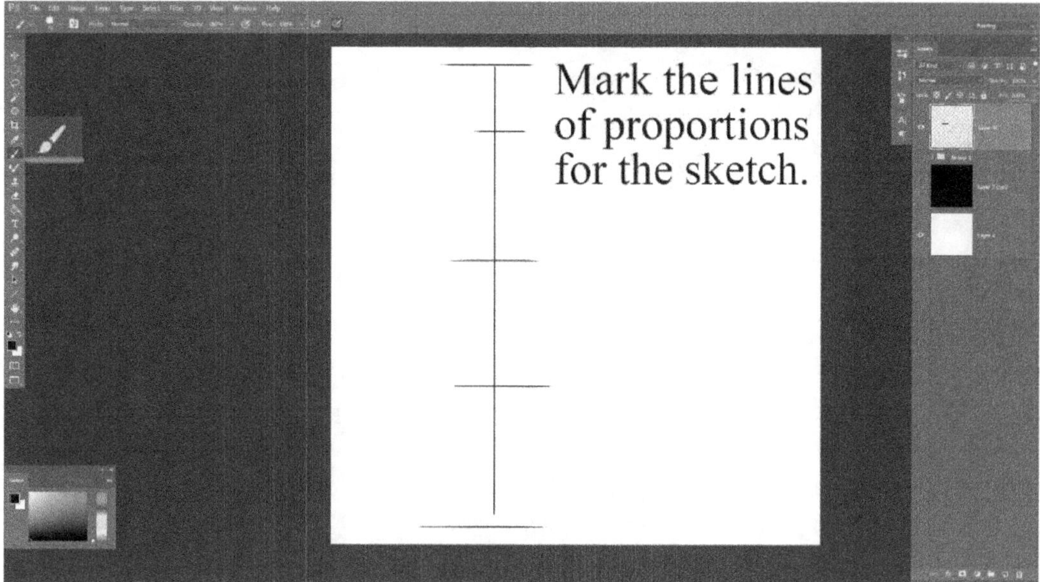

2. Sketch the head of the man. Just draw the general shape of the head. Do not include too many details yet.

3. Draw the shoulders and the torso.

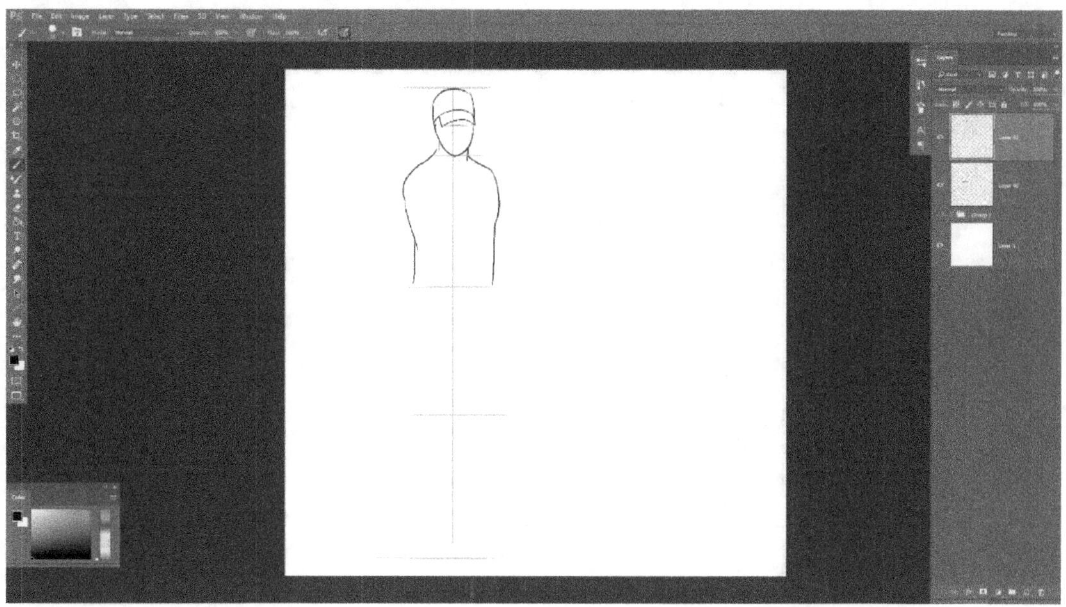

4. Draw one of the legs. Draw the leg that is directly facing the viewer.

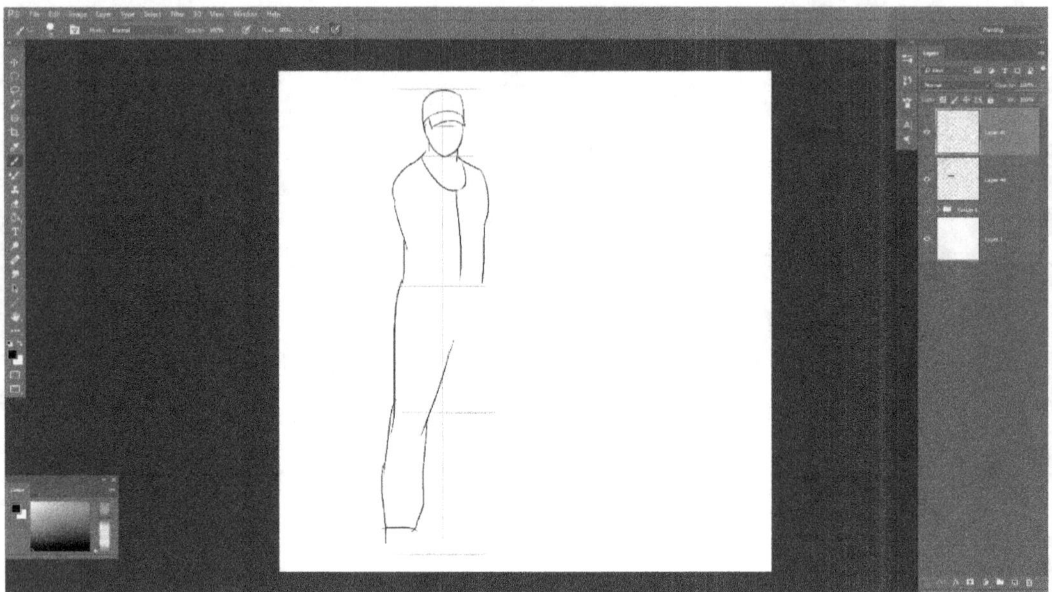

5. Draw the other leg. Draw it slightly facing away from the viewer.

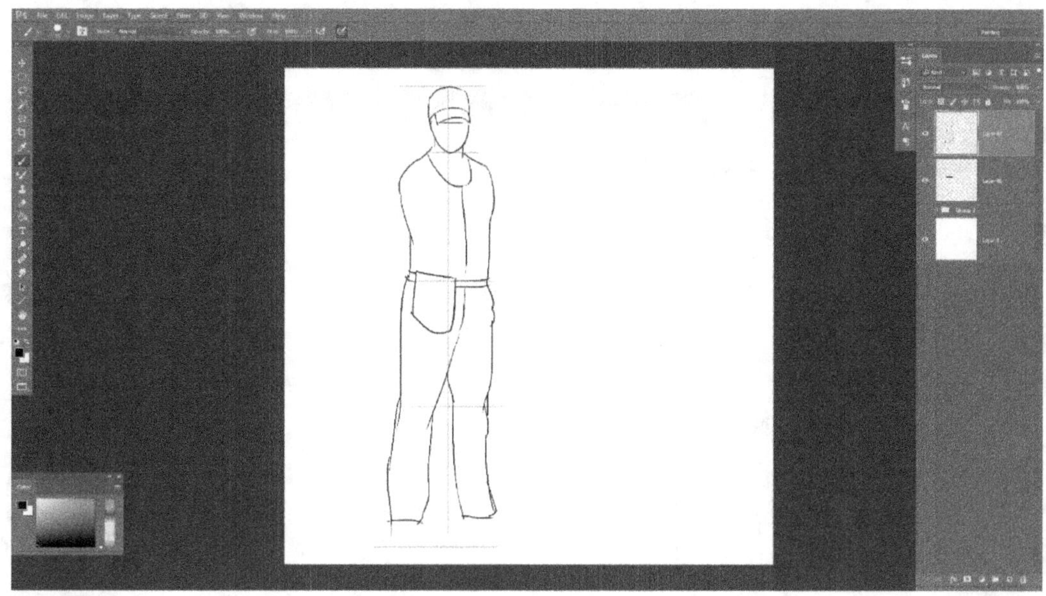

6. Draw the one arm and hand. These may take any pose you like. Just be aware of the principles of foreshortening or the distortion in the general shape of the object the closer it is to the viewer.

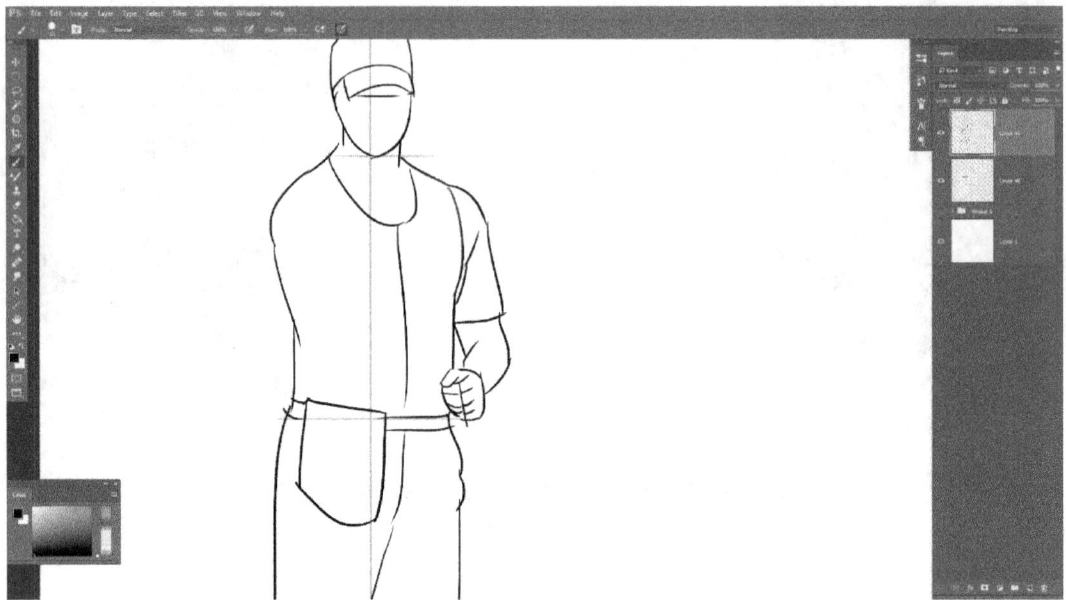

7. Draw the other arm and hand.

8. Draw the feet of the figure.

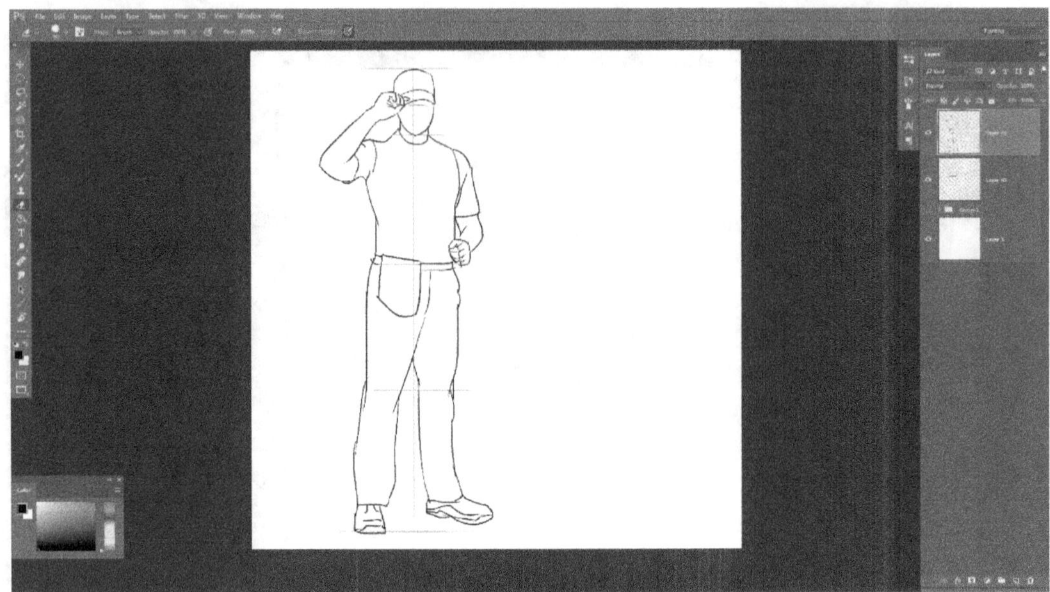

9. Draw the details of the figures clothing.

10. Draw the details of the figure's face. You can draw it in any expression you like.

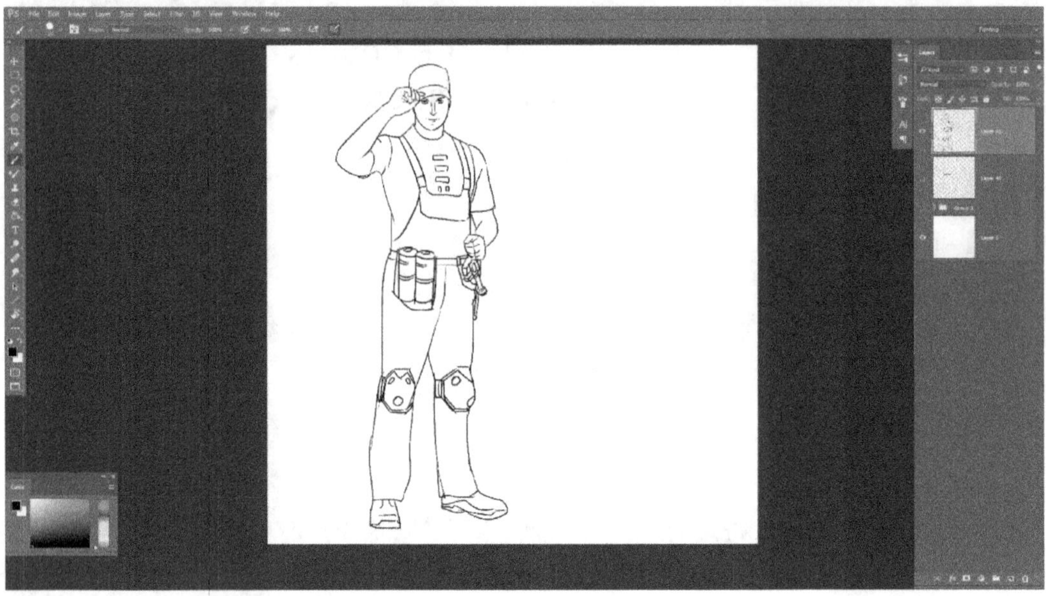

11. Make a new layer for the colors. Fill the pants of the figure with a color using the Brush Tool.

12. Using the Eraser Tool, remove any excess color from areas that you do not want to be colored.

13. On the same layer, fill in all the parts of the figure that have the same color.

14. Create another layer for the coloring in the shoes. Use the Brush Tool in Behind Mode and with 100% Opacity. Paint the main color, own shadow, and highlights of the shoe.

15. Make another layer and fill in the shirt of the figure.

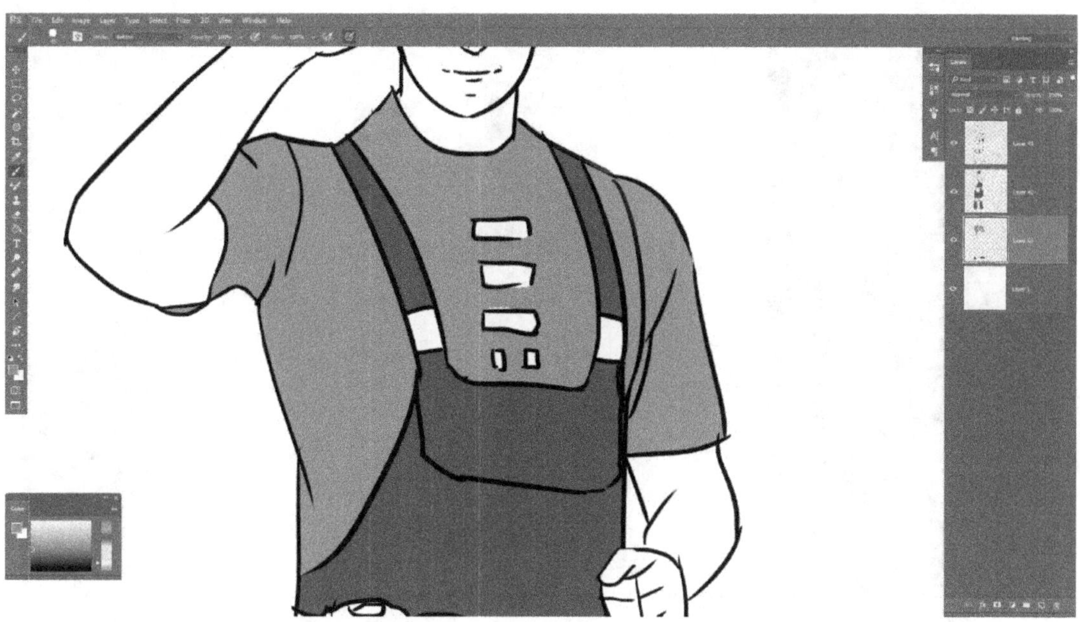

16. While on the same layer, fill in the parts and details of the figure's suit.

17. Make a new layer and fill in human's skin. Draw in the shadows and highlights as well. Use the Brush Tool with the following parameters: Behind Mode and 100% Opacity.

18. Fill in the rest of the figure's exposed skin. Use the same parameters for the Brush tool.

19. Lock the layer of the figure's suit. Draw the own shadows of the suite. Use a color that is darker than the original color.

20. Draw the own shadows for the rest of the figure's clothing. Draw the own shadows for the details as well. The details may have highlights. Draw them too.

21. While the Brush Tool is still selected, click the right mouse button anywhere on the workspace area to pull up the brush details window. Select one of the textured brushes and change its size to the desired level.

22. Change the parameters of the Brush tool to Normal mode and with opacity of 26%. Draw multiple lines with two colors to blend them. Soften the lines between the light and the shadows.

23. Do this for all the figure's pieces of clothing.

24. Using the same technique, soften the shadows and highlights of the areas with exposed skin.

25. Do the same for all the details of the figure's clothing.

26. Click on the Dodge Tool and change the Range to Midtones and the Exposure to 68%. Add highlights to the details of the clothes.

27. Lock the layers with colors. Use the Dodge Tool to highlight other areas of the figure.

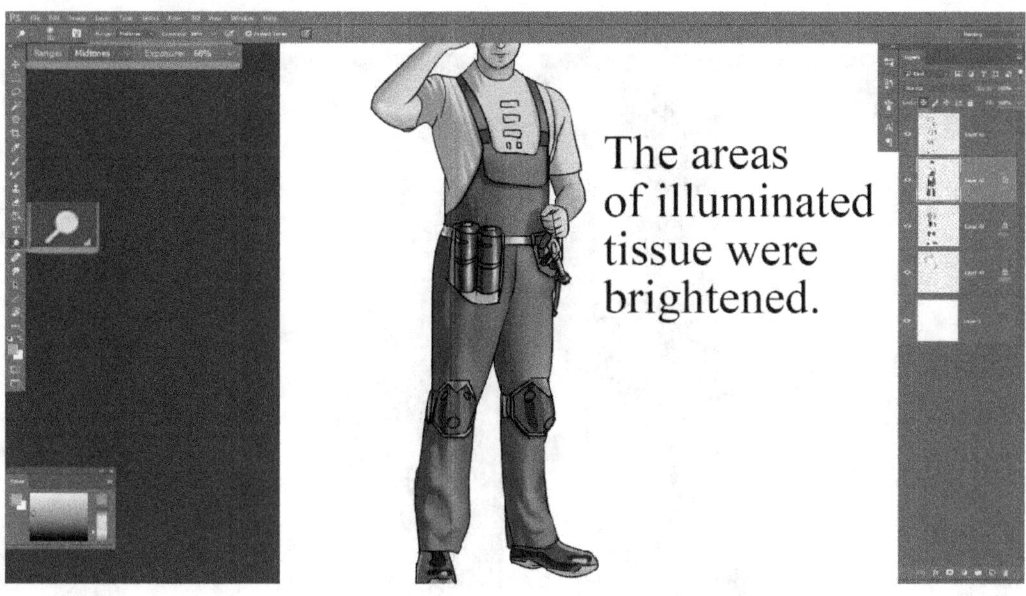

28. Click on the Smudge Tool and change its parameters to Normal Mode and 82% Exposure. Smudge the areas between light and shadow to soften the transition.

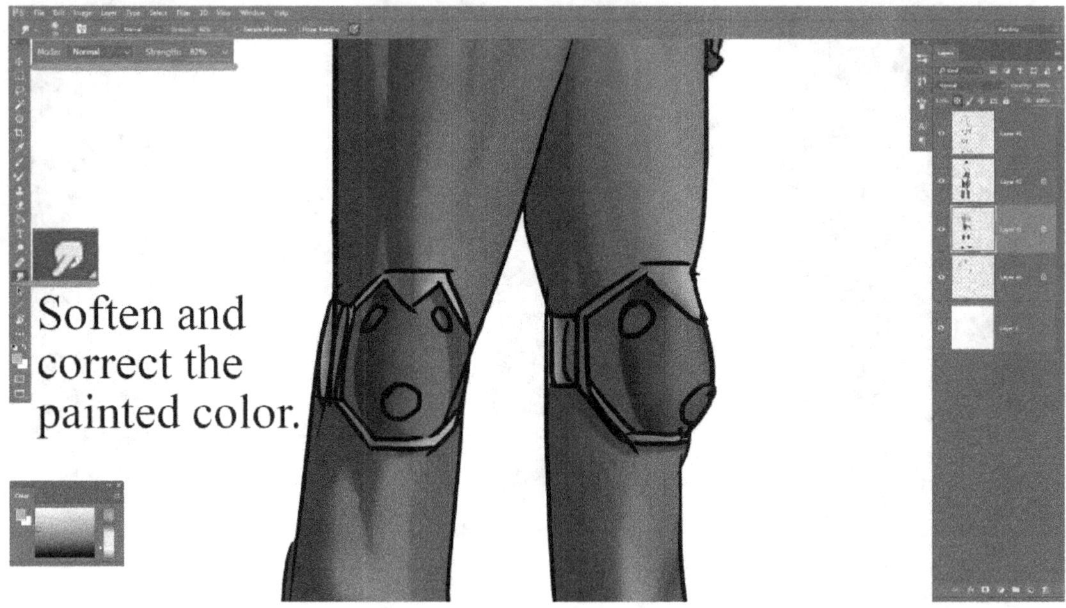

29. Click on the Dodge tool and highlight areas of the details of the figure's suit. Use Midtones for Range and set the Exposure to 68%.

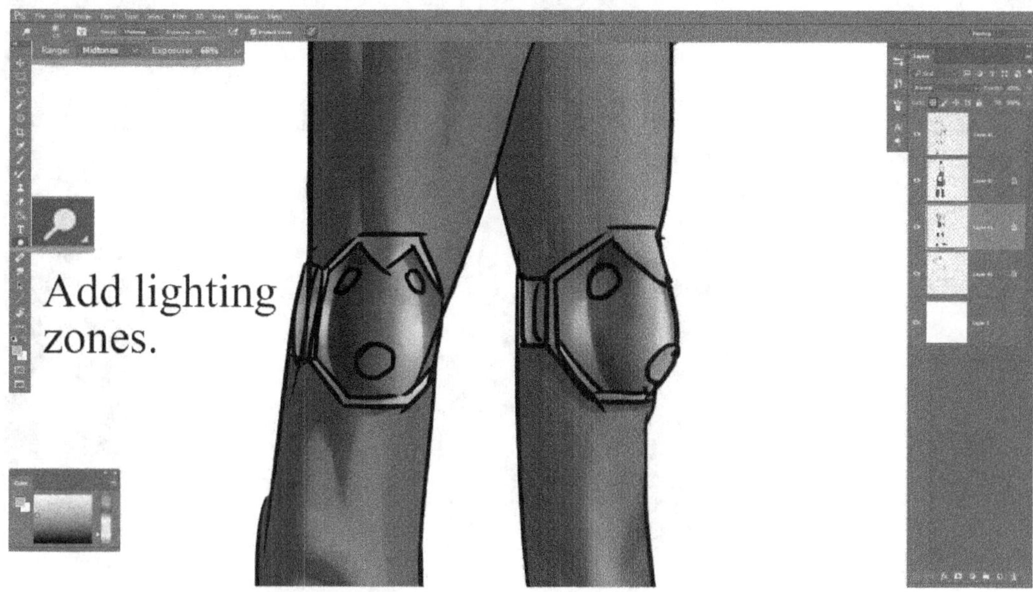

30. Click on the burn tool and darken the areas of the shadows.

31. Lock the layers of the details and use the Smudge Tool to soften the transitions between light and shadow.

32. Select and lock the layer of the original sketch. Use the Brush tool to paint over the lines of the original sketch. Use colors that are close to the color of that part.

33. Paint over the lines close to the skin of the figure. Draw over the details of the face and hands of the figure.

34. Paint over the pants and details of the suit.

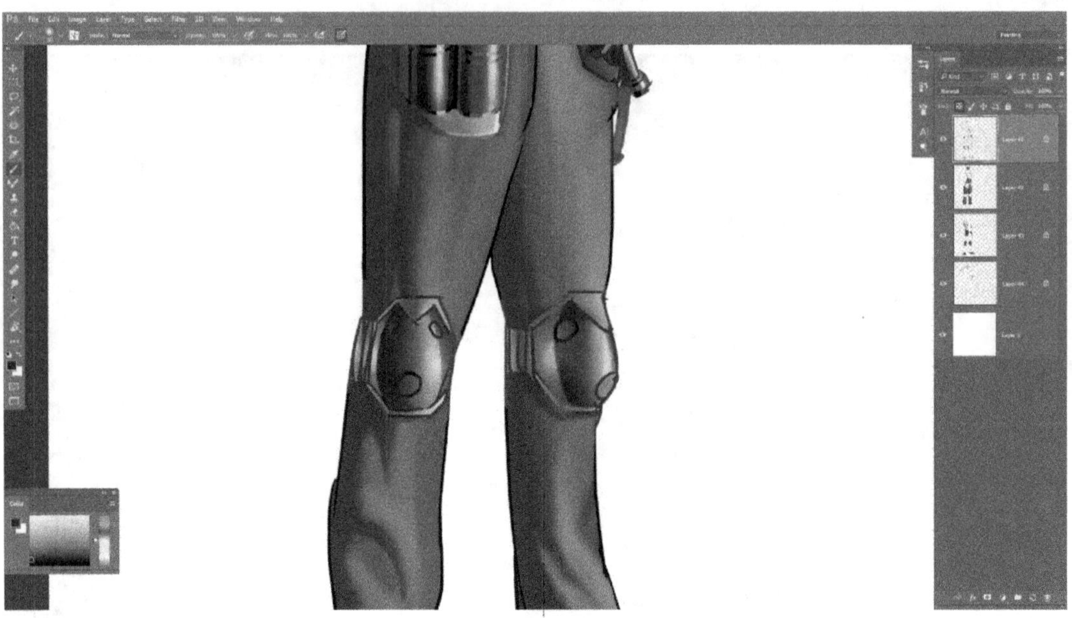

35. The figure should look like this after the change of color of the sketch.

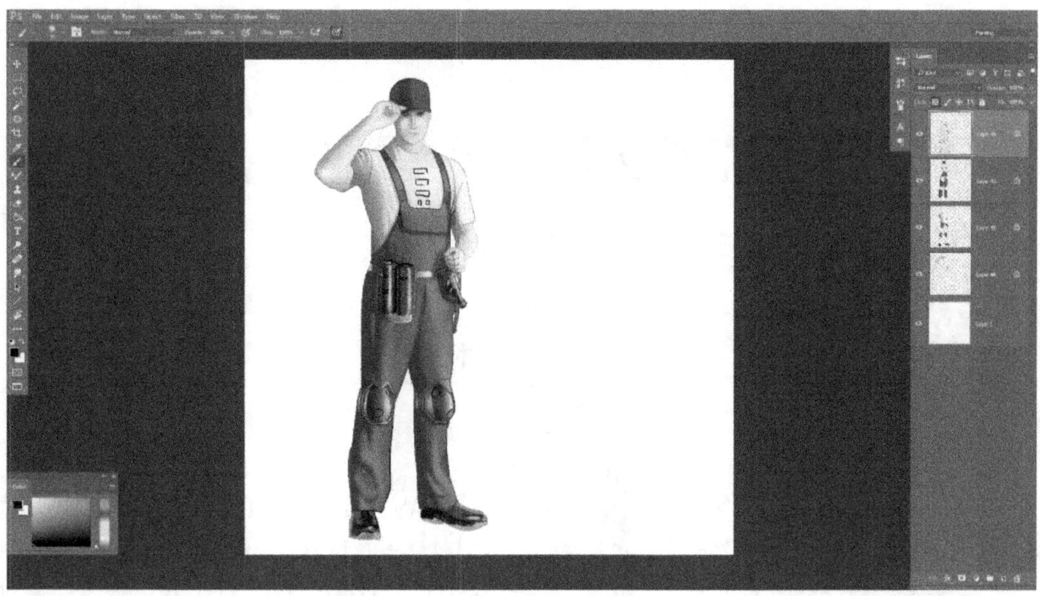

36. Select the Brush Tool and change it to Color Dodge Mode and adjust its Opacity to 100%. Paint over the areas that are the source of efflorescence or the light sources. Change the color of the lines of the sketch around them as well.

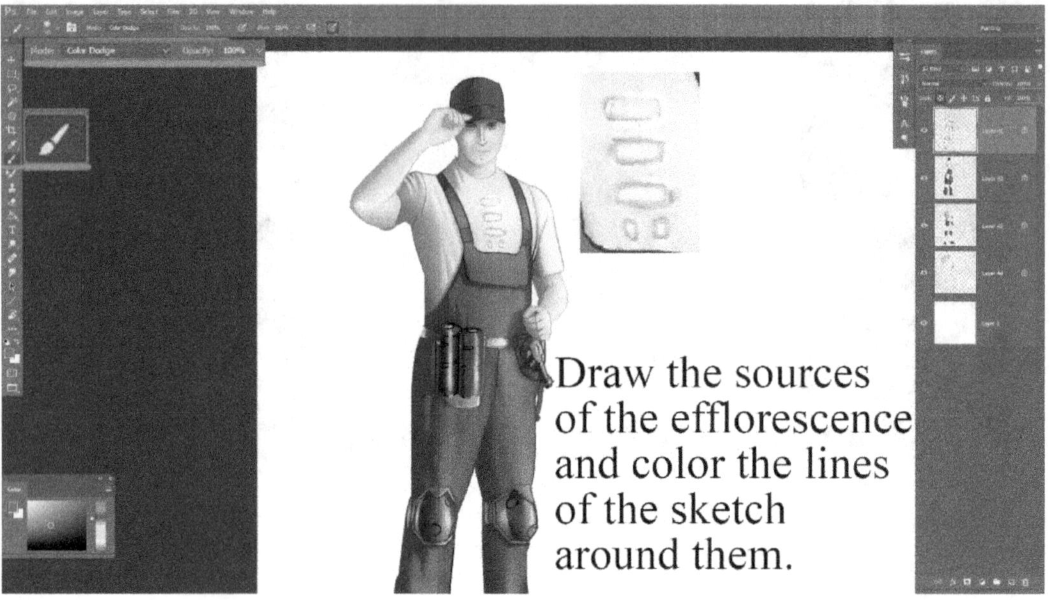

37. Paint over the other light sources.

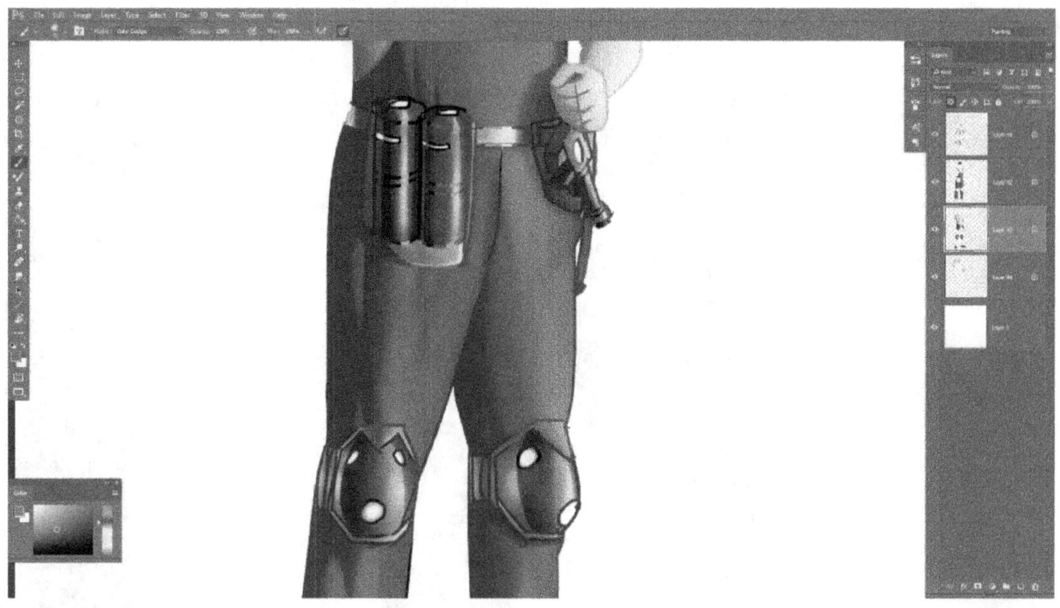

38. Change the Brush Tool to Color Dodge Mode. Click on the icons for the layers of the original sketch and the suit of the figure. Paint over the areas illuminated by the light sources.

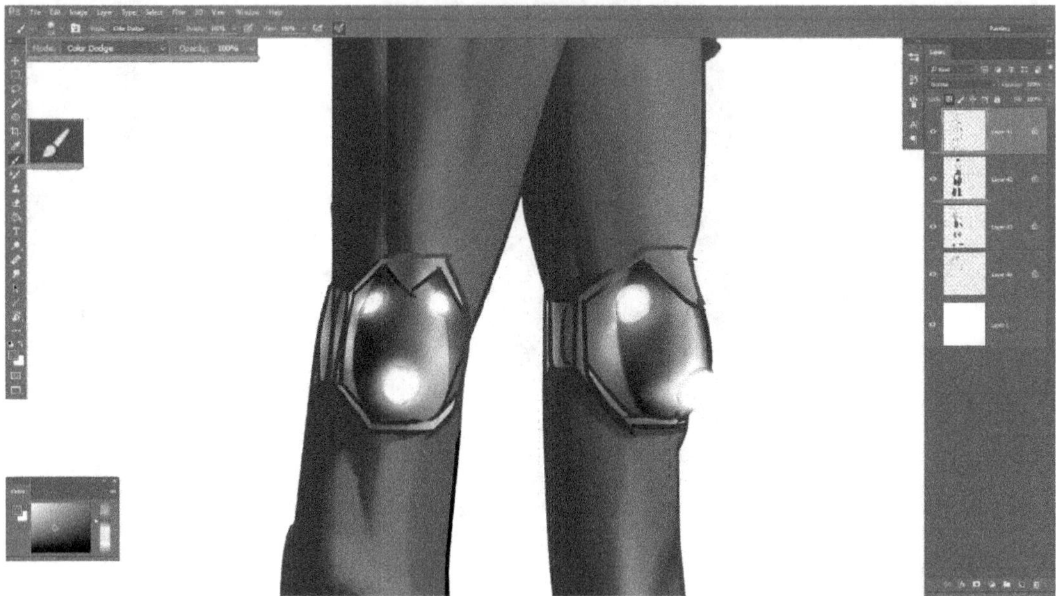

39. Select the layer for the details of the suit. Using the Brush tool with the same parameters as before, draw the reflections created by the light sources.

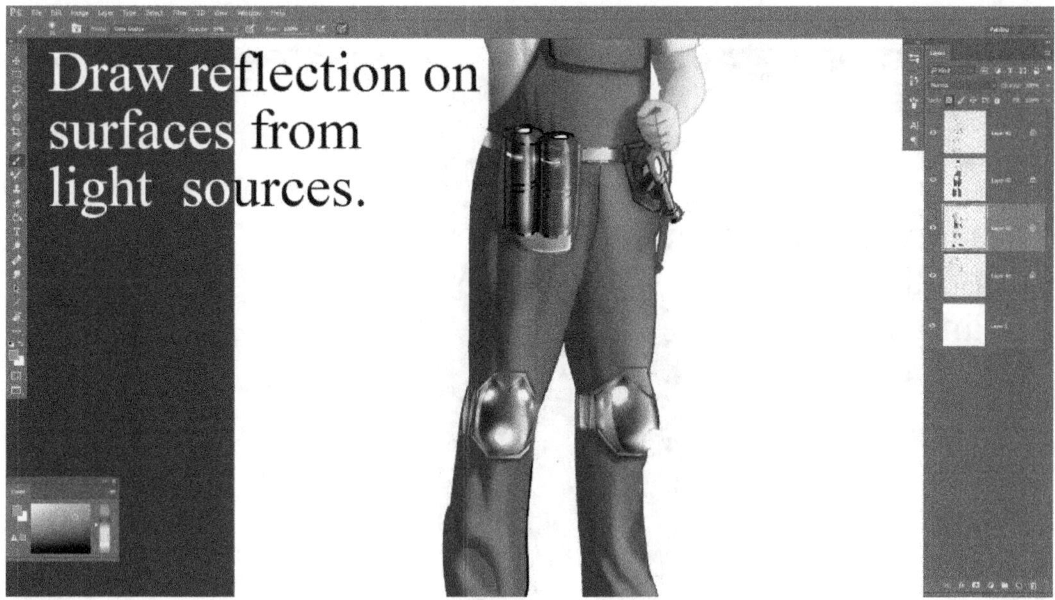

40. Change the Opacity of the Brush Tool to 25%. Lock all the layers except for the background. Draw the reflections created by the light sources on the surfaces of the suit and on the skin.

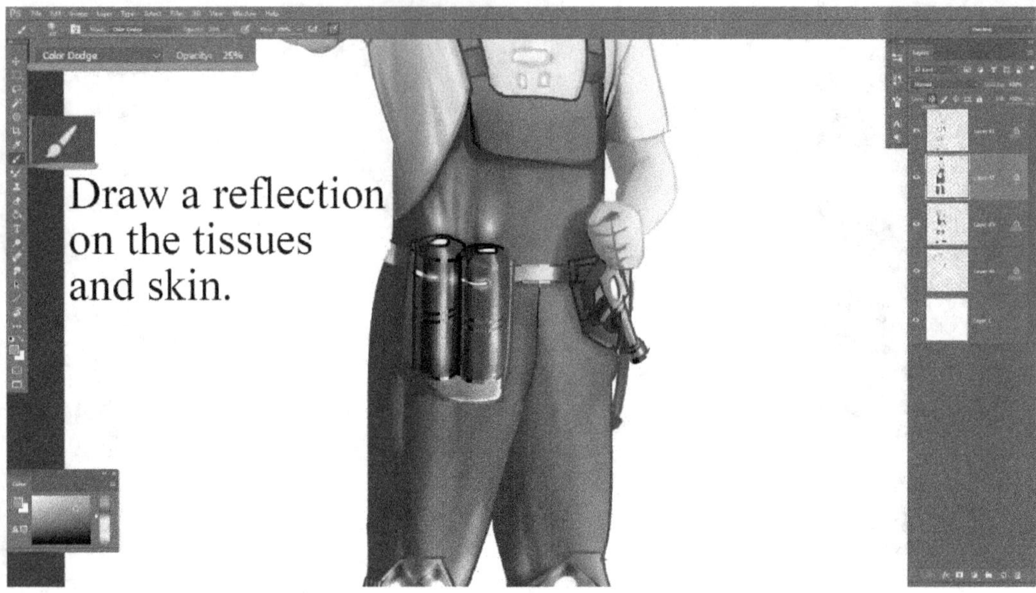

41. Select all of the layers and click on the Crop Tool. Adjust the size of the workspace in relation to the figure drawn.

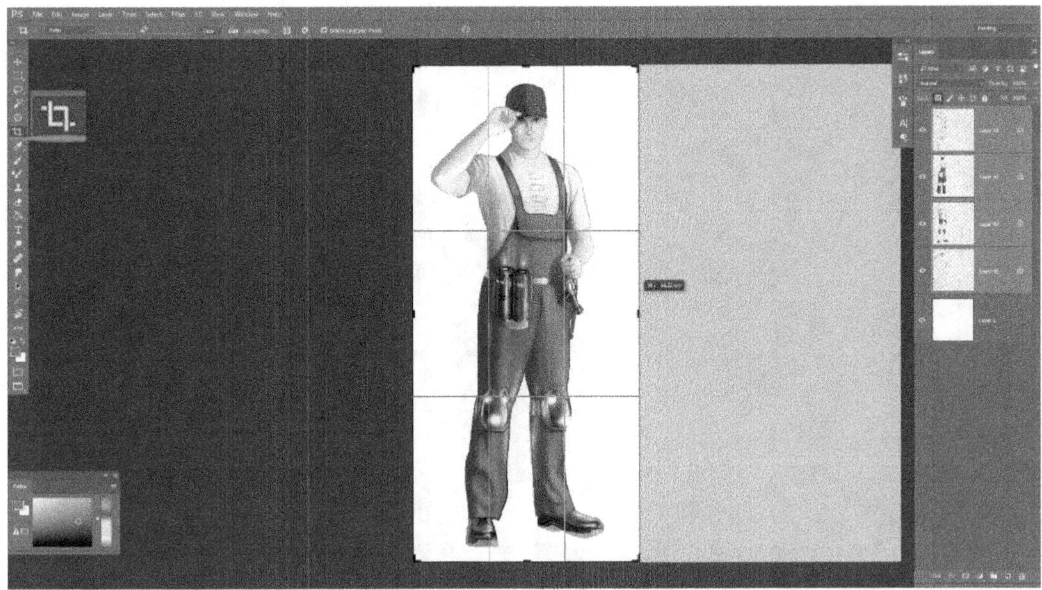

Sitting woman

1. Make a new layer. Using the Brush Tool, draw two oblique lines. To make sure that they are perfectly straight, hold the Shift key while drawing them.

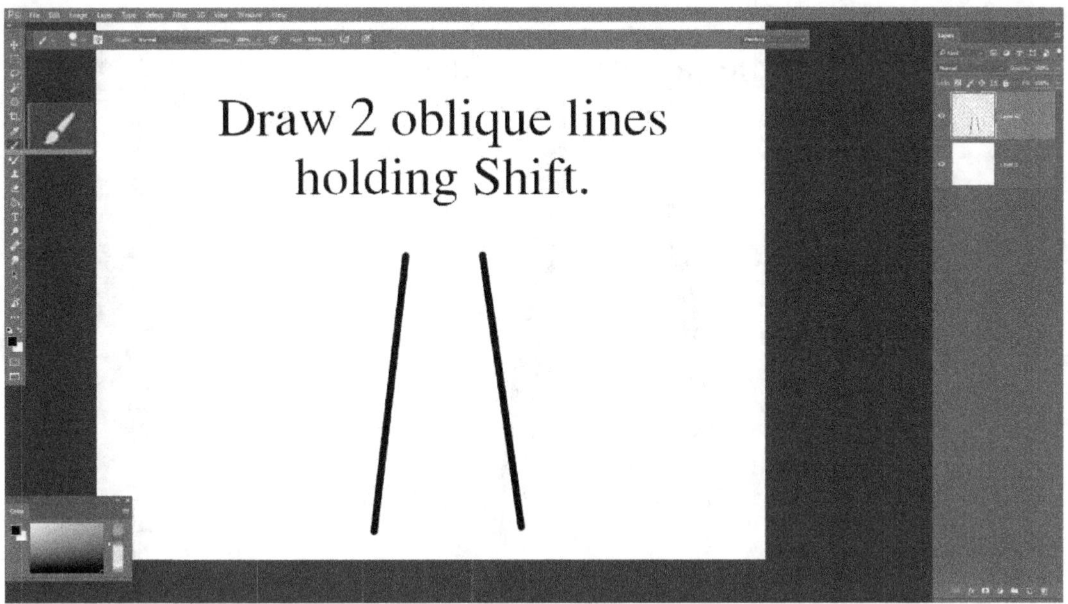

2. Copy the layer of the lines, then press Ctrl+T. Adjust the scale and position of the new lines to make them appear as if they are further away.

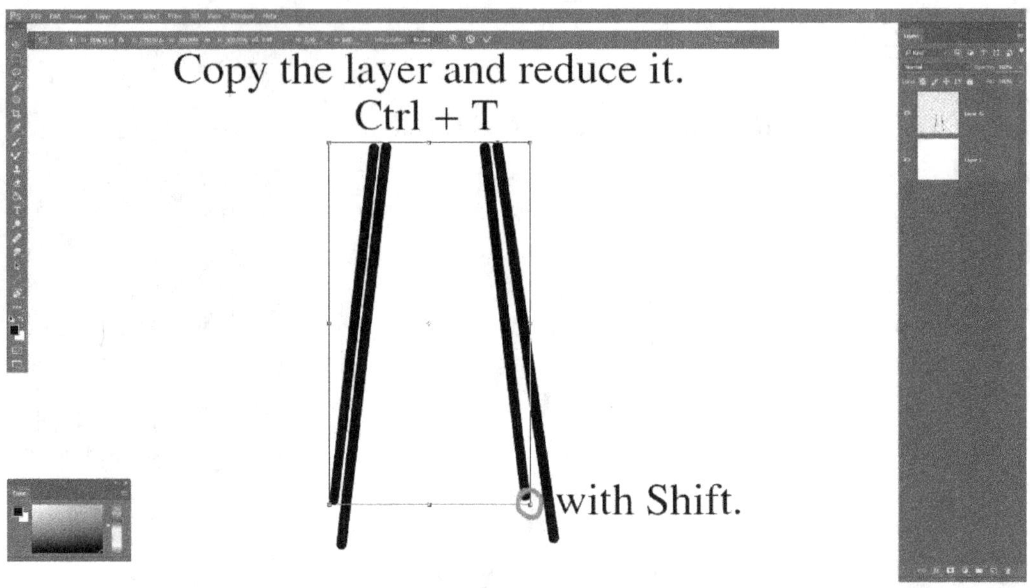

3. Select both the layers and press the Right Mouse button. Merge both the layers.

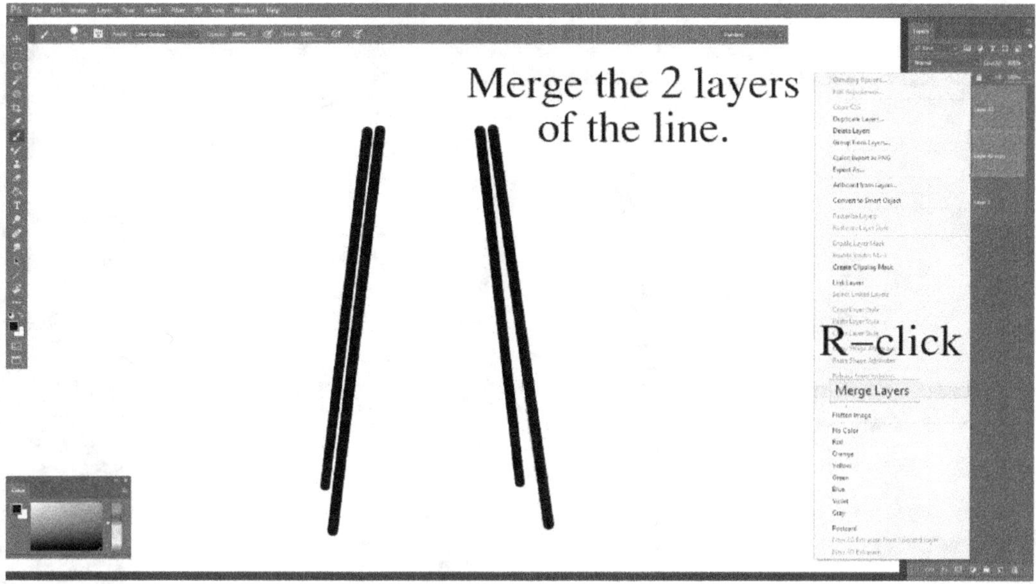

4. Click on the Lasso Tool. Select the icon of the layer of the lines. Make another layer. On this layer, press the Right Mouse Button and on the popup menu select Stroke.

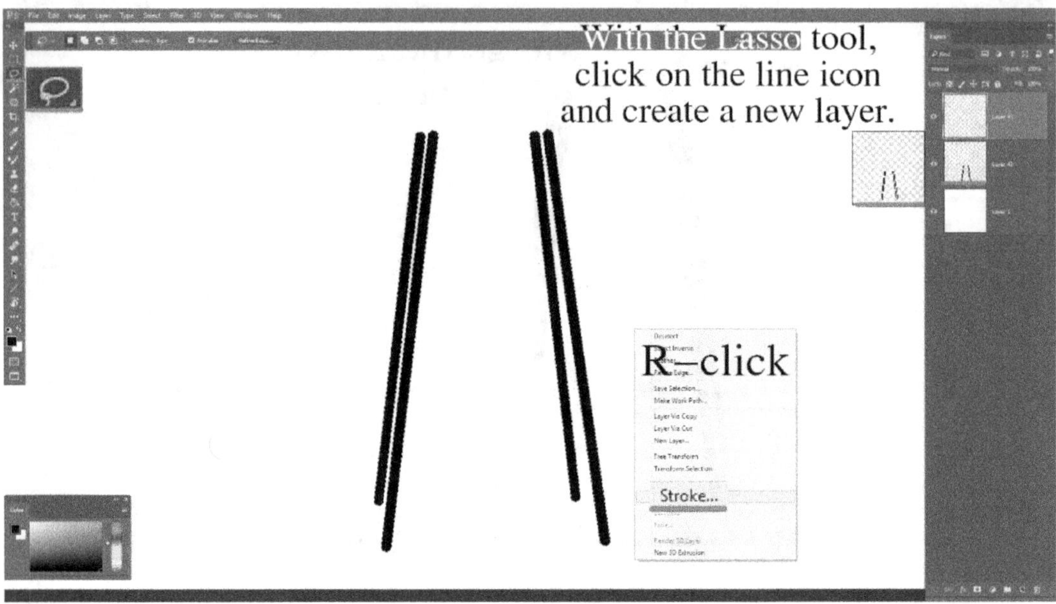

5. This will create a stroke version of the lines on the new layer.

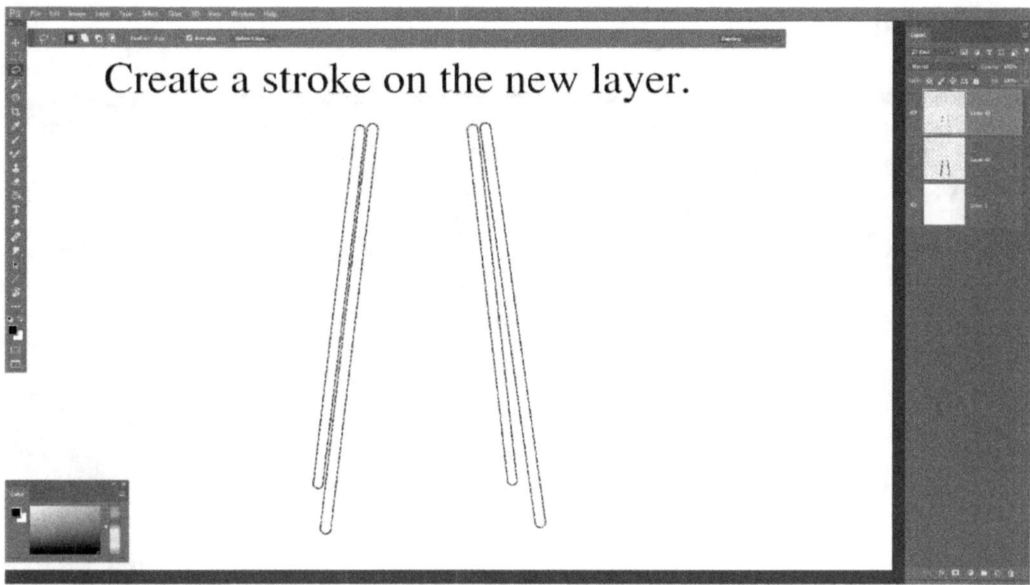

6. Delete the old layer and leave the stroke. Make a new layer and draw a horizontal line. To ensure the straightness of the line, press the Shift key down while drawing it.

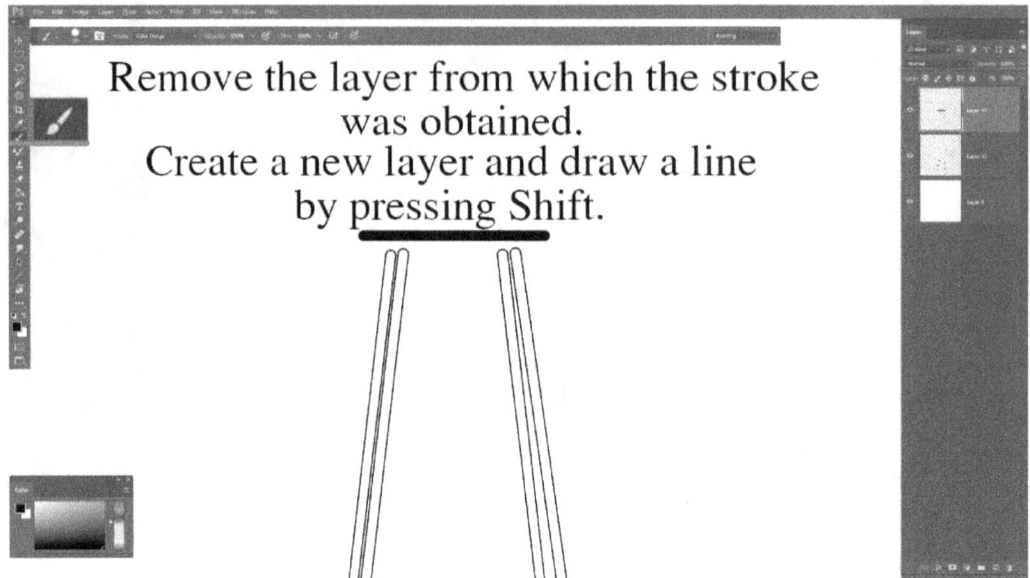

7. Press Ctrl+T to select this horizontal line. Press the Right Mouse Button. On the popup menu, select Warp.

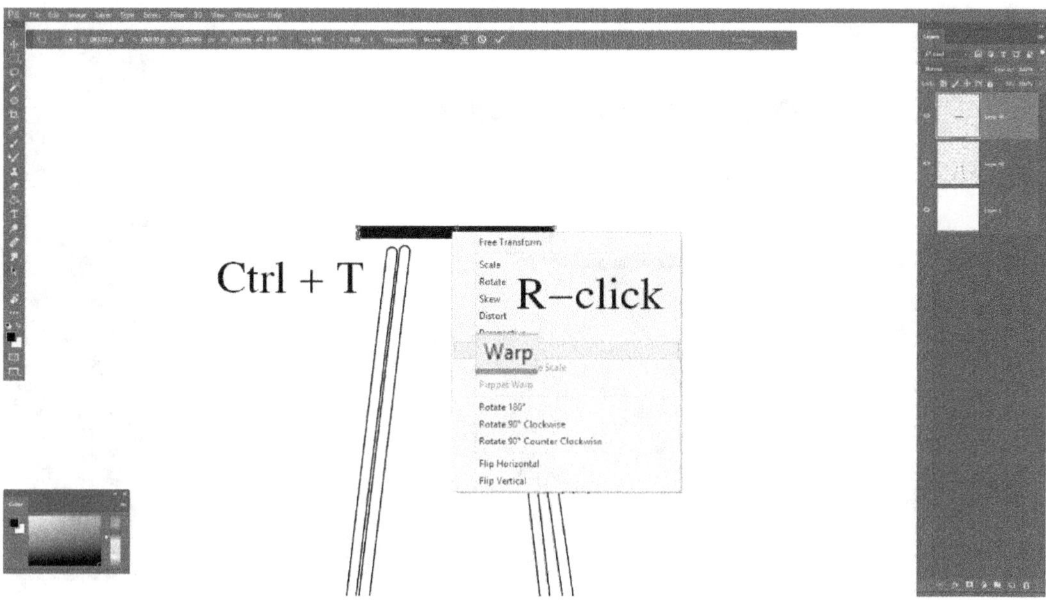

8. Distort the shape of the horizontal line by dragging the small black circles of the Transformation Box downwards.

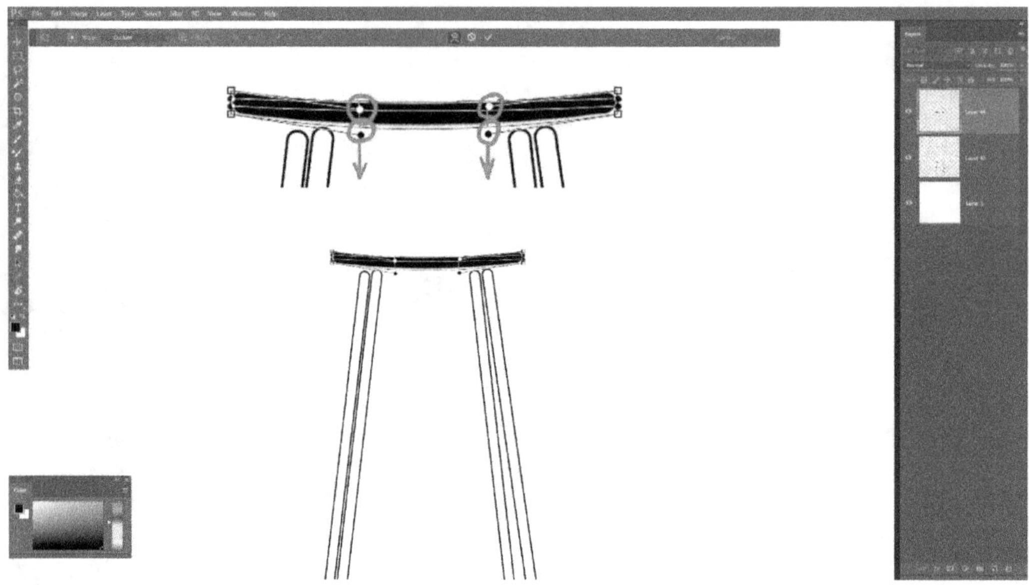

9. Copy the layer for the horizontal line and press Ctrl+T. Press the right mouse button while on the workspace and select Flip Vertical on the pop-up menu.

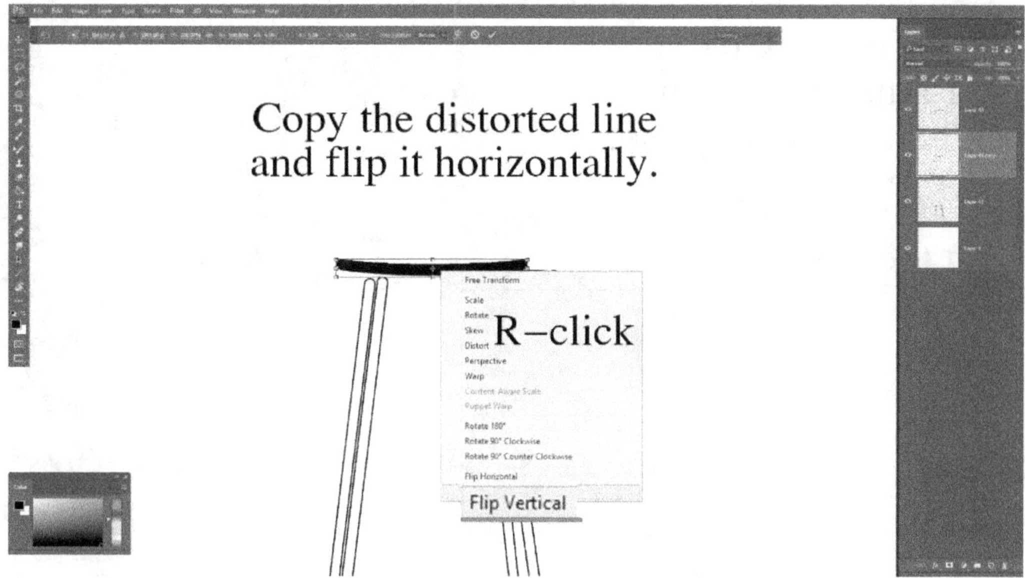

10. Make a new layer and create a stroke of 5.0px width for the horizontal lines. These will be the top of the stool.

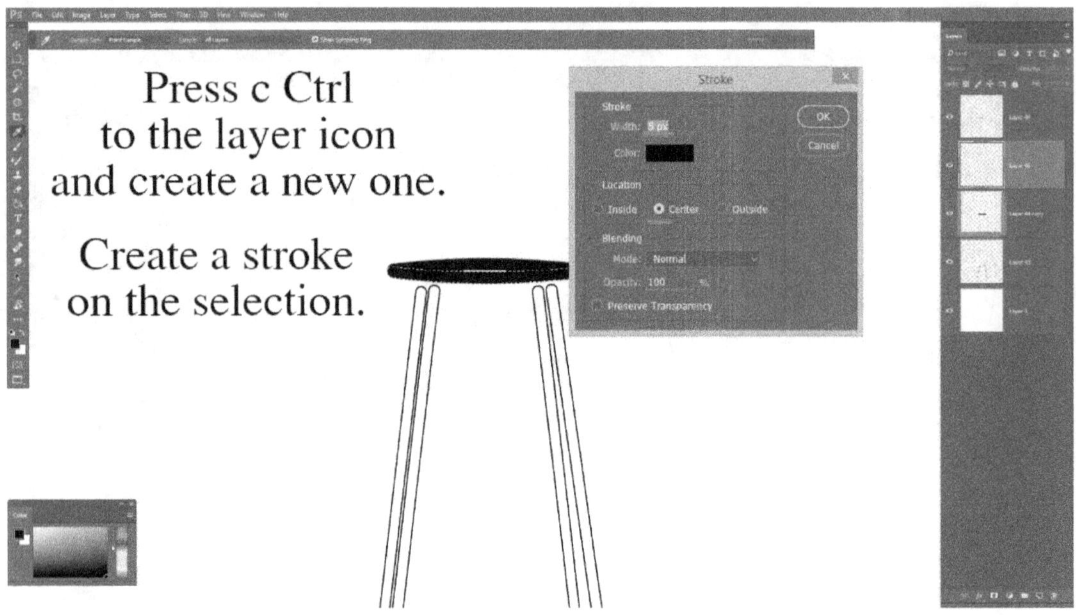

11. Delete the layers of the original horizontal lines and merge the layers for the strokes.

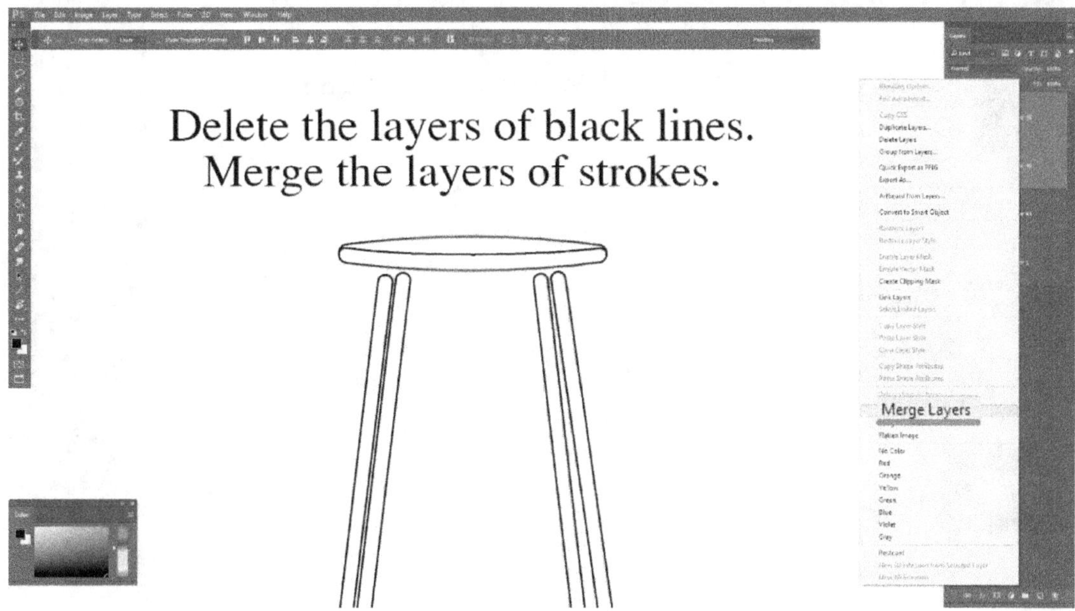

12. Using the Eraser Toll, remove any overlapping lines.

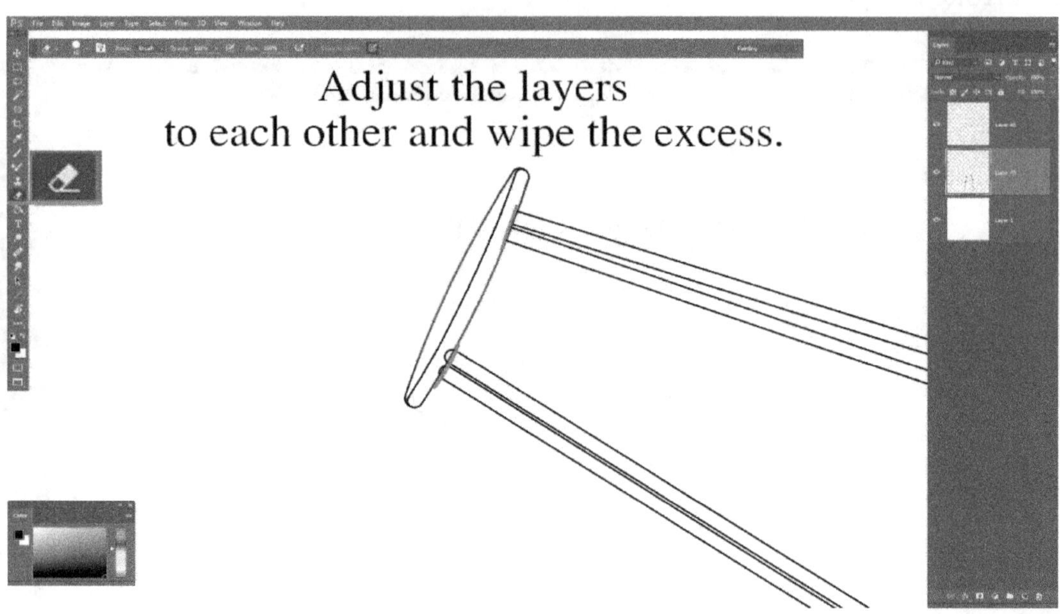

13. Select both layers and merge them.

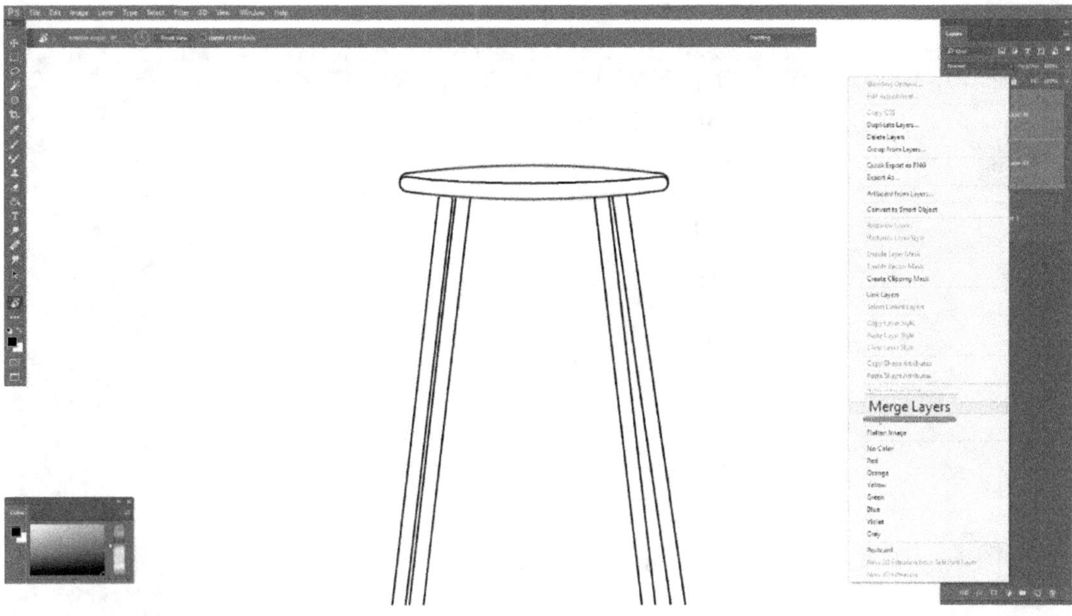

14. Draw the stool connections using the Paint Brush Tool. Convert them to strokes as well.

15. Make a new layer. Draw the outline for the body and thighs of the figure. Use a basic stick figure. Note the proportions and distances between the body parts.

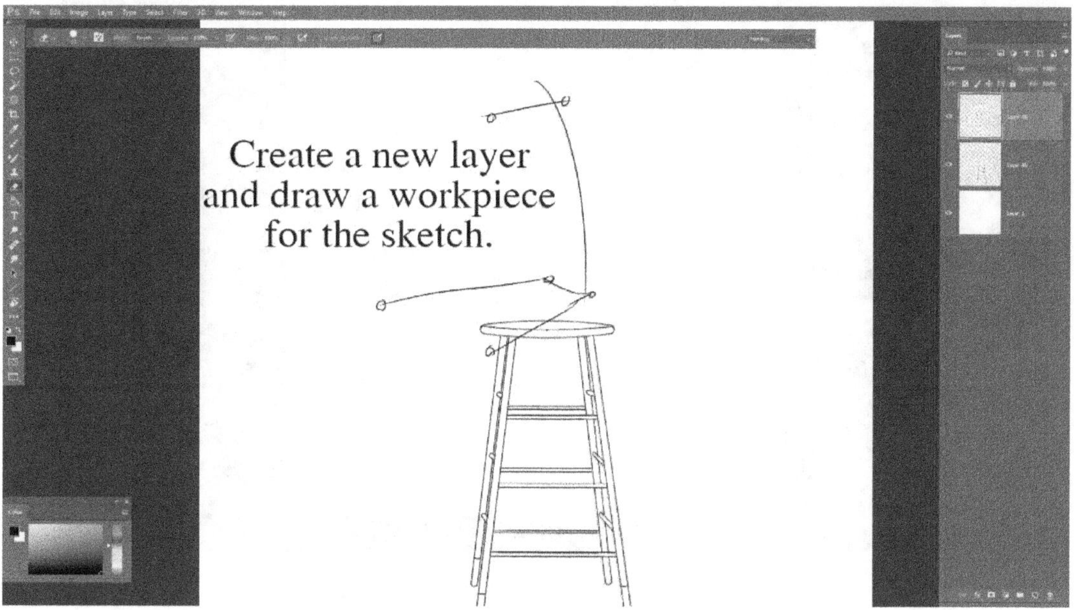

16. Make a new layer and "flesh out" the figure using the skeleton as a frame. Draw the outline for the head, arms and legs.

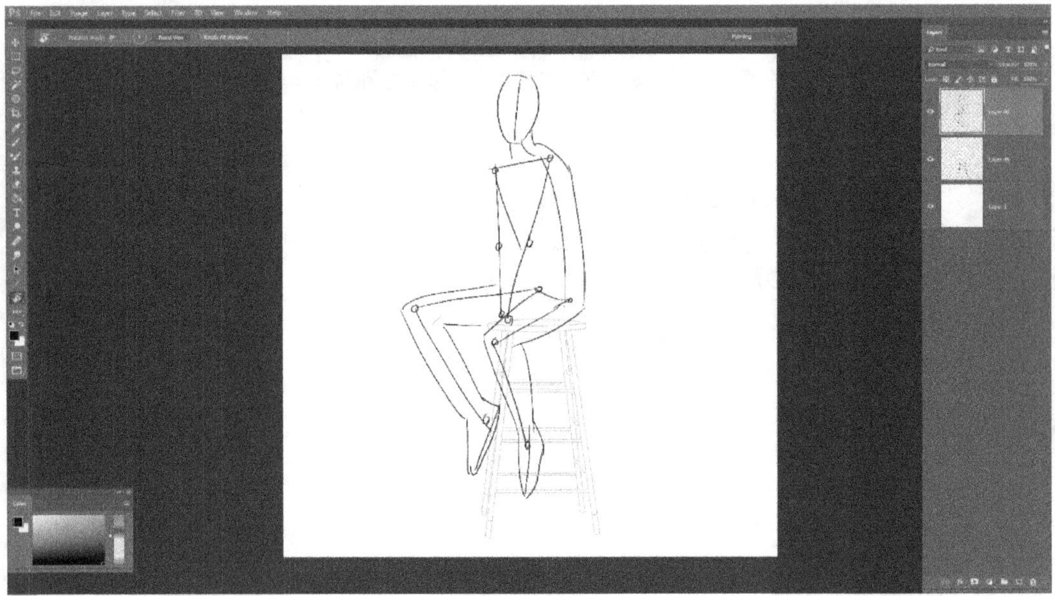

17. Add details for the arms and the head.

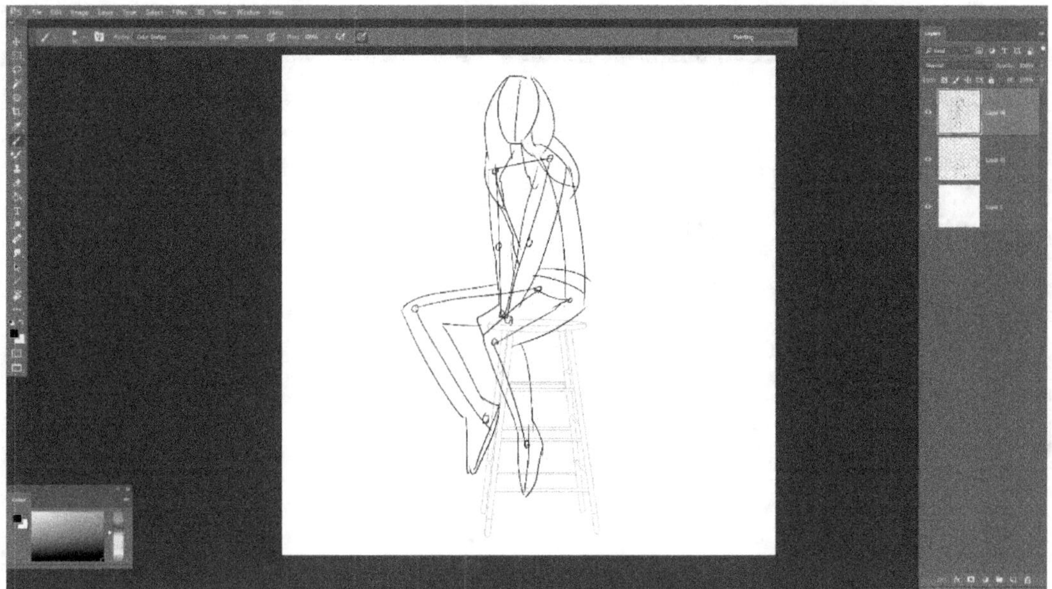

18. Delete the layer for the outline.

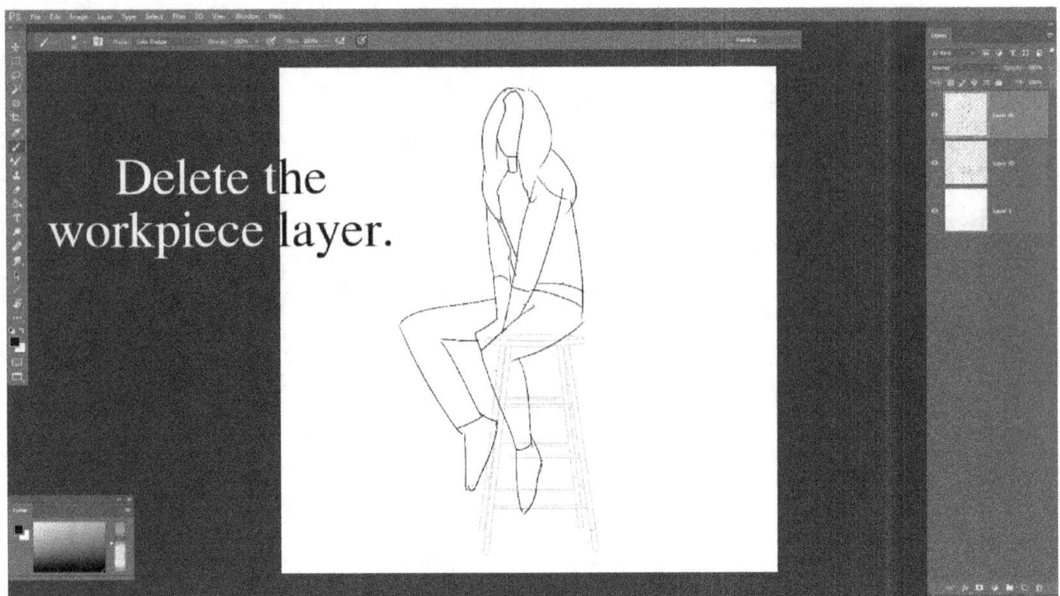

19. Create another layer. Reduce the transparency of the first sketch. On the new layer, draw a more detailed sketch using the Paint Brush Tool.

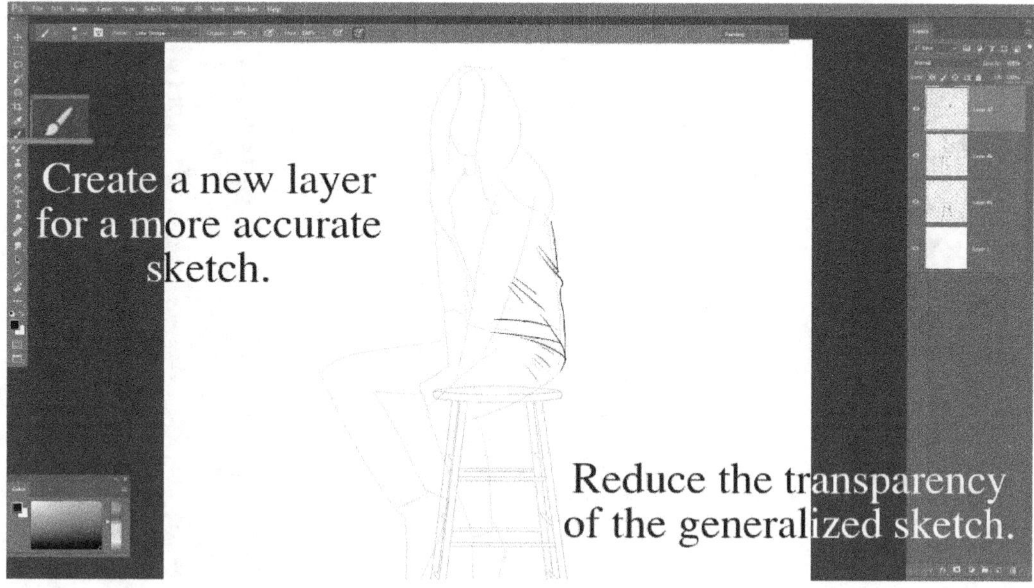

20. Continue drawing in the details of the sketch. Take note of the folds of the subject's clothes.

21. Draw the pants of the figure.

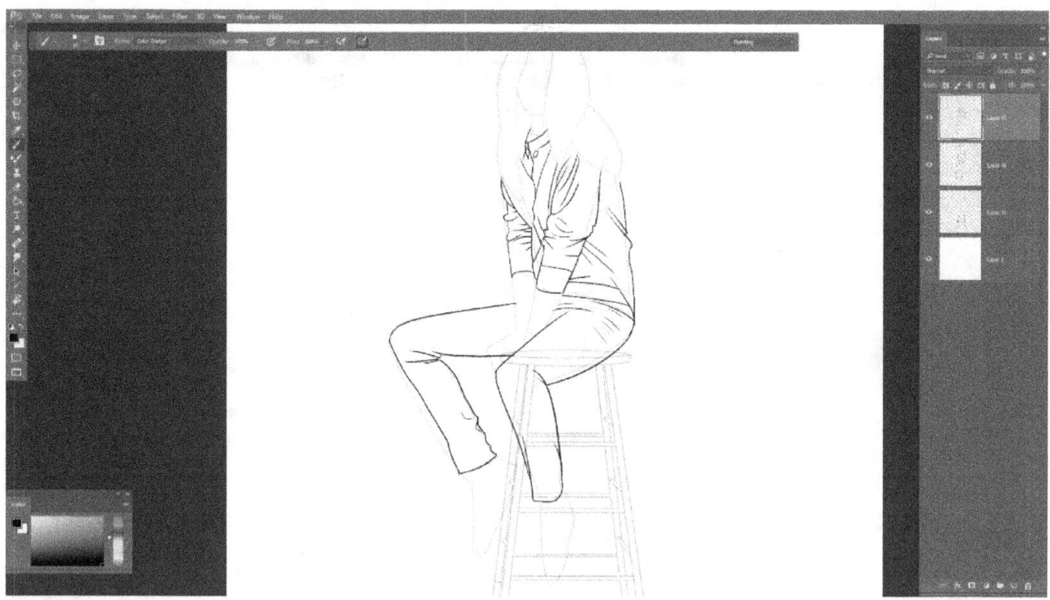

22. Draw the shoes and arms of the figure. Take note that the more detailed sketch does not have to follow the original sketch's lines exactly.

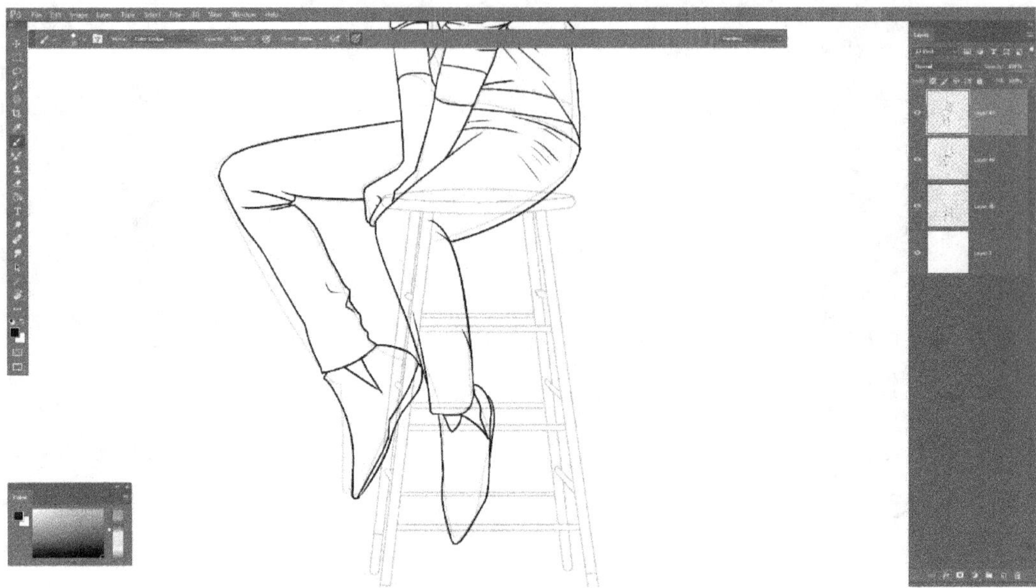

23. Draw the rest of the figure. Draw the face and the hair.

24. The finished sketch should have all the details.

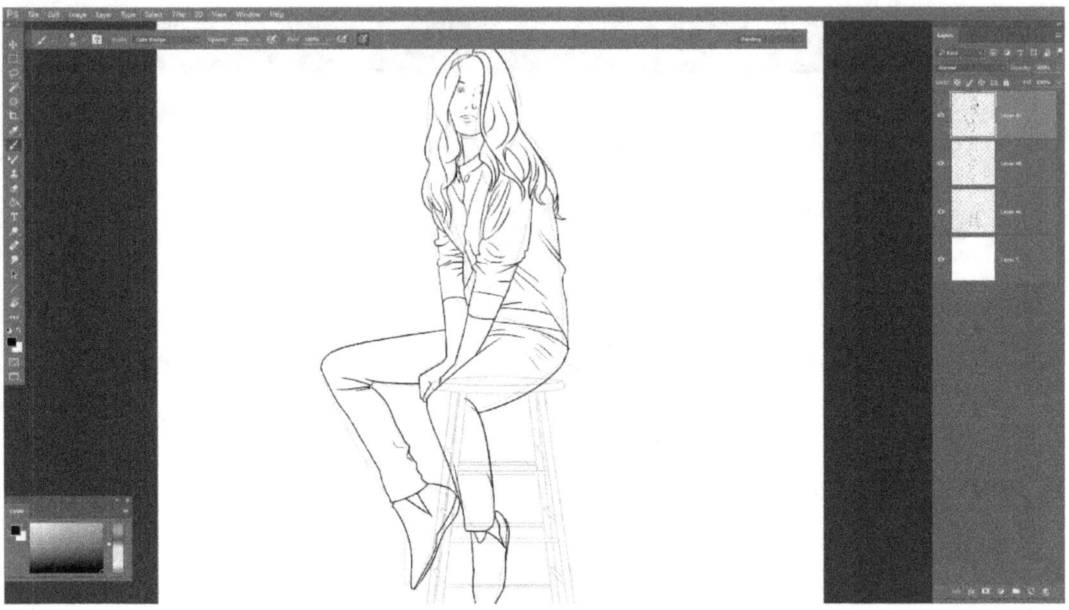

25. Delete the first sketch and select the layer of the stool.

26. Erase any parts of the stool that overlap the figure with the Eraser Tool.

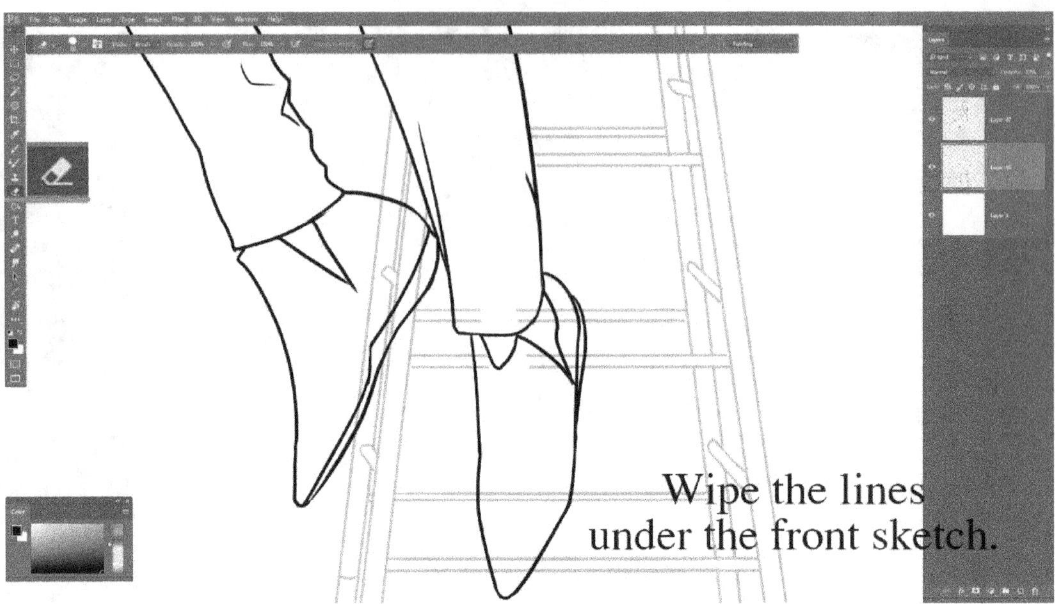

27. For convenience in erasing these overlapping lines, reduce the opacity of the figure to 21%. Select all the layers and merge them.

28. Make another layer and fill in the sketch with any color of your choice.

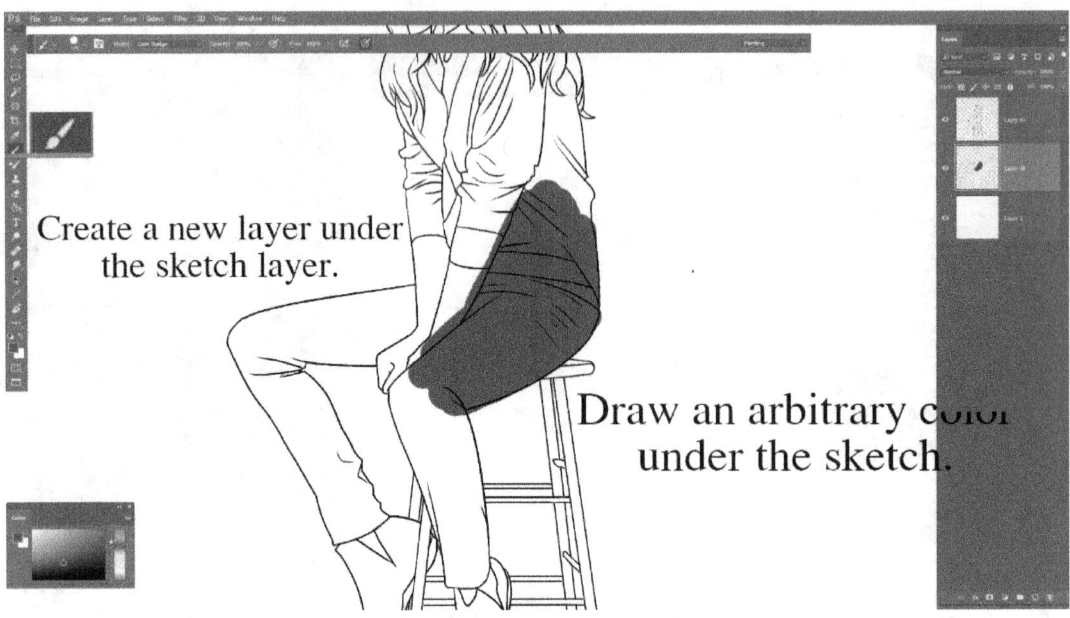

29. Fill in the rest of the figure's clothes.

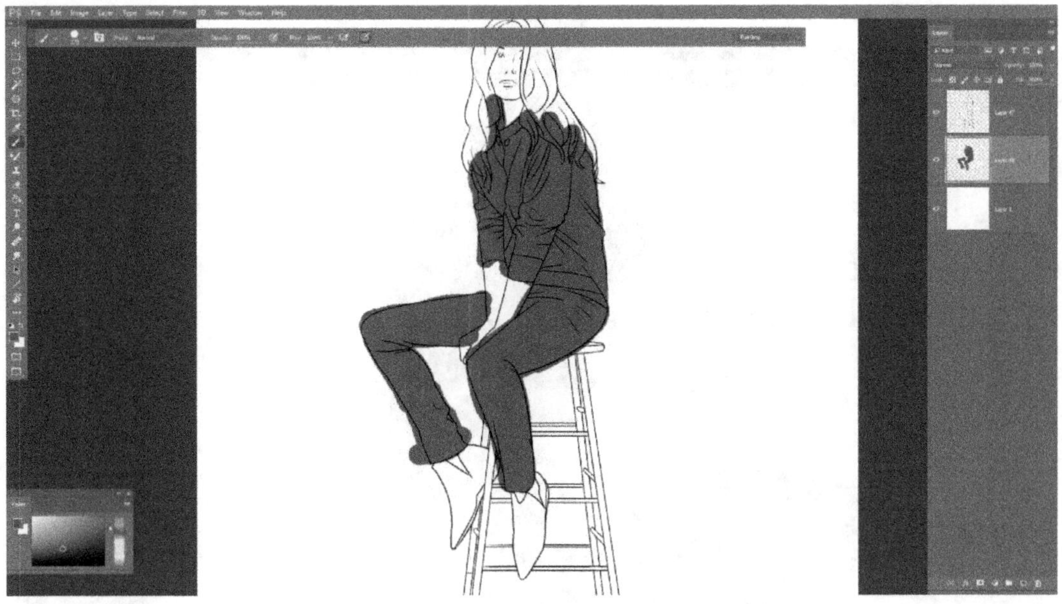

30. Wipe out any color that exceeds the bounds of the sketch with the Eraser Tool.

31. You can flip, rotate and zoom in on the figure to erase all excess colors.

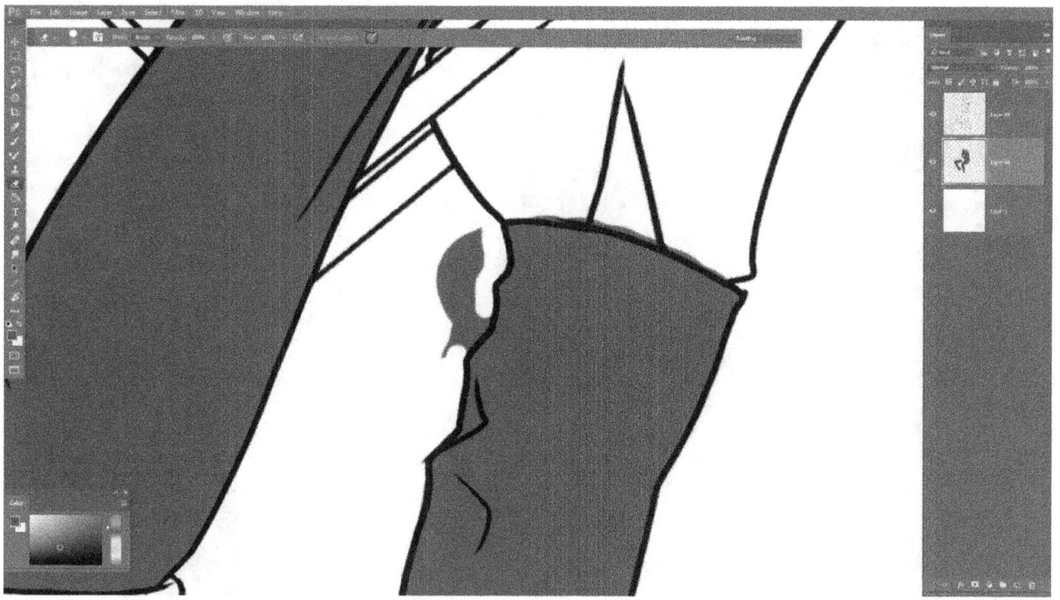

32. The colored-in figure should be like this.

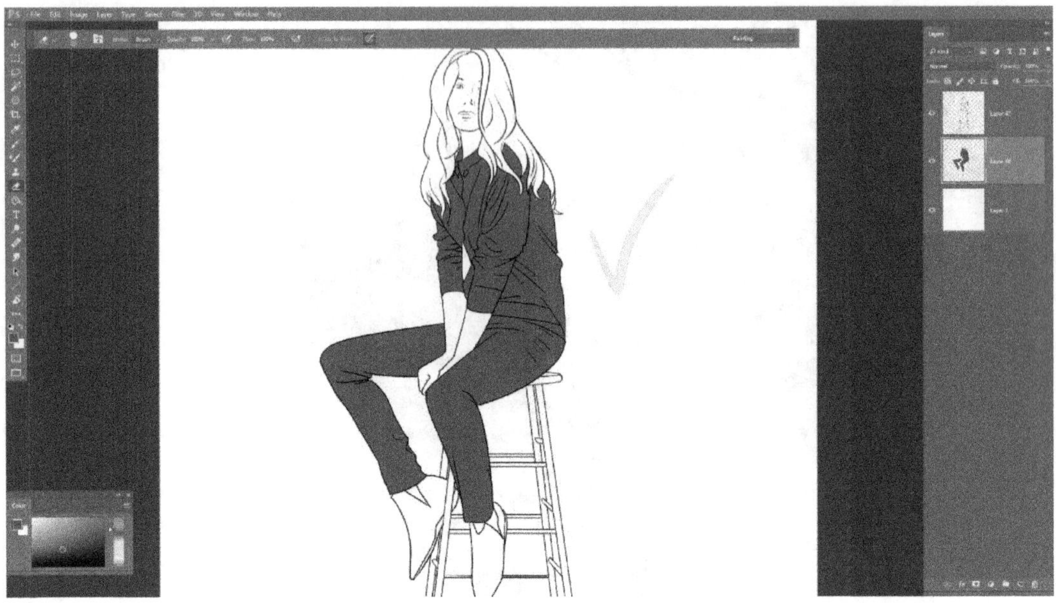

33. On a new layer, color in the face and any exposed skin.

34. Use a new layer for different parts of the figure. In this example, one layer is used for the hair and shoes together, and another for the stool.

35. This is the figure colored in with its basic colors.

36. Lock the layer for the exposed skin and select the Brush Tool. Change it to Color Dodge mode at 6% Opacity. Choose a color that is lighter than the skin color. Draw the highlights on the face.

37. Click on the Burn Tool with an Exposure of 36%. Draw the shadows of the face.

38. Draw the highlights and shadows for the arms. Use the technique in shading a cylindrical shape.

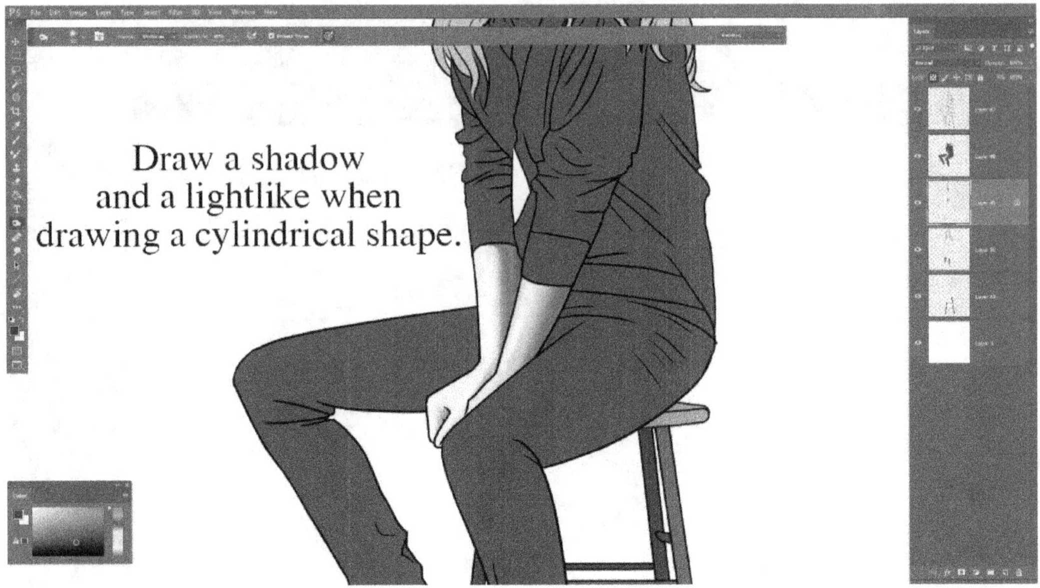

39. Lock the layer for the hair and shoes. Use the Dodge Tool to highlight the areas of the shoes that are hit by direct light. Use the following settings: Highlights for Range and 29% for Exposure.

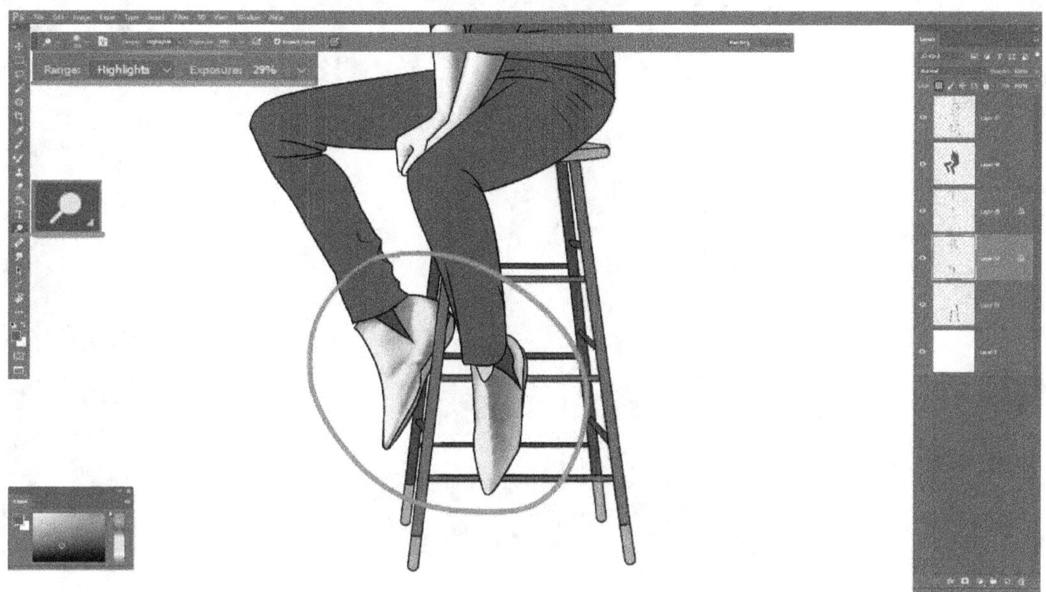

40. Click the Brush Tool and select Normal Mode and 27% Opacity. Use a color that is darker than the hair and draw the shadows for it.

41. Using the same settings for the Brush Tool, select a light color. Paint the highlights of the hair.

42. Select the Smudge Tool and change the Strength to 82%. Smudge the edges between the light and shadow.

43. Lock the layer for the clothes. Click the Brush Tool and use it to paint the shadows of the clothes. Select a color that is a bit darker than the clothes.

44. Add the shadows for the rest of the shirt.

45. Paint in the shadows for the pants as well.

46. Increase the Brush Tool's Opacity to 32% and chooses a light color. Draw the highlights of the subject's clothes.

47. Select the Burn Tool and paint over the highlighted areas to make them larger.

48. Click on the Smudge Tool and smoothen the transition from light to shadow.

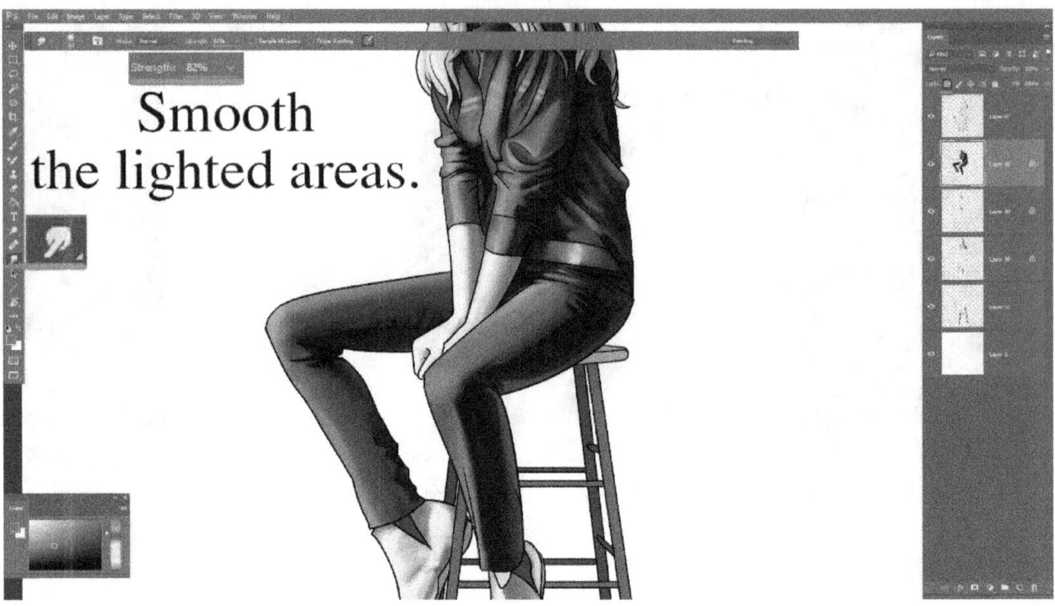

49. While still on the same layer, press Ctrl+U to open the Hue/Saturation window. Adjust the Saturation level to -23.

50. Press Ctrl+L and change the left level to 223.

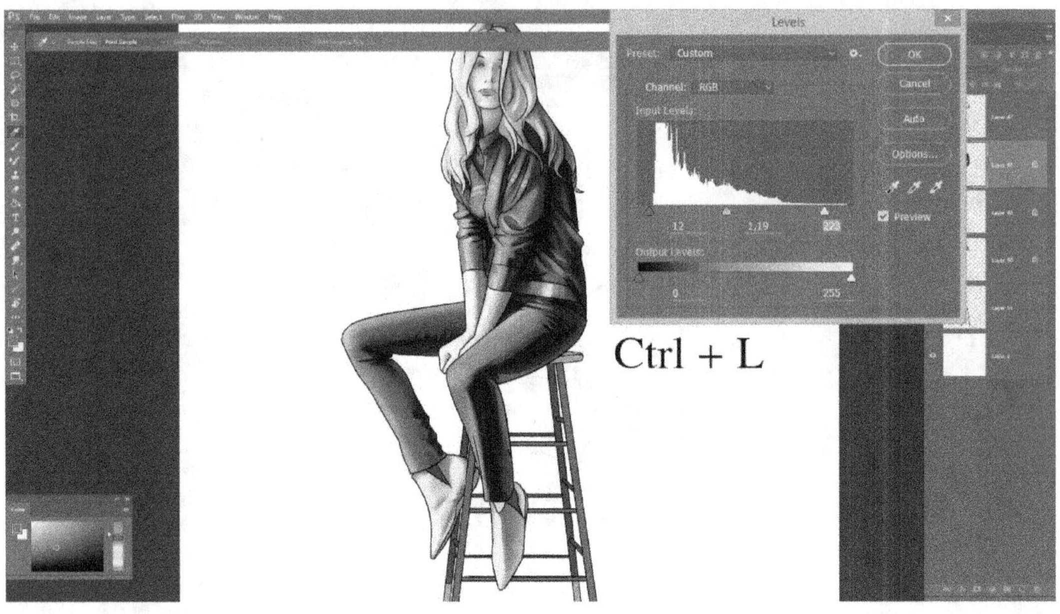

51. Select the layer of the original sketch and lock t. Select the Brush Tool. Change the color the lines of the original sketch with a color that is a bit darker that the one next to it.

52. Do the same for all the parts of the sketch. Note the reflections of color on the stool and the feet.

53. The lines of the sketch are now hidden.

54. Select all of the layers and click on the Move Tool. Drag the image to the side of the workspace.

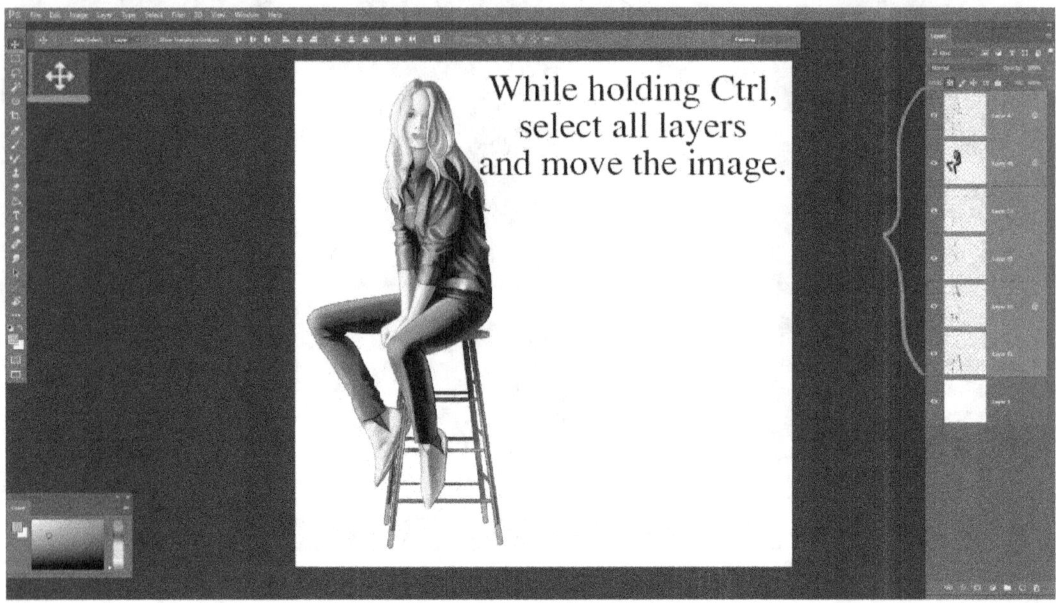

55. Merge all the layers and press Ctrl+C. Crop the canvas to make it narrower.

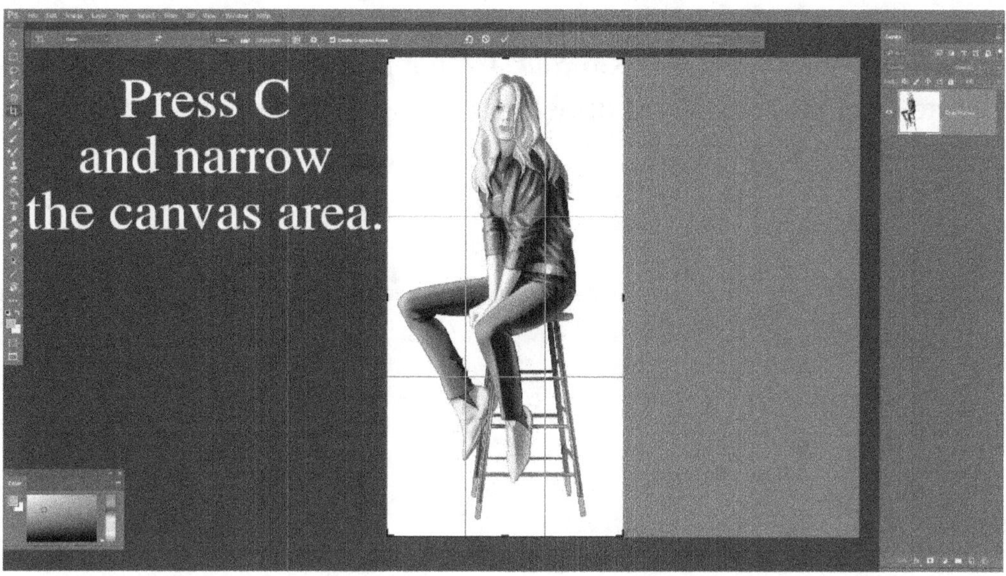

Creating Animal Portrait using Adobe Photoshop

Animals are a different category in drawing altogether. Every form of animal is different from another. Drawing a cat does not use the same shapes as drawing a fish or a bird, for example. In this part of the book, we will show you some examples of ways of drawing animals using Adobe Photoshop.

Some Examples of Animal Portrait

Running Cheetah

1. Make a new layer and select the Brush Tool. Draw the sketch for the cheetah's shape. This is the neck and chest area of the cheetah.

2. Draw in the rest of the cheetah's body. Rotating the canvas may help in making this step easier? You can do this by pressing the R key.

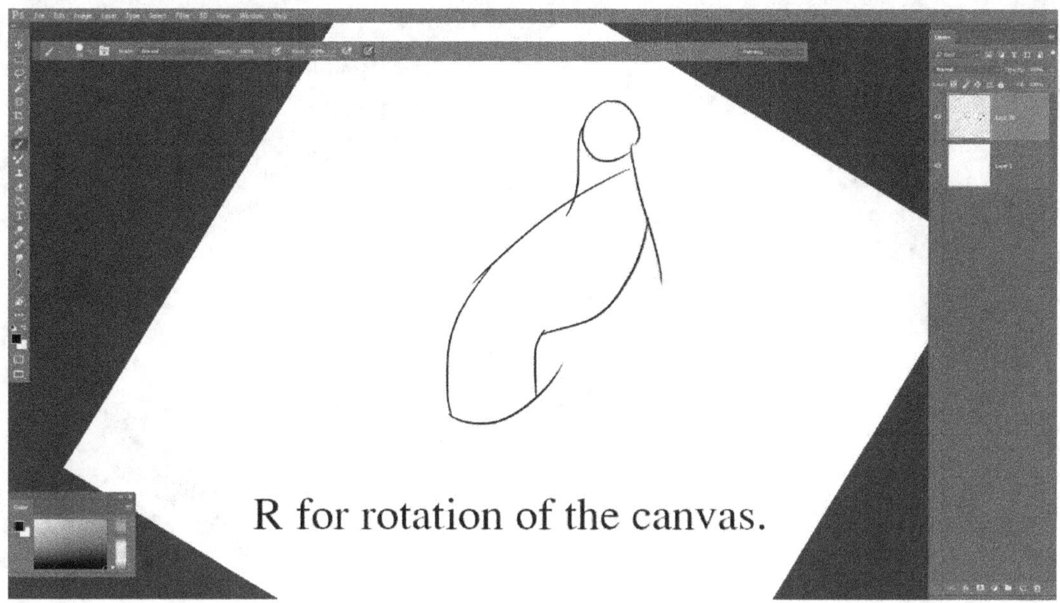

3. Draw the snout and the forelegs.

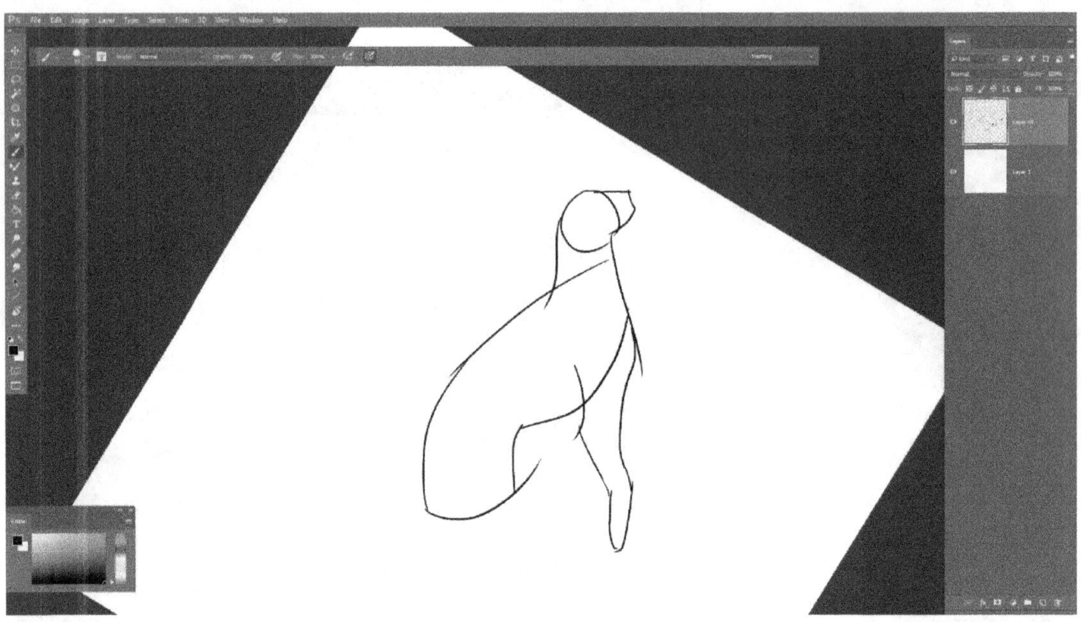

4. Draw the hind legs and the claws.

5. Draw the tail and the other legs.

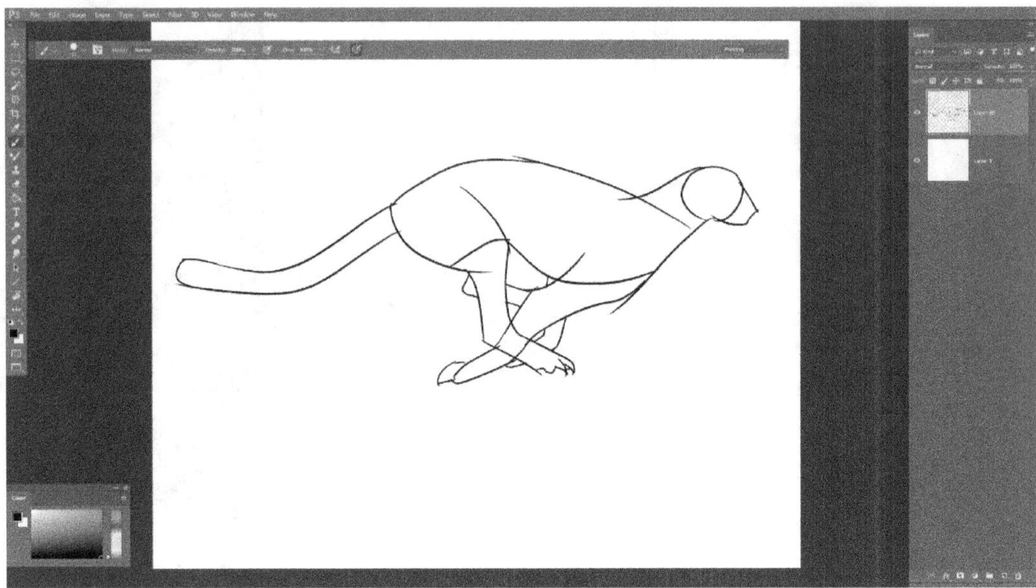

6. Add some details to the drawing, especially to the head. Draw the ears, eyes and nose.

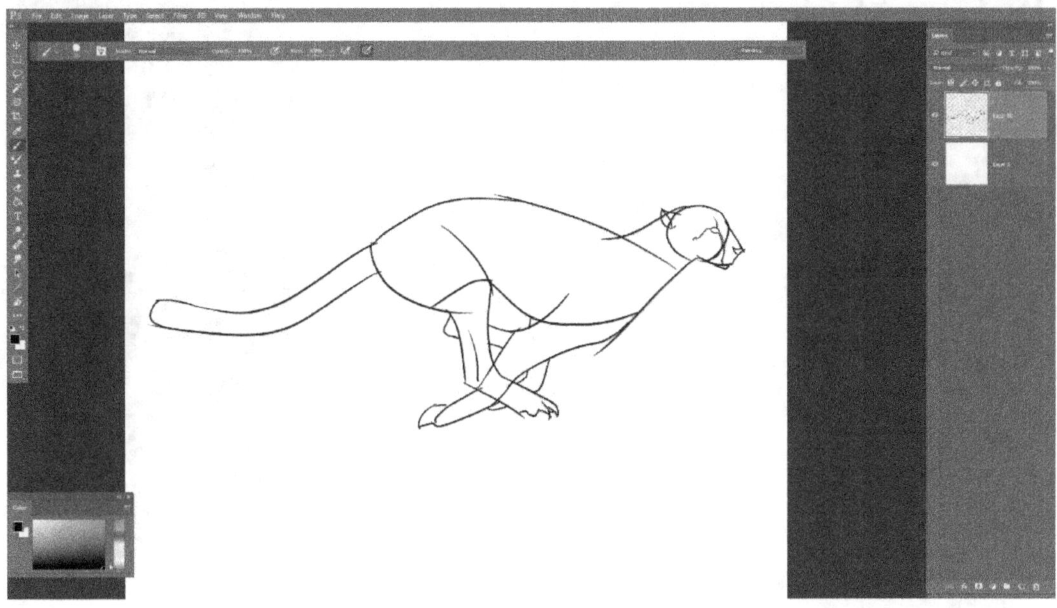

7. Use the Eraser Tool to remove excess lines in the sketch.

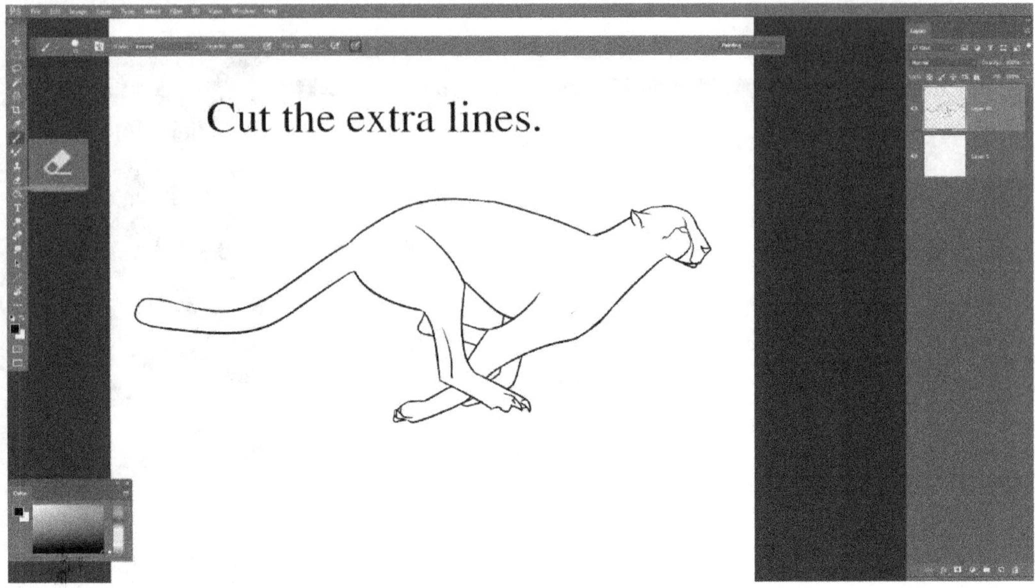

8. Add some details to the drawing like the fur and claws.

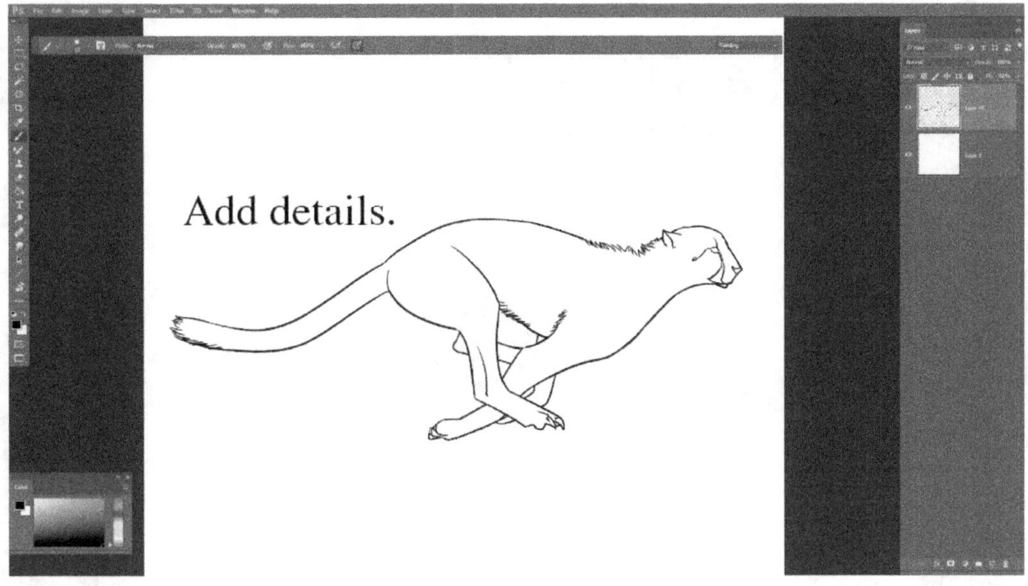

9. Deactivate the display of the sketch layer. To do this, click on the eye next to the layer icon. Make a new layer to create the texture for the cheetah's fur.

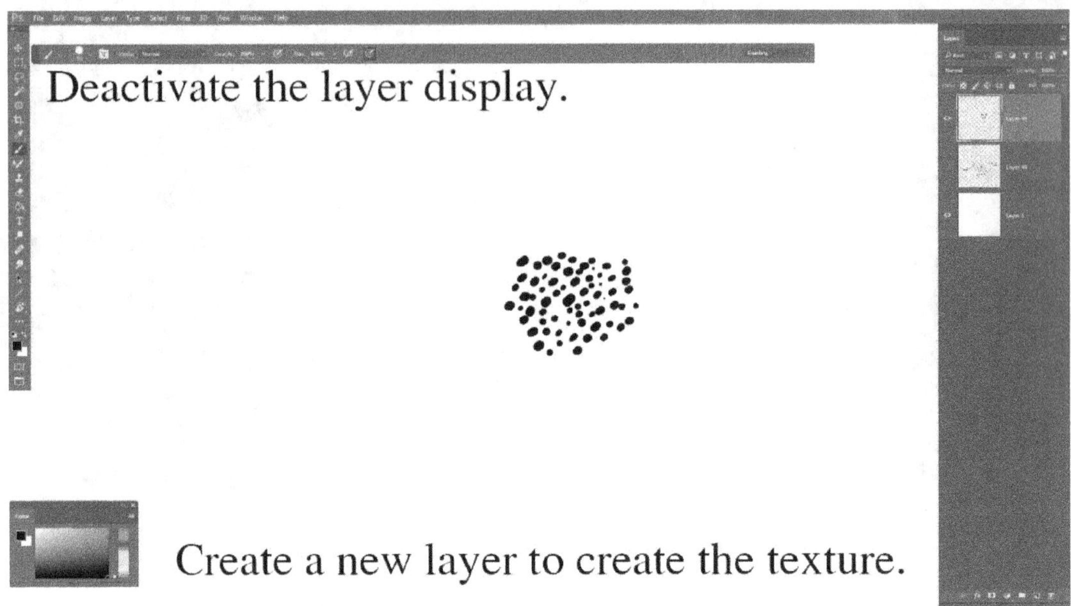

10. With the brush Tool, paint the color of the cheetah's fur. Use the Behind Mode and 100% Opacity for the Brush Tool.

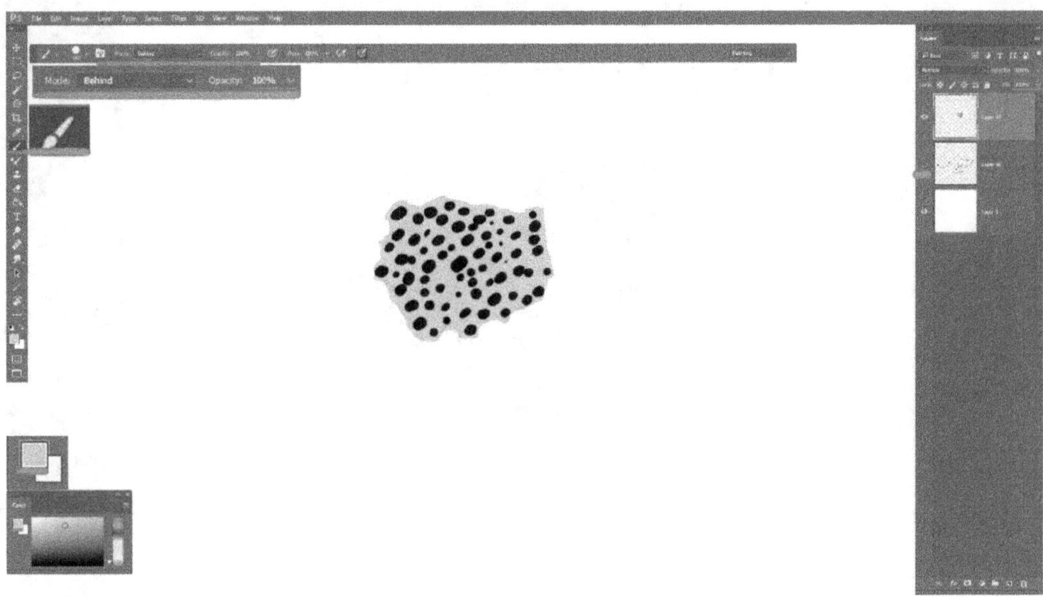

11. Copy the layer of the color and move them to spread them out.

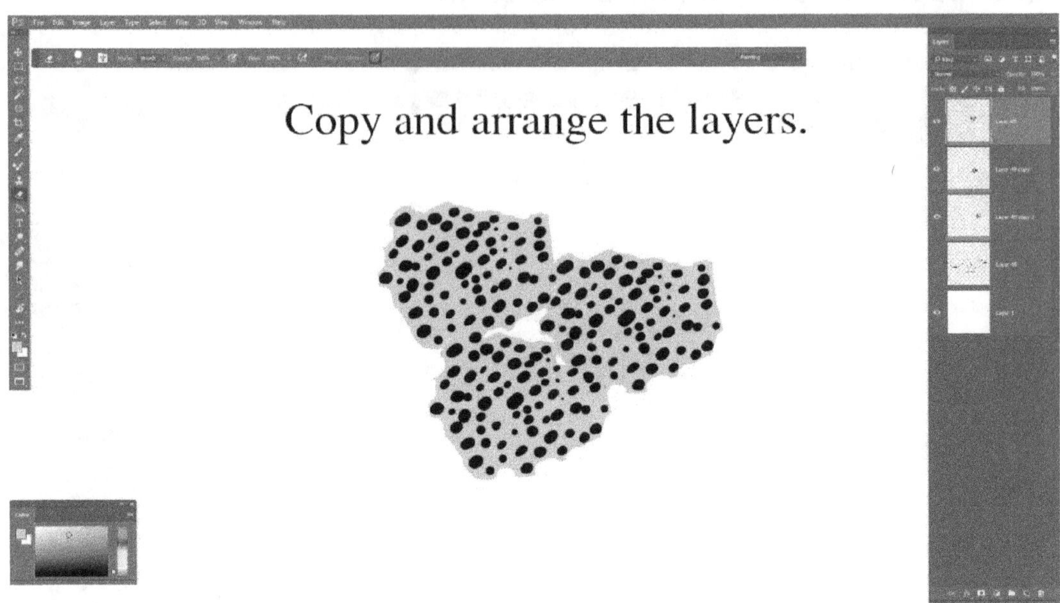

12. Select al the layers and press the Right Mouse button. Select Merge Layers on the pop-up menu.

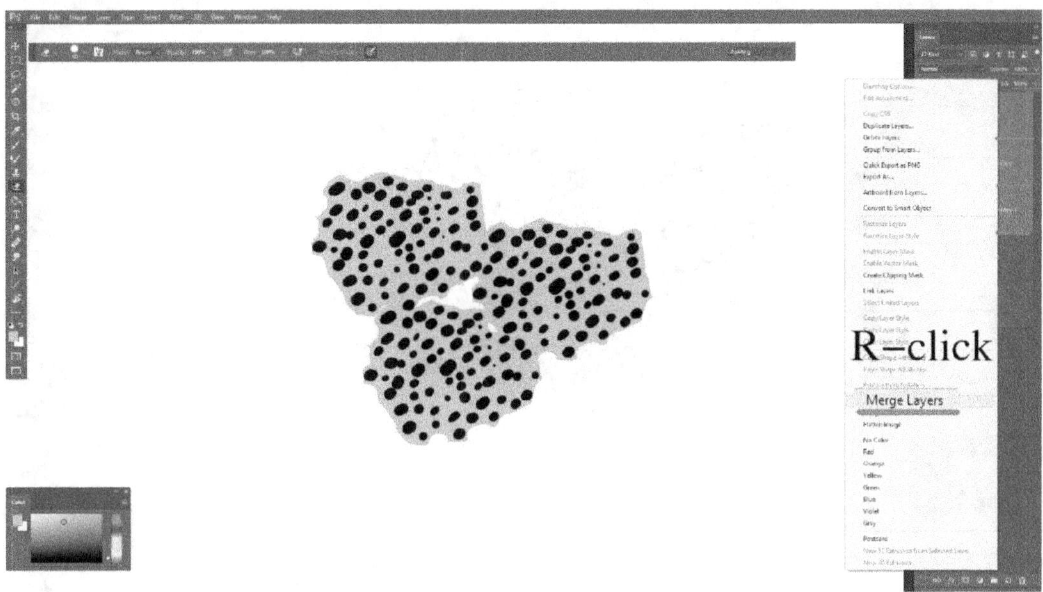

13. Copy the layer and spread them out again. Merge the layers again.

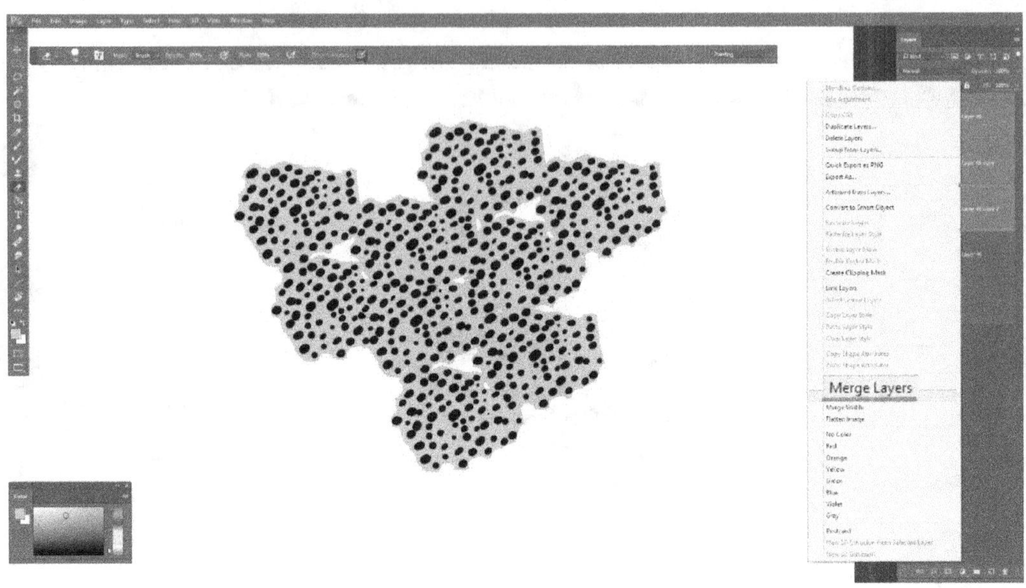

14. Do the steps another time until you think the whole sketch will be covered by the pattern? Make sure that any blank areas are covered.

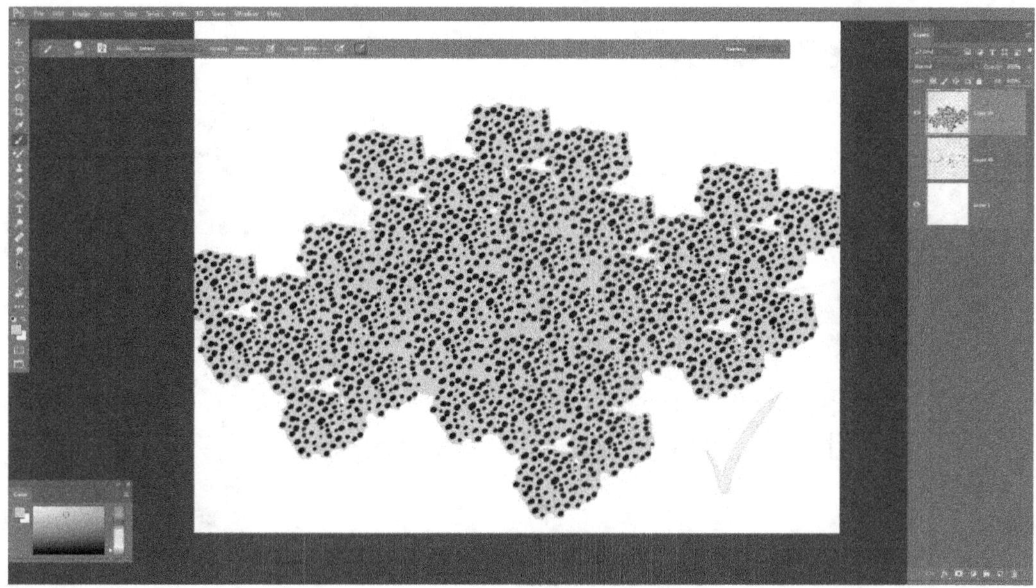

15. Make the layer of the sketch visible again and hide the pattern's layer. Click on the Magic Wand Tool. Click on the areas outside of the sketch.

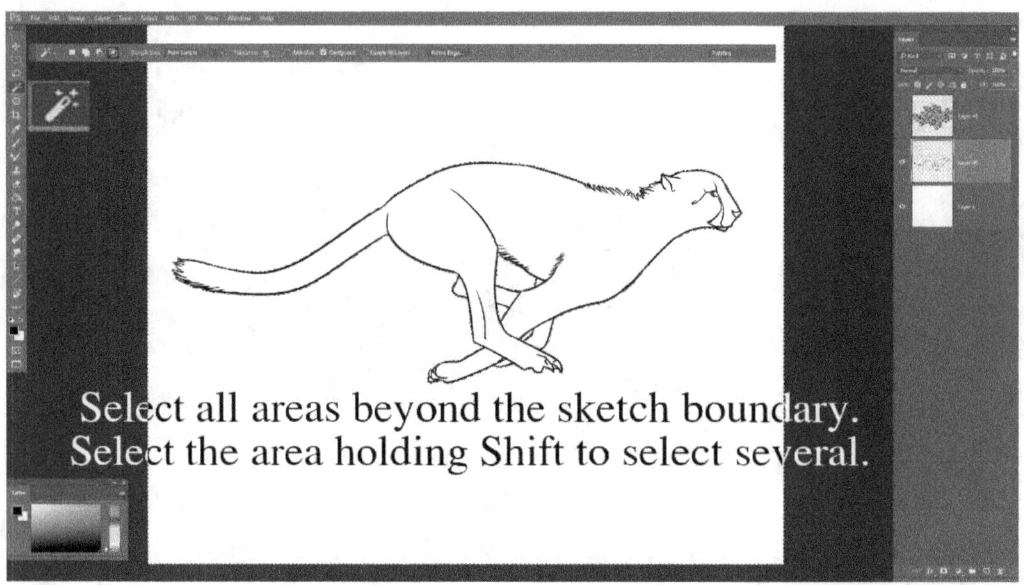

16. Make the pattern's layer visible again and select it. Press the Del Key to delete any excess areas of the pattern.

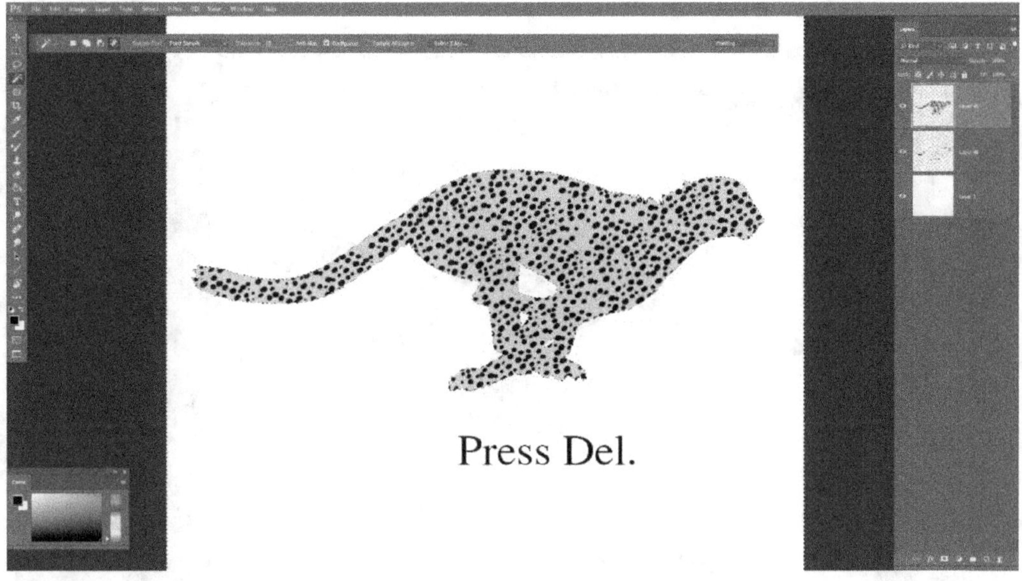

17. Move the layer of the pattern under the sketch. Click the Brush Tool and change it to Overlay Mode with 60% Opacity. Select a color lighter than the color of the body. Highlight the areas hit by a light.

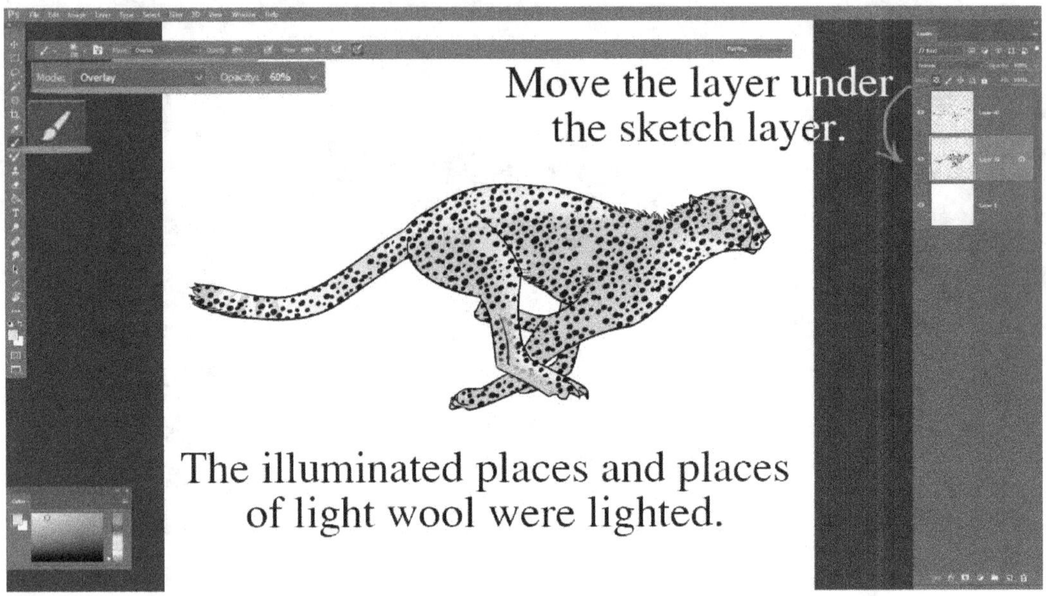

18. Lock the layer of the pattern. Change the Brush Tool's Mode to Normal and the Opacity to 33%. Hide some spots with a lighter color.

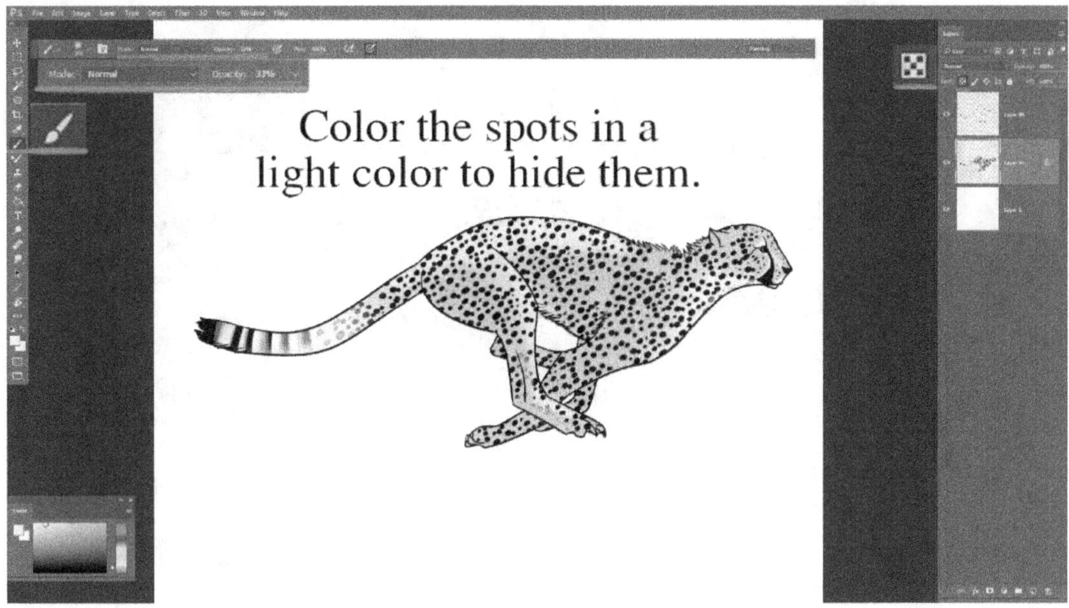

19. Click the Burn Tool and change its Range to Shadows and its Opacity to 36%.

20. Click on the layer of the sketch and lock it. Click on the Brush Tool and paint over the lines of the sketch. Color it with a color close or darker to the one next to the line.

21. Make the layer of the pattern invisible to make coloring over the lines easier.

22. Merge all the layers together and press Ctrl+C. Crop the size of the canvas to fit the image.

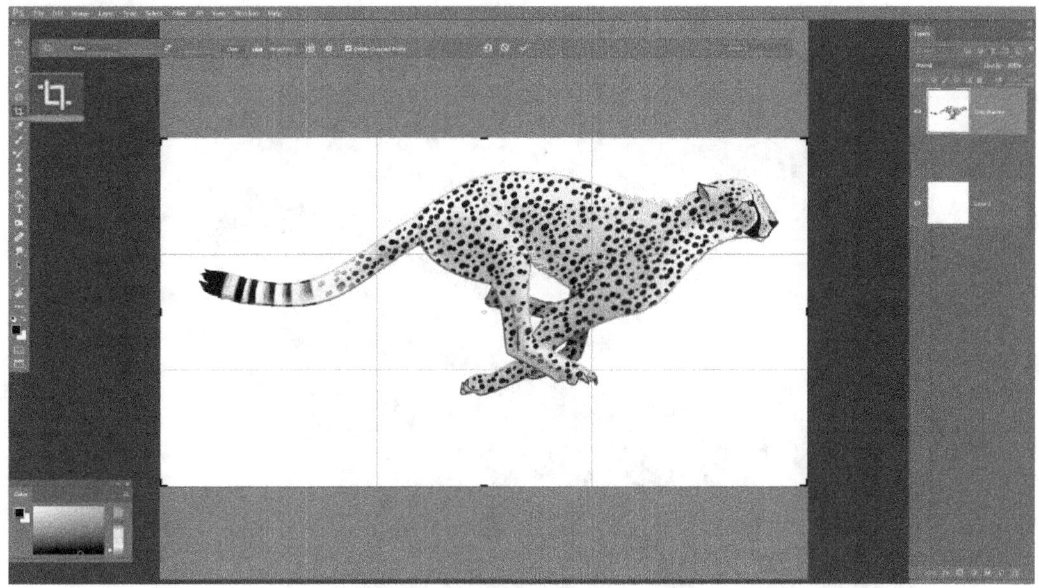

Bug

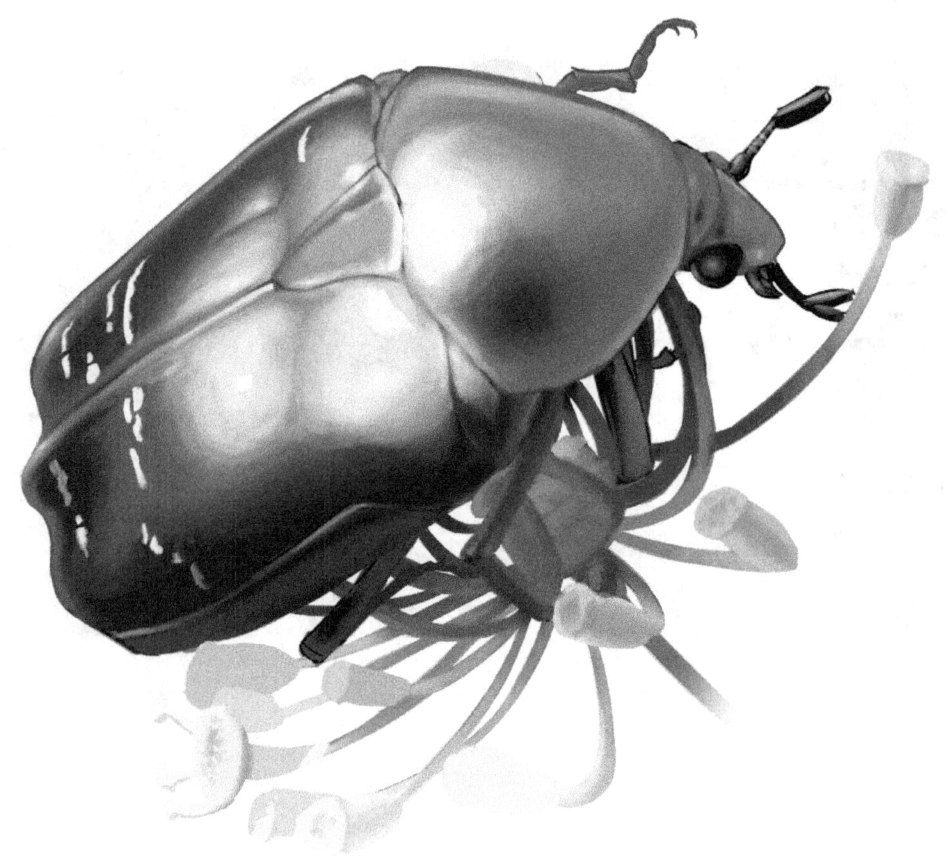

1. Make a new layer. Draw a sketch of a bug's shape.

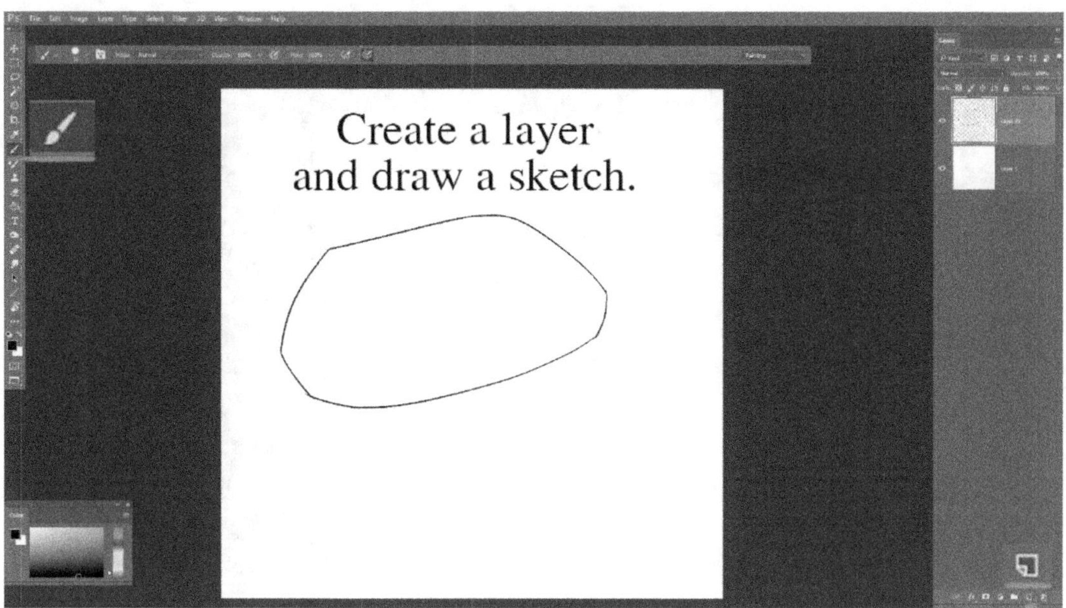

2. Refine the shape and add the dividing line on the body.

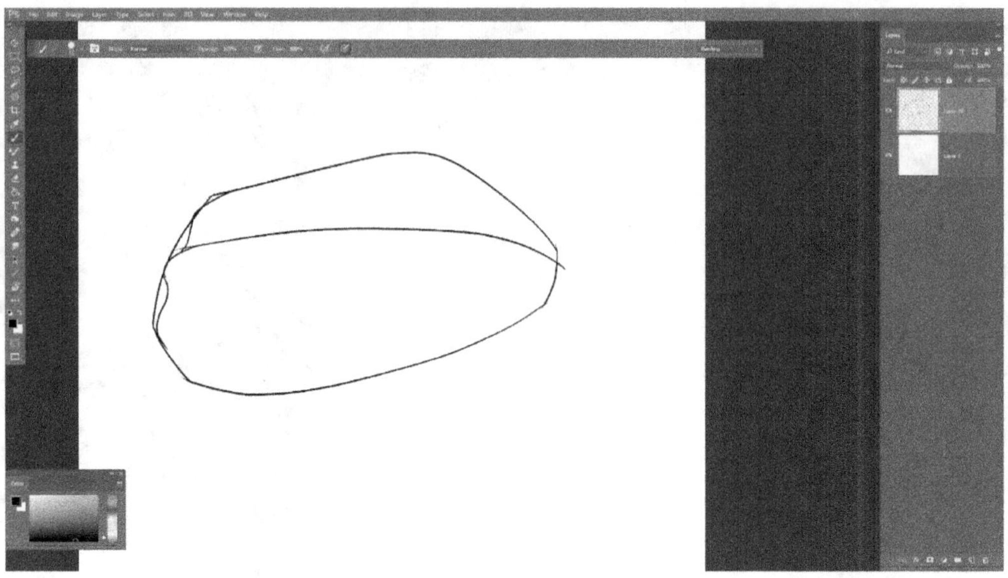

3. Add the lines for the thorax and the head of the bug.

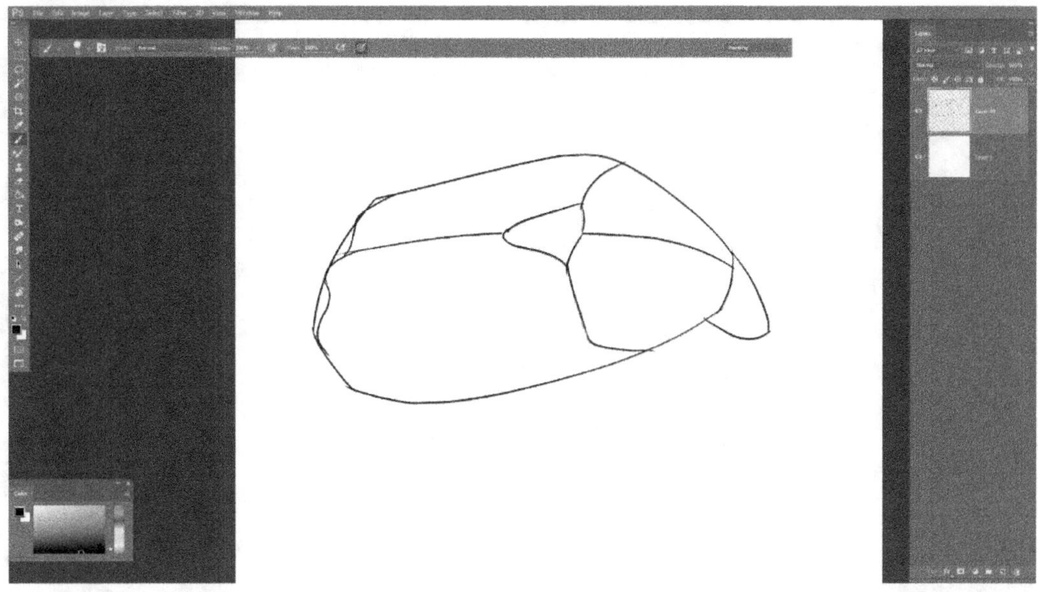

4. Erase the center line for the thorax and erase any excess lines.

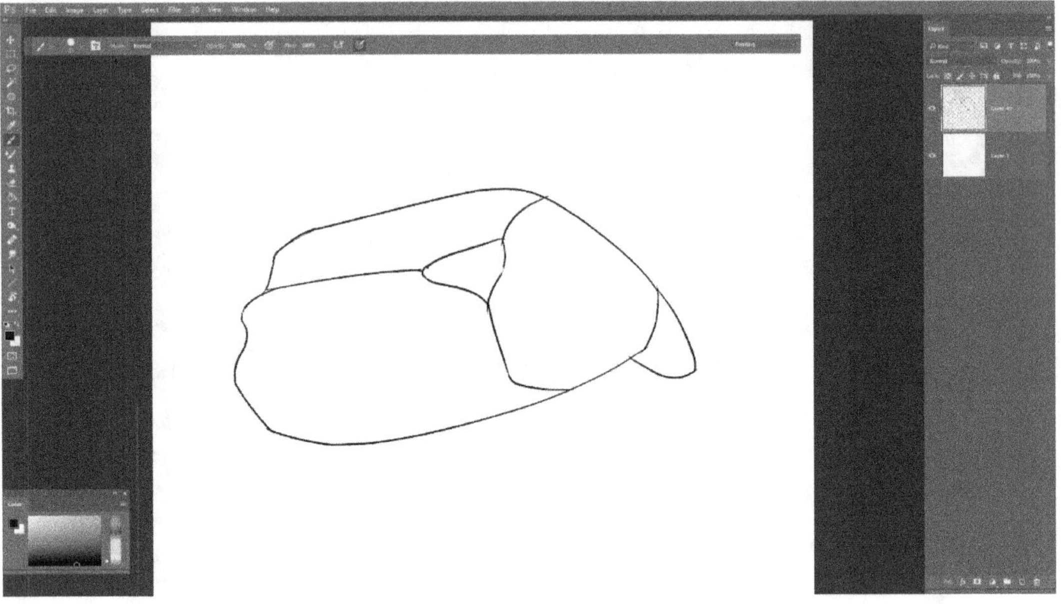

5. Add details for the stomach and the eyes.

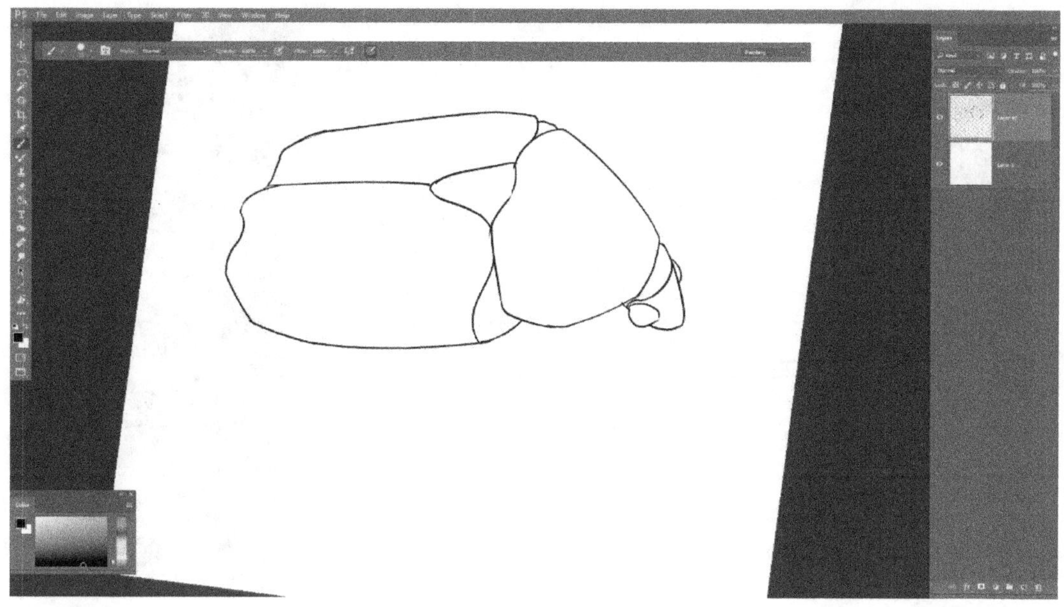

6. Draw the legs, feelers and antennae.

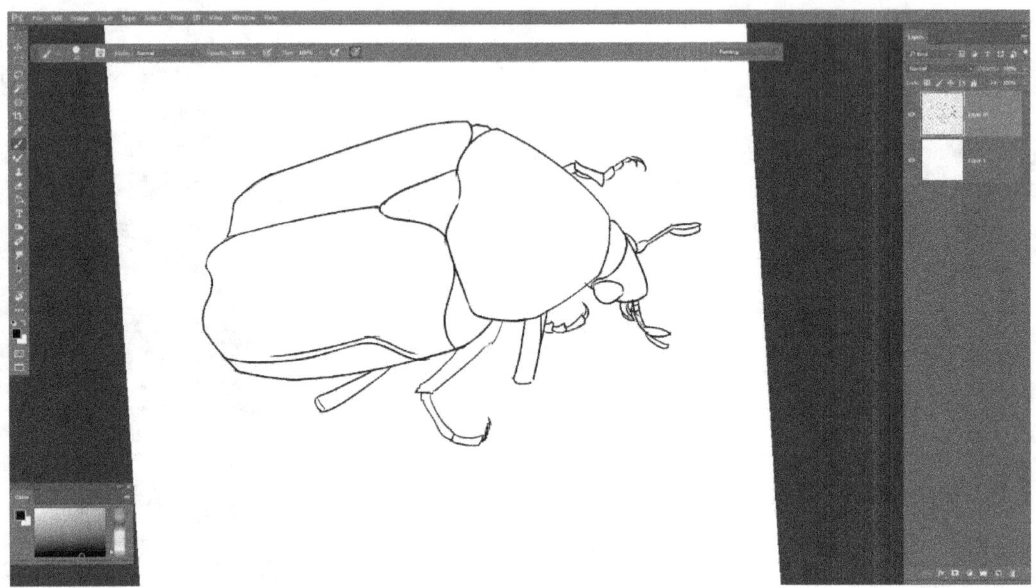

7. On another layer, draw a flower underneath the bug.

8. Make another layer and fill in the flower with any color.

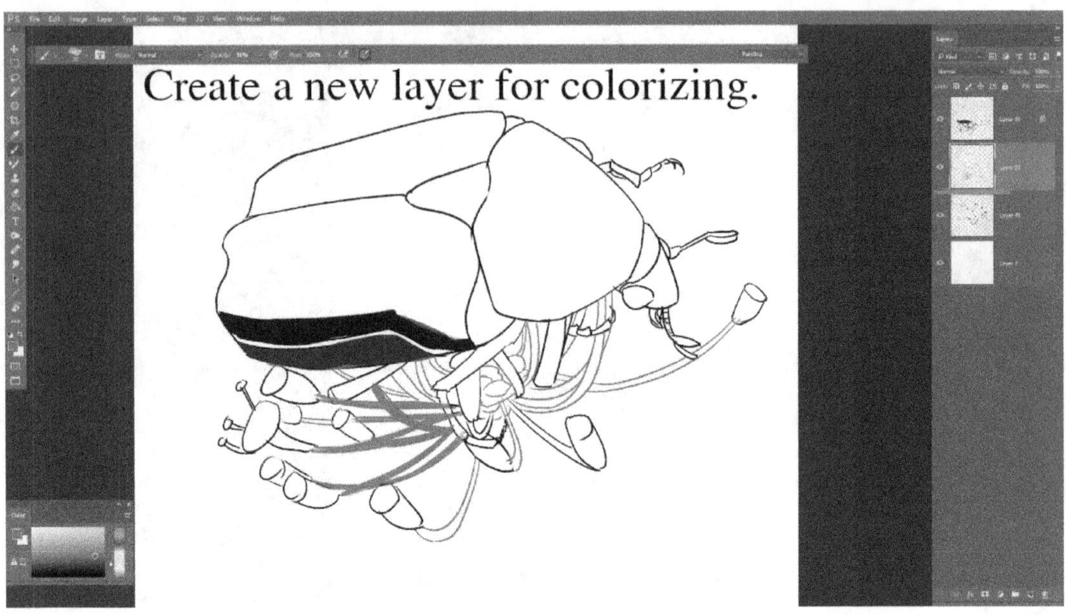

9. Continue coloring the flower. You can choose a different color for other parts of the flower.

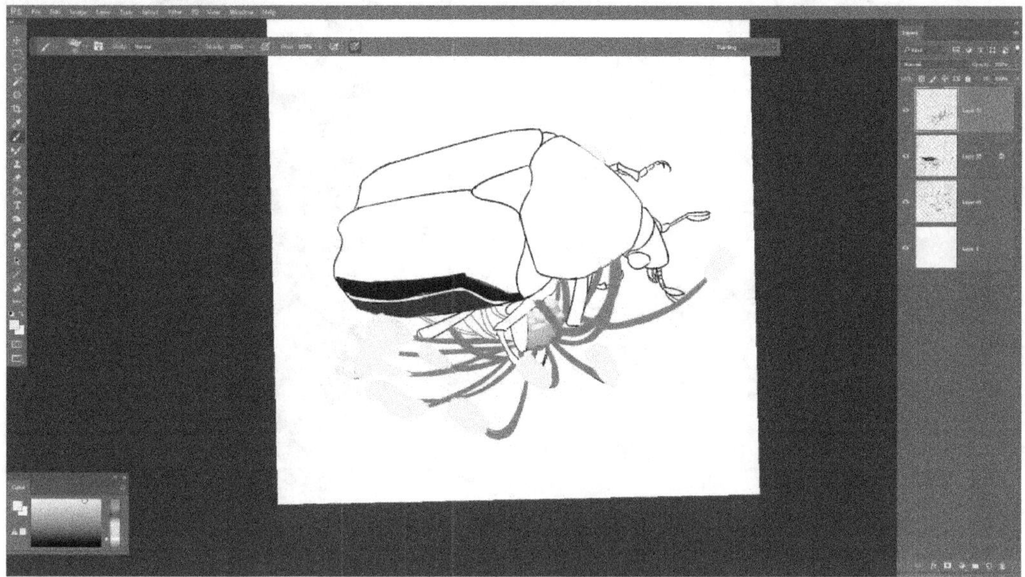

10. Merge all the layers.

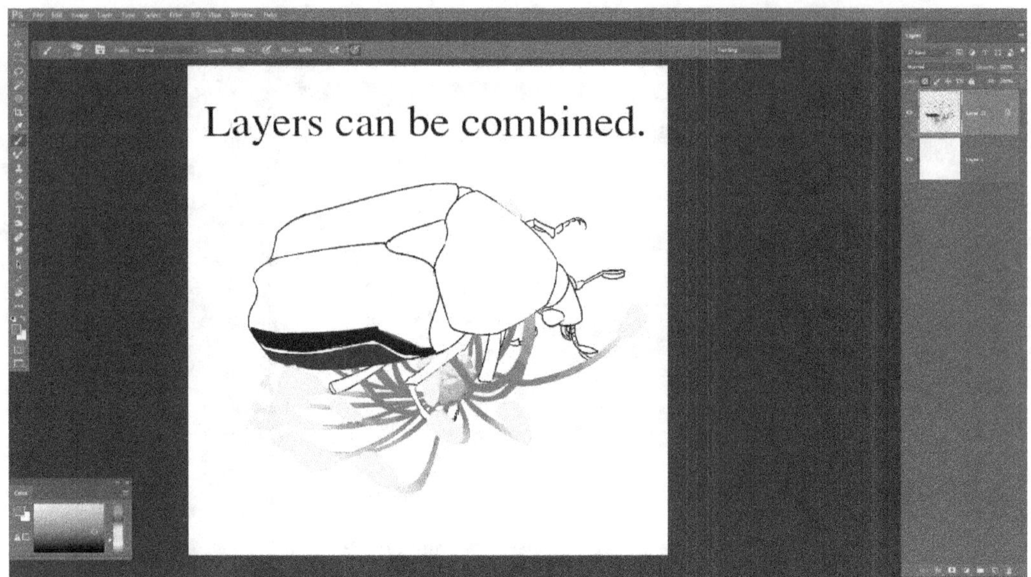

11. Create another layer and paint the colors for the bug. Use local colors.

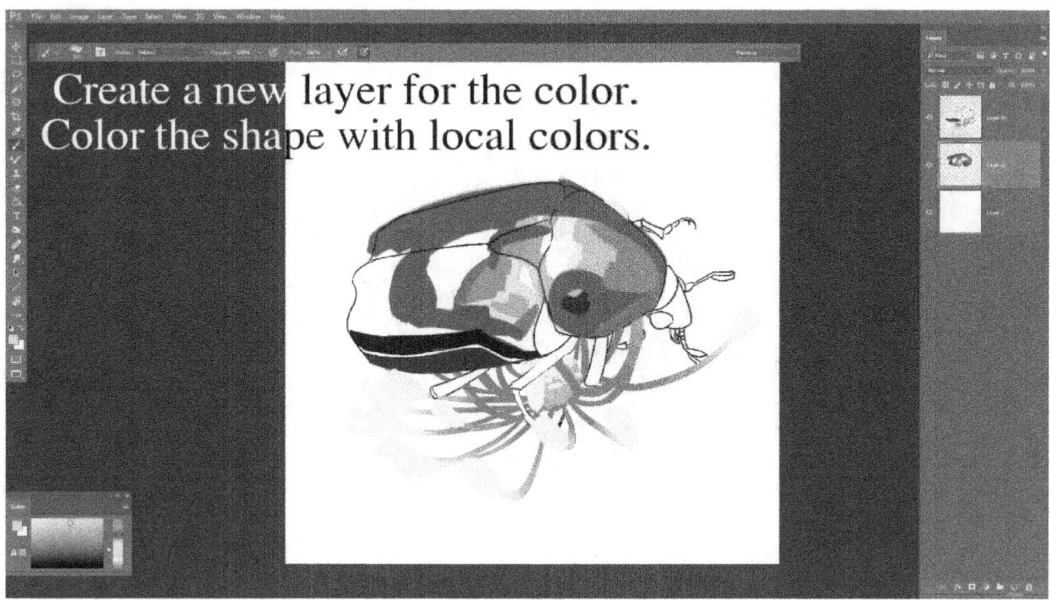

12. Fill in the color the head and the rest of the body.

13. Use the Eraser Tool to remove any excess color.

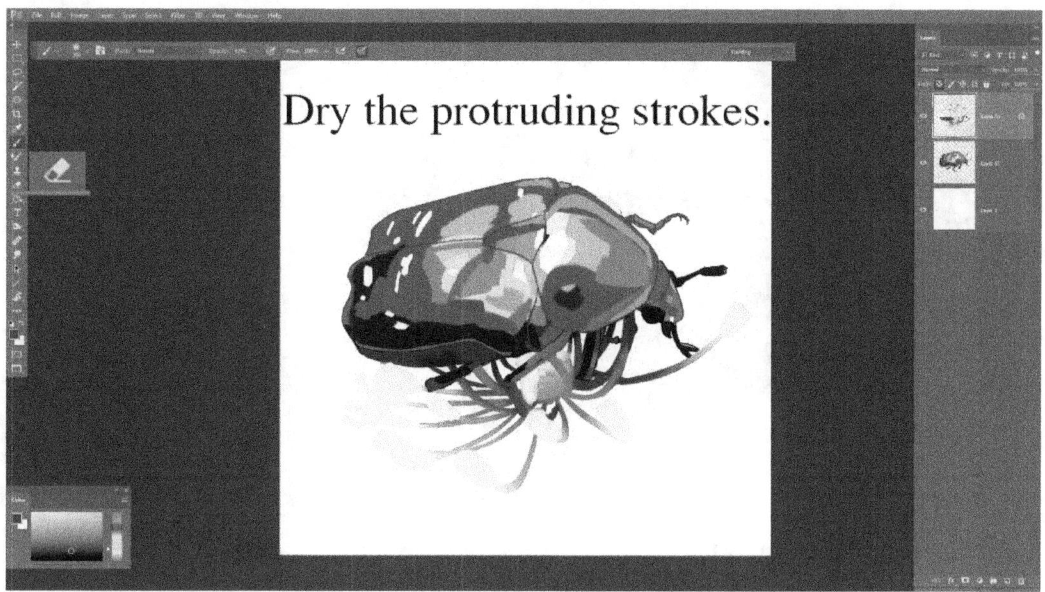

14. Merge the layers. Smooth the transition between the local colors.

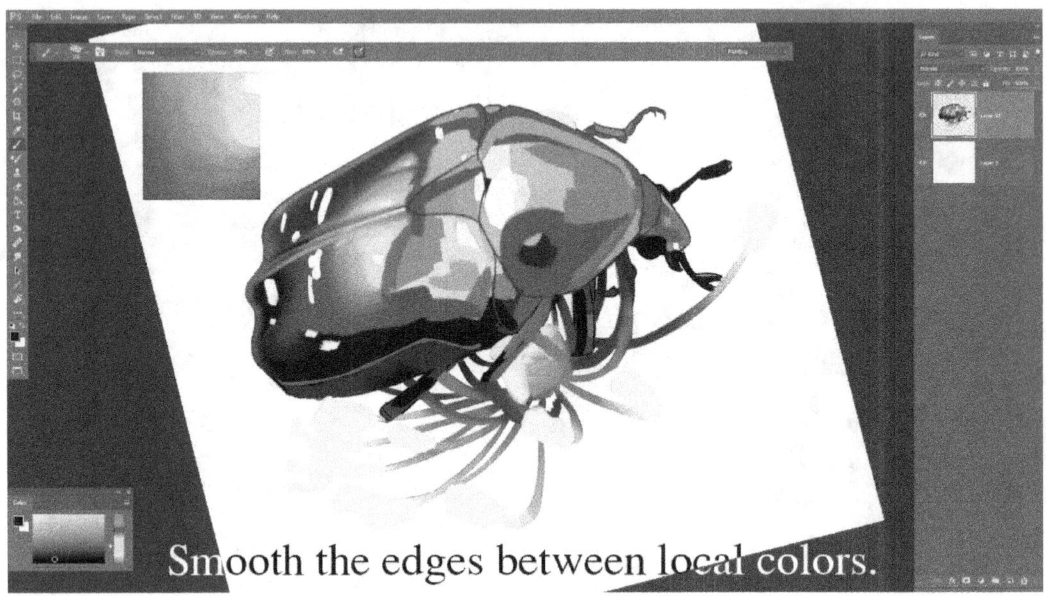

15. This is how the smoothing method is done. Click the Brush Tool. Change its Opacity to 30% and its Mode to Normal. Draw two vertical lines of different colors: a light one and black. Because of the Opacity of the brush, you will need multiple brush strokes to get a solid color.

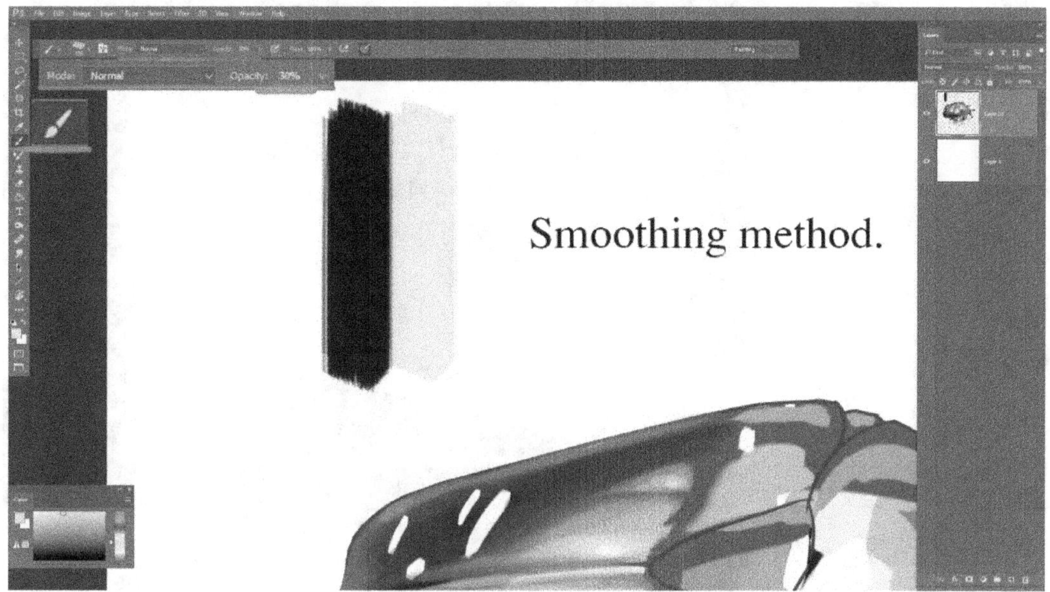

16. Brush the light color a little bit over to the black side. Hold the Alt Key and click on the mixed color to copy that color.

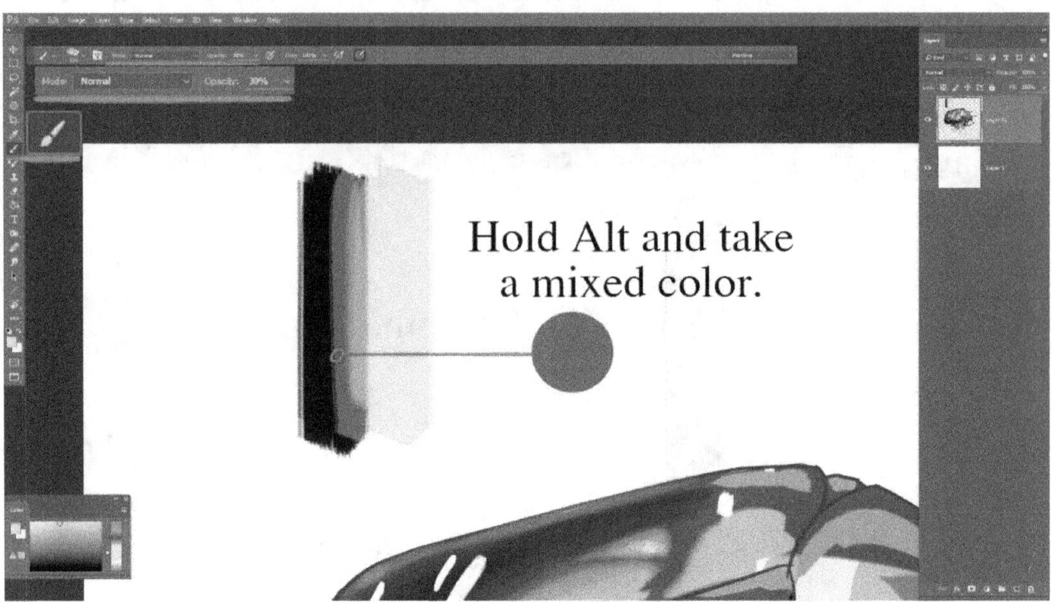

17. Lower the Brush Tool's Opacity and continues the same process until you get a smooth transition between the colors.

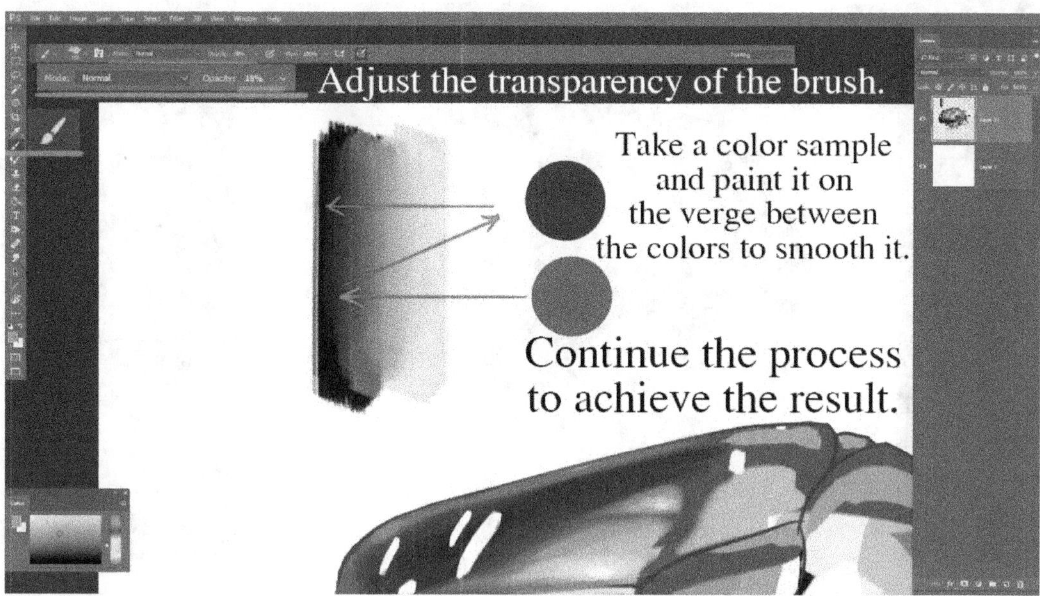

18. This is the piece with the colors unmixed yet.

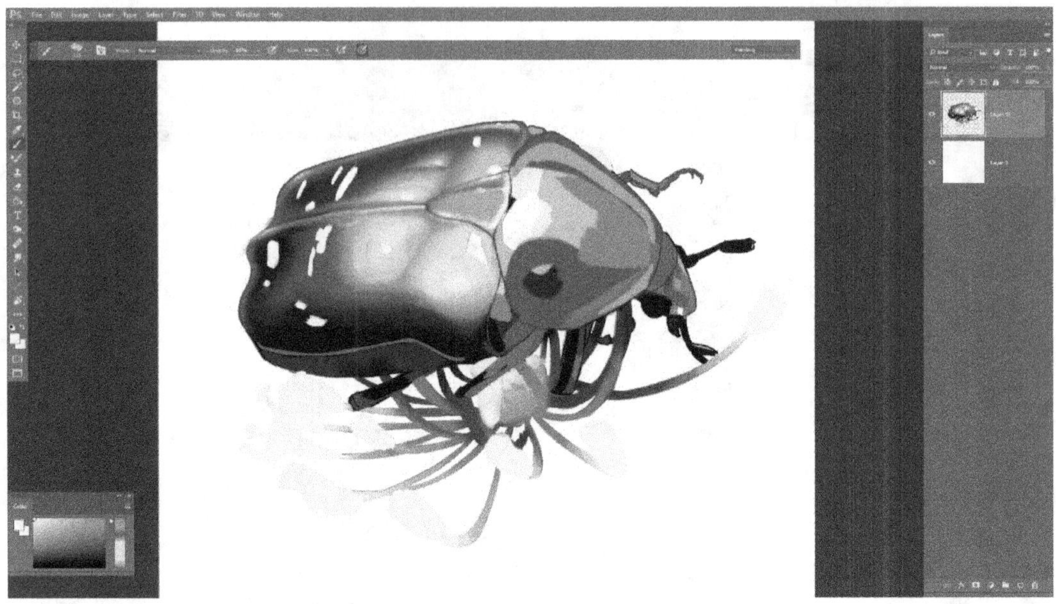

19. Apply the smoothing method shown above to the thorax as if you were drawing a sphere. Notice the color smoothing applied.

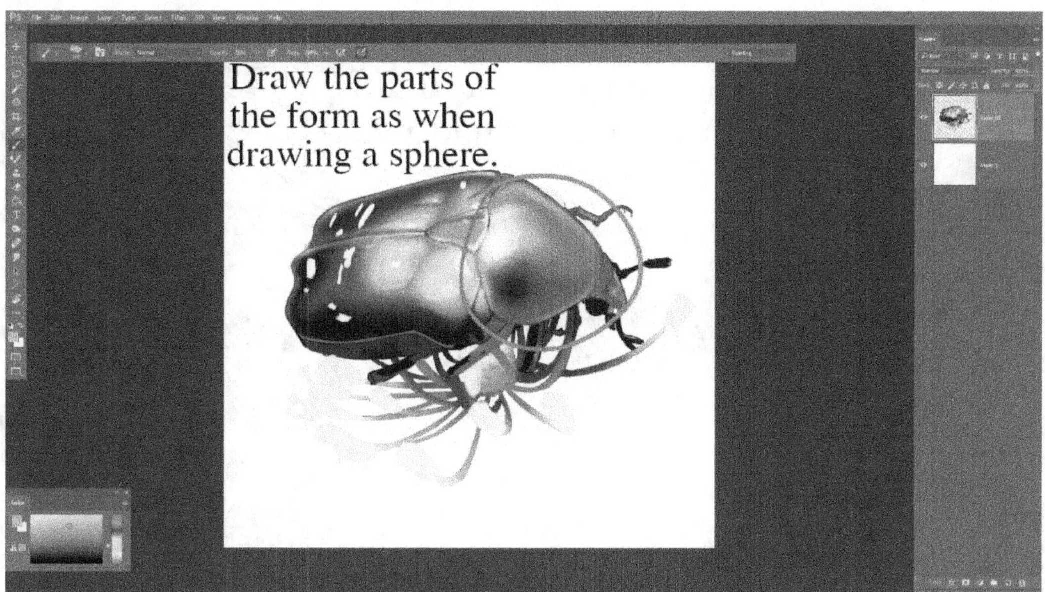

20. Use the Brush Tool with a dark color to darken any areas of the scattered shadow.

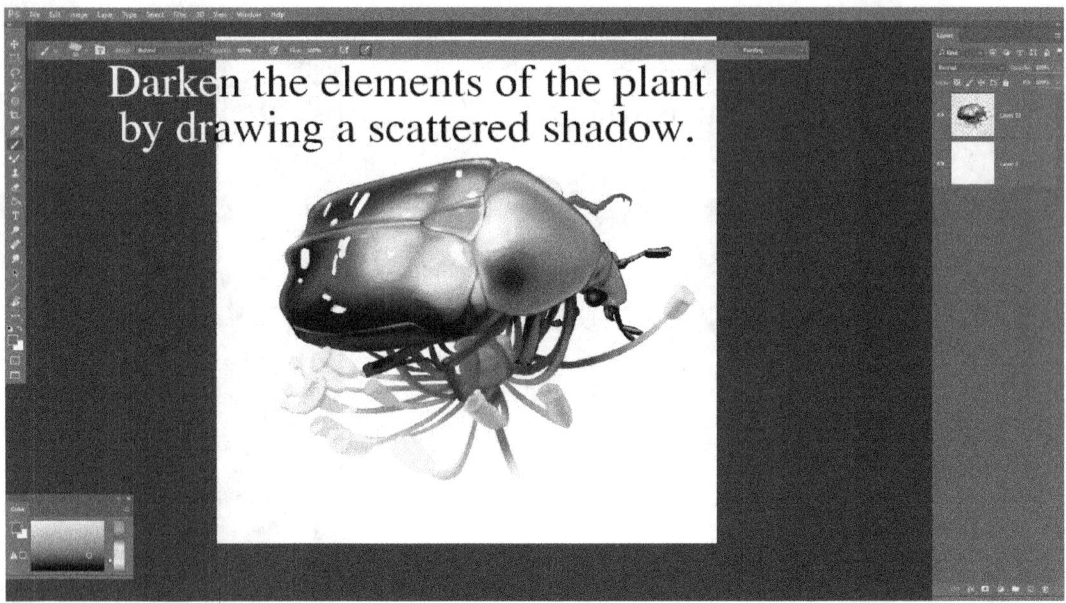

21. Use the Smudge Tool with 91% Strength to smoothen out any blots in the piece.

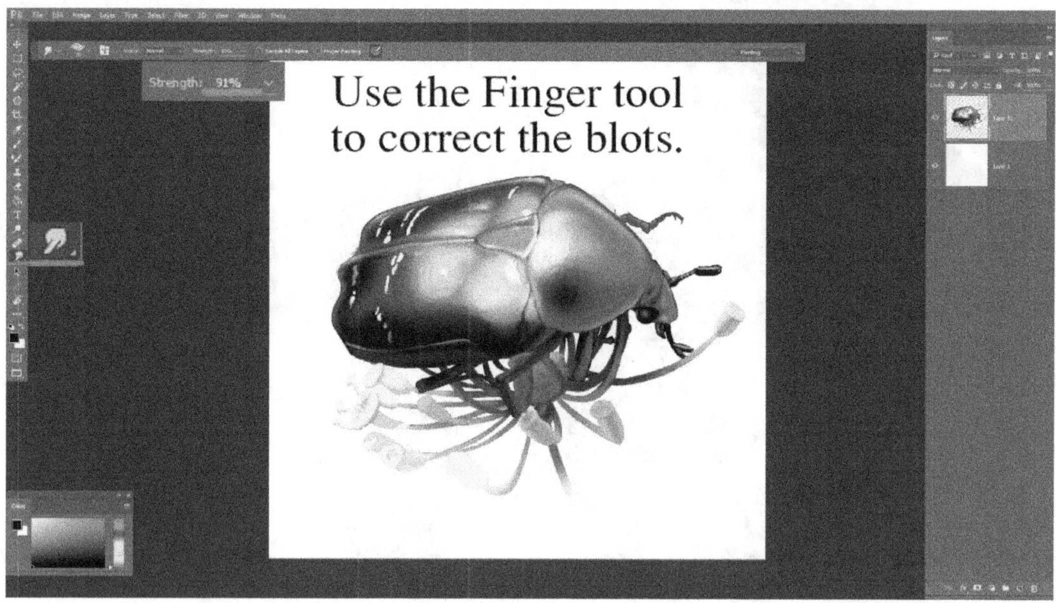

Dinosaur

1. Make a new layer. Start sketching the main body and the tail of the dinosaur.

2. Begin drawing the neck and the head.

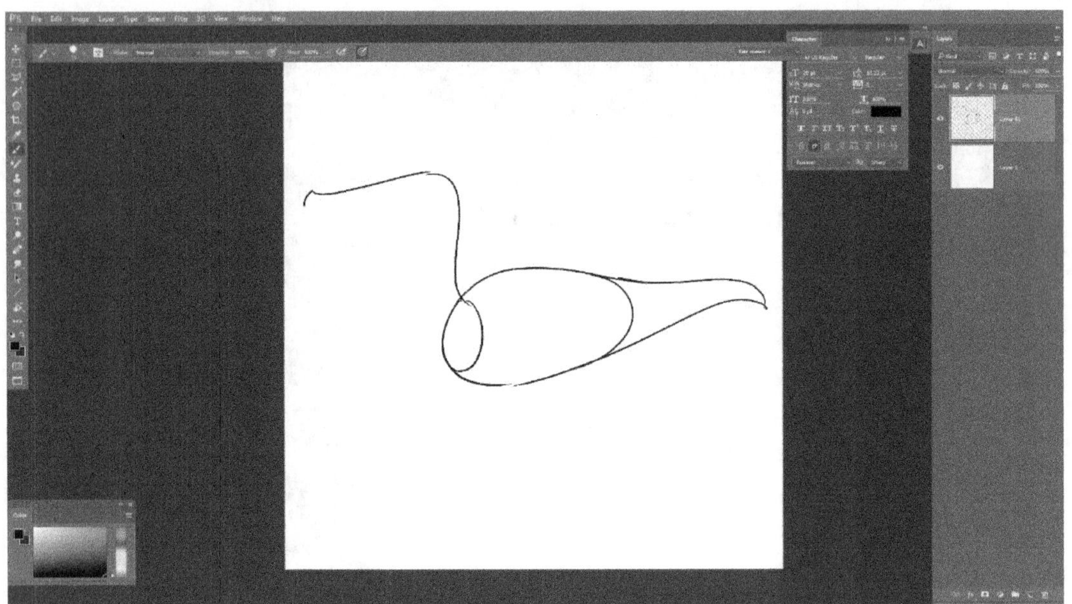

3. Draw the rest of the neck and the lower jaw.

4. Draw the front legs, or arms, of the dinosaur.

5. Sketch the hind legs.

6. With the Eraser Tool, erase any excess lines. Add details to the sketch like the claws and hands.

7. Refine the sketch more. Add folds on the skin and eyes.

8. Draw the teeth.

9. Make a new layer. Use the Brush Tool to paint color over the sketch.

10. Use the Eraser Tool to remove colors that exceed the bounds of the sketch.

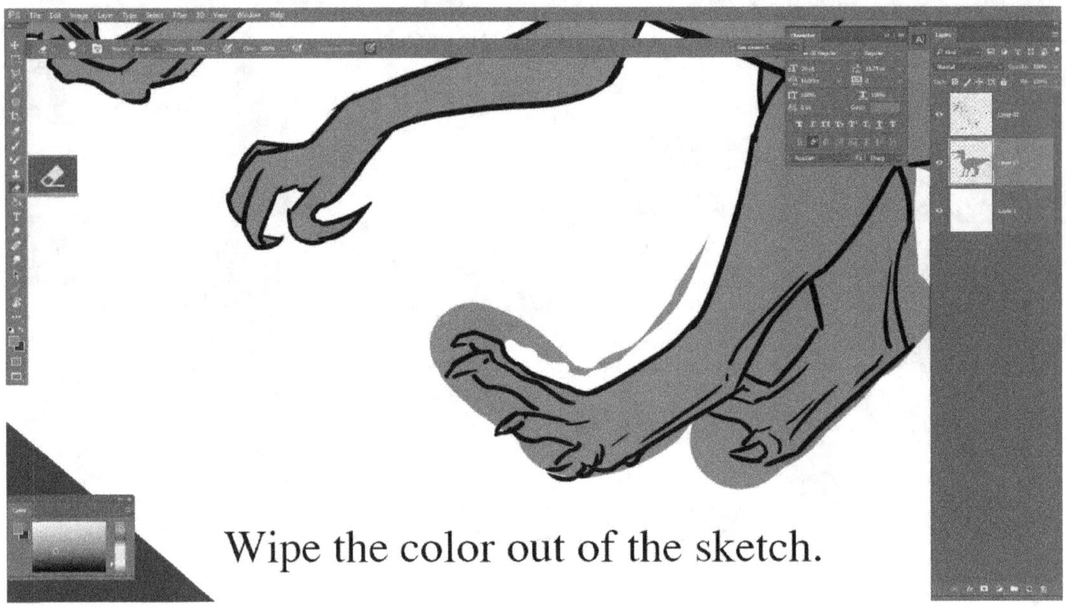

Wipe the color out of the sketch.

11. The dinosaur filled with color and the excess areas removed.

12. Paint the insides of the mouth in a different layer. Click on the lasso
Tool. Draw an area around the legs in the background. Press Ctrl+L to pull
up the Levels Window. Darken the legs by lowering the middle level to 0.61.

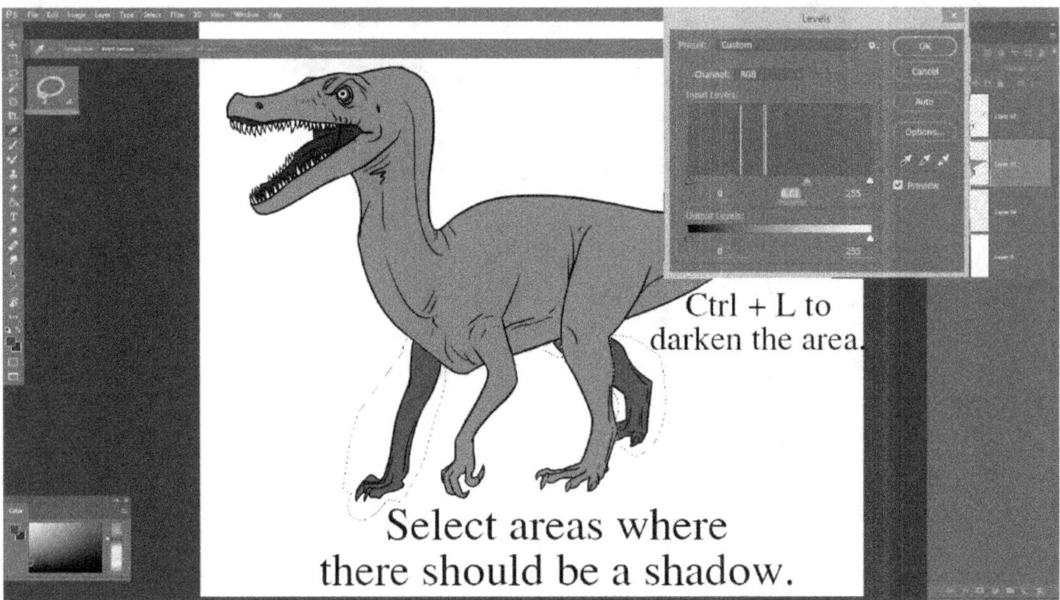

13. Select an area under the belly and behind the front leg of the dinosaur. These are the parts of the supposed shadow. Darken these areas as well.

14. Select other areas of the supposed shadows and darken them as well. Click on the Smudge Tool. Change its Mode to Normal and its Strength to 43%. Smooth the transition for the shadows.

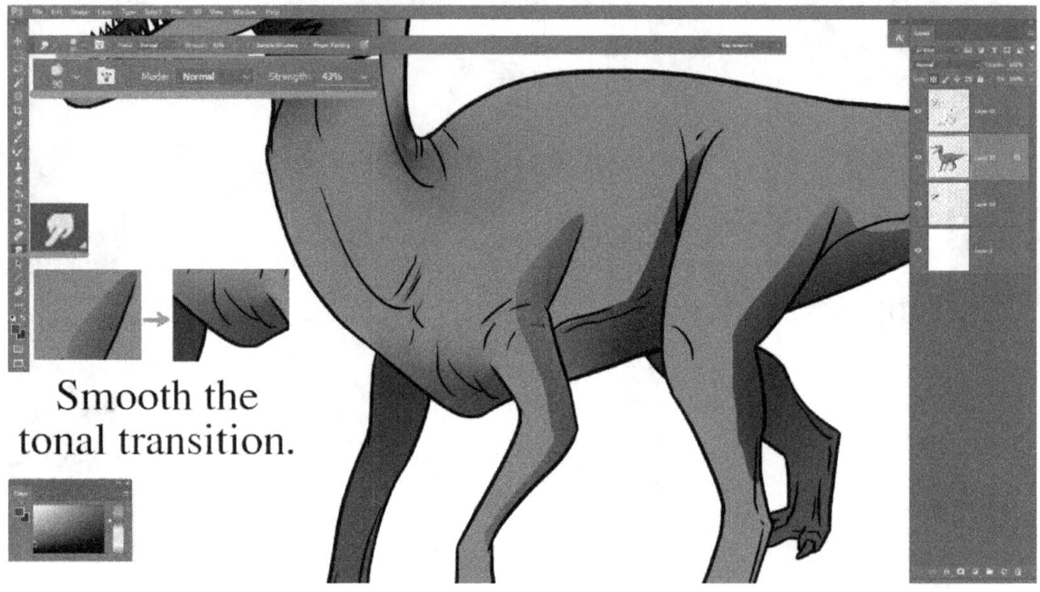

15. Increase the Strength of the Smudge Tool to 75% and spread any areas of the shadow to accentuate the folds of the skin.

16. Click on the Lasso Tool and mark out an area around the claws of the dinosaur. Click the Right Mouse button over the area. Select "Feather..." from the pop-up menu.

17. Open the Hue/Saturation window by pressing Ctrl+U. Change the Hue and Saturation of the area to your desired level. On this piece the Hue was changed to -180 and the Saturation was adjusted to +35.

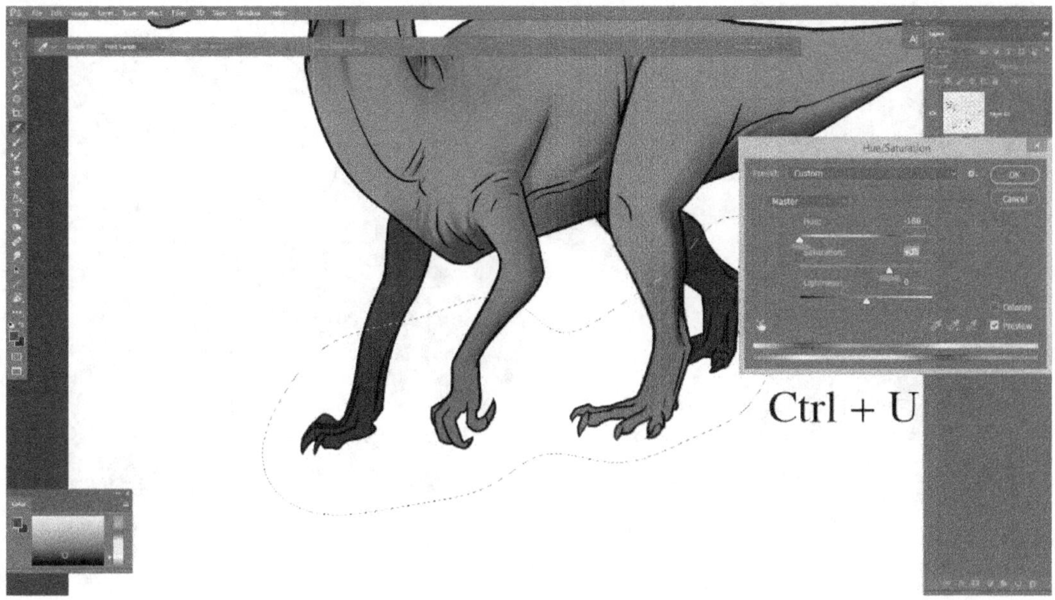

18. Select an area around the head and do the same process.

19. Click the Smudge Tool and spread the areas of color to any areas you may desire.

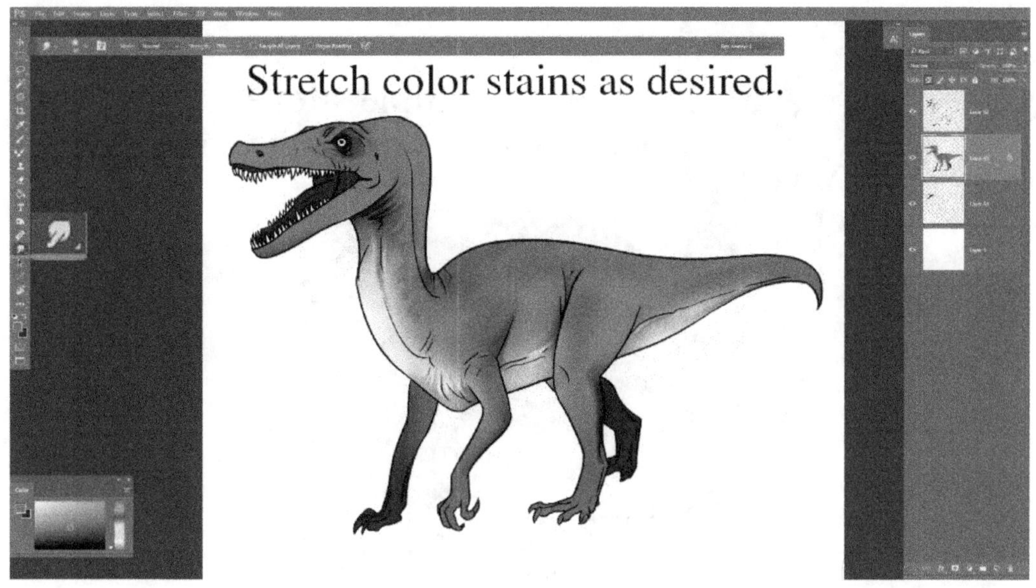

20. Select the Brush Tool in Normal Mode and with Opacity of 33%. Paint areas on the dinosaur to add some measure of texture.

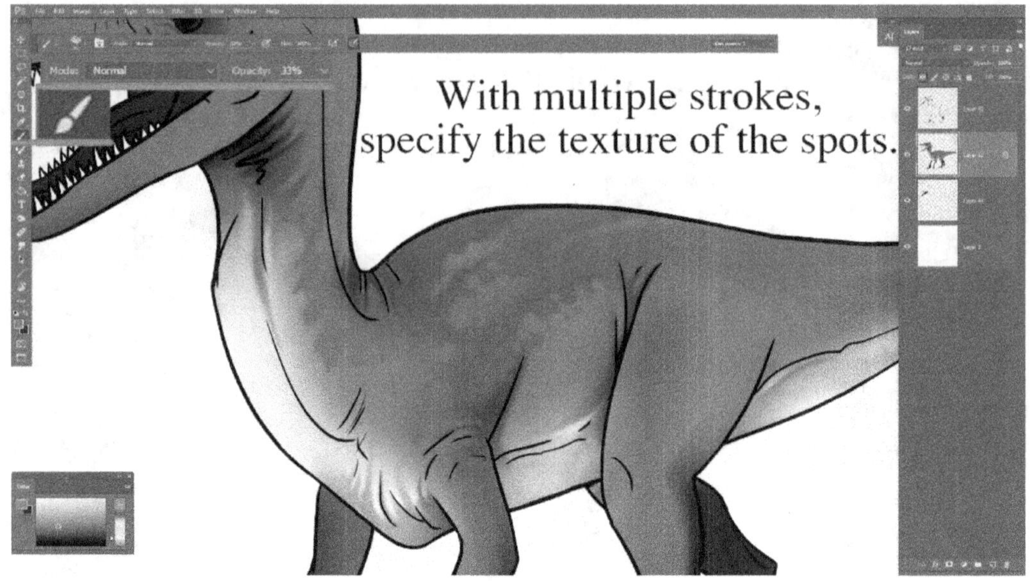

21. Change the Opacity of the Brush Tool to 23%. Paint areas with a lighter color to add highlights and a darker color to add shadows.

22. You can change the Color of any area by drawing a selection area around it using the Lasso Tool and changing the Hue and Saturation levels of the said area.

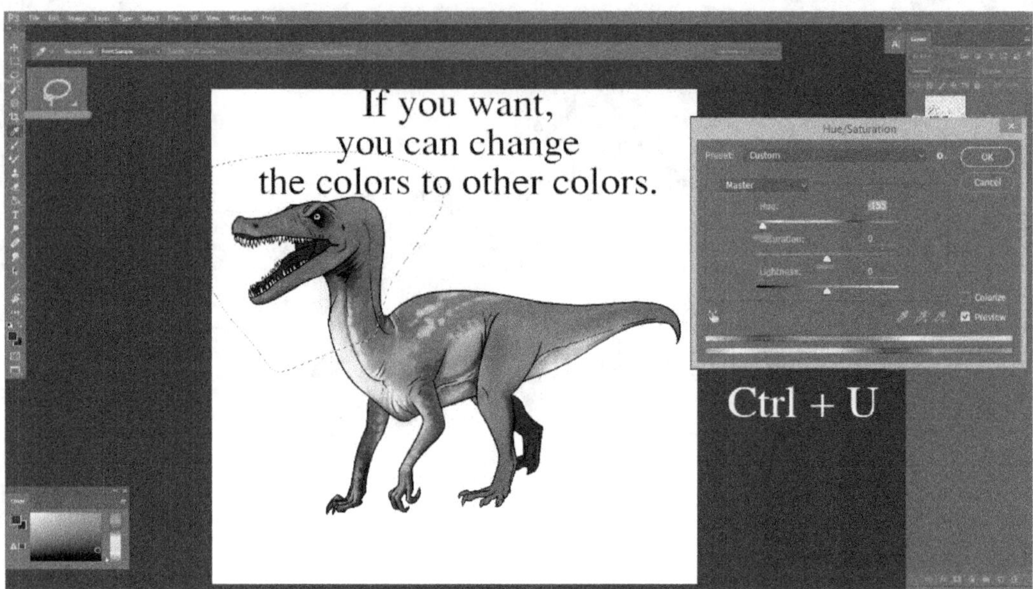

23. Continue the process of adding shadows and highlights on the piece until you are satisfied with the results.

24. Select the layer of the original sketch and lock it. Change the opacity of the Brush Tool to 43%.

25. Paint over the lines colors to hide its sharp strokes. Choose colors that are close to the color next to it.

26. The area of the tail with the sketch lines still unchanged.

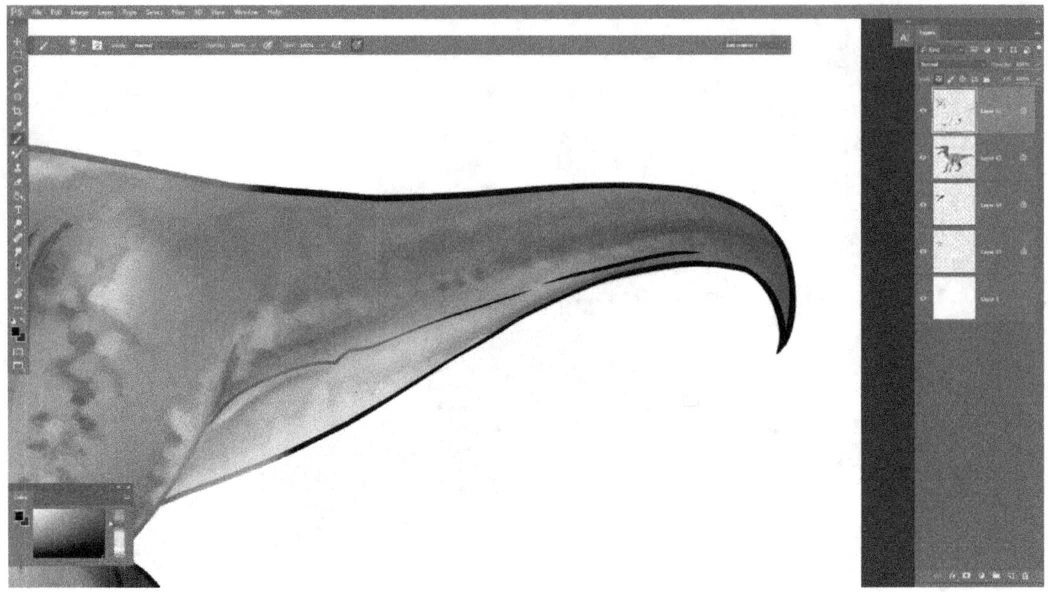

27. The colors shown are the ones directly next to the line. Paint the sketch lines with these colors in areas where the line is next to them.

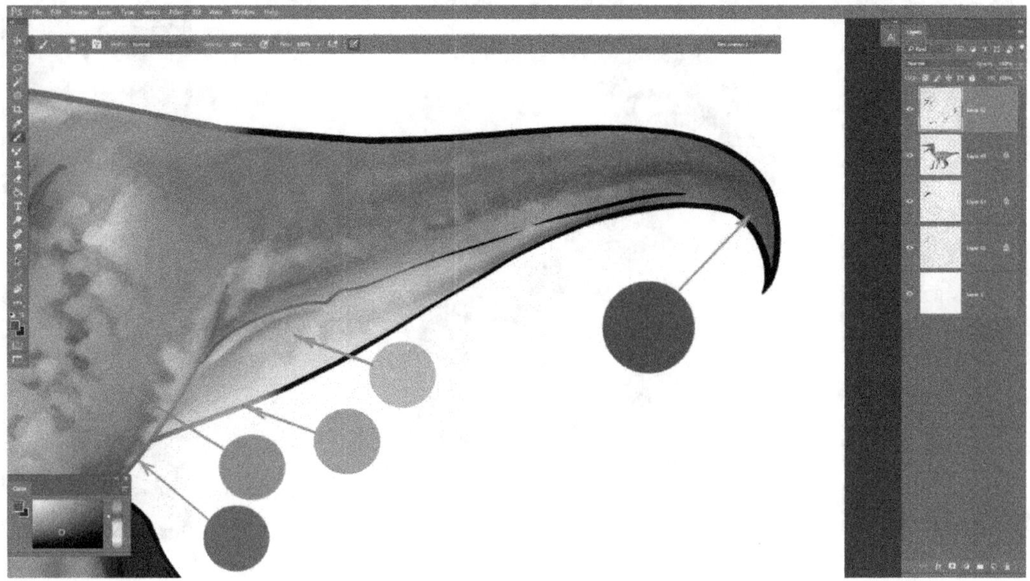

28. The finished dinosaur drawing.

Important Tricks and Reminders in Creating Images using Adobe Photoshop

Here are some reminders and tricks in creating images in adobe Photoshop.

- **Always work in layers:**

Layers are an essential part of drawing in Photoshop and it makes the drawing and painting process a whole lot easier. Try to master the use of layers in painting.

- **Change the Brush Size faster**

You can change the brush size quicker by holding the Right Mouse Button and the Alt key at the same time. Then slide the mouse to the right to increase the Brush size and to the left to decrease it. You can also change the hardness by moving the mouse up or down.

- **Presets**

Save a lot of time by setting the tools and brush settings you use often as a Tool Preset. You can find and edit your presets by going to Edit> Presets>Preset Manager.

- **Keyboard Shortcuts**

The keyboard can be a lifesaver when speed is essential for the job required. Make sure to master the most common keyboard shortcuts used to streamline the drawing process.

- **Accurate Brushes**

You can make the painting with the Brush Tool more accurate by activating the crosshairs feature. Go to Edit>Preferences>Cursors to pull up the Cursors window. Select the "Show Crosshair Brush Tip" and click OK.

Conclusion

Painting and drawing in Adobe Photoshop is very similar to the traditional way of doing it but there are also drastic differences. Mastering this tool will take a long time to do, but it is not impossible. Just like anything in this world, anything can be mastered as long as you put in time and effort in it. And, if you love what you are doing, it will make it even more enjoyable.

Just like any other tool Adobe Photoshop needs a lot of practice for one to be proficient with it. Make sure to experiment. Find your comforts and challenge them. Make sure to always challenge yourself to be better and learn more about the tool.

Thank you!

Thank you for choosing our book.

If you liked the book, please leave your feedback on **AMAZON.COM**

We would really appreciate this!

If you would like to have a bonus – **FREE BOOK**, please send the screenshot or the link of your review to this e-mail:

gloria.kemer@gmail.com and we will send you a **FREE BOOK** in PDF as a **GIFT!****

If you want to receive coloring book, please mention it in your message.

**** in the e-mail subject please mention the name of the book you reviewed and the author.**